THE LANDS IN BETWEEN

THE LANDS
IN BETWEEN

*Russia vs. the West and the New
Politics of Hybrid War*

MITCHELL A. ORENSTEIN

OXFORD
UNIVERSITY PRESS

Oxford University Press is a department of the University of Oxford. It furthers
the University's objective of excellence in research, scholarship, and education
by publishing worldwide. Oxford is a registered trade mark of Oxford University
Press in the UK and certain other countries.

Published in the United States of America by Oxford University Press
198 Madison Avenue, New York, NY 10016, United States of America.

© Oxford University Press 2024
© Oxford University Press 2019 First published 2019
First published in paperback 2024.

CIP data is on file at the Library of Congress

ISBN 978-0-19-776935-5

DOI: 10.1093/oso/9780197769355.001.0001

Printed by Marquis Book Printing, Canada

In a more volatile and uncertain world, in which power is more diffuse, the weight of the hedging middle is growing—economically, politically, and militarily. Democracies and autocracies, developed and developing economies, and countries from the Global South and other parts of the globe, are intent on diversifying their relationships in order to expand their strategic autonomy and maximize their options.

—WILLIAM BURNS, "A World Transformed,"
Ditchley Annual Lecture, July 1, 2023

CONTENTS

FIGURES

ACKNOWLEDGMENTS

I have incurred many debts in writing this book. First, I would like to acknowledge my students at Johns Hopkins University School of Advanced International Studies (SAIS), Northeastern University, and the University of Pennsylvania, who helped me to form and refine ideas through many conversations, questions, and interactions inside and outside the classroom. Thanks to Jacob Cohen, whose research assistance and senior thesis on Russia's oil trade with Europe provided valuable insights, and to Nicholas Emery and Alexander Schrier at Penn. I owe a special thanks to all the SAIS students who accompanied me on several wintry trips to Russia and Eastern Europe to study international relations in the region and helped to set up and conduct interviews; it is always a pleasure to hear from you and follow the progress of your careers. I would like to extend thanks to our local partners, colleagues, and hosts on these trips as well. In particular, thanks to Ramūnas Vilpišauskas of Vilnius University, who helped facilitate the organization of one trip to Lithuania and Belarus, and to the students and faculty from Vilnius University. I learned a lot from you all. I appreciate Oleg Kravchenko (decd. 2020), then chargé d'affaires of the

Belarusian embassy in Washington, DC, and Victor Shadurski, dean of international relations at the Belarusian State University, for helping to organize a fascinating and unforgettable trip to Belarus. My appreciation goes also to the European Humanities University in Vilnius for providing an alternative perspective. Thanks to the Washington, DC European Union Center, particularly director Dan Hamilton and Gretchen Losee, who helped to sponsor, administer, and advise us on these trips. I am grateful to all my interlocutors on the faculty at Johns Hopkins SAIS who helped to enhance my understanding of the diplomacy of the region.

Special thanks to my many colleagues and interviewees in Belarus, Bulgaria, Hungary, Latvia, Lithuania, Romania, Russia, Ukraine, and Brussels during research trips to the region over ten years. It has always been my pleasure to speak with you, whether or not the interview went well. I have a great deal of respect for the government officials, academics, think tank analysts, businesspeople, political fixers, drivers, and translators with whom I have met, often together with student groups, and thank you for your gracious willingness to spend time discussing your perspective and the perspective of your organization. Even the small number of difficult encounters taught me a lot. A particular shout-out to Ilian Cashu, my former student at the Maxwell School of Syracuse University and member of the city council of Chisinau, Moldova, for helping to arrange my trip to Chisinau and explain the ins and outs of Moldovan politics, as well as to Valery Yakubovich, who accompanied me on a fascinating trip to Kyiv, Berdichev, Pavoloch, and Odessa, Ukraine, and served as a sometime translator, and to Viktoria and Ostap Sereda in Lviv.

I owe a special thanks to US ambassador Adrian Basora, with whom I organized a conference on democratic backsliding in Central and Eastern Europe in Washington, DC, in 2007, in cooperation with the Foreign Policy Research Institute (FPRI) and the German Marshall Fund, the first of many undertakings together. I have been proud to serve with you in the Project on Democratic Transitions and the Eurasia Program at FPRI, as well as with John Haines, Chris Miller, Maia Otarashvili, Bob Hamilton, Alan Luxenberg, Rollie Flynn, Aaron Stein, and the rest of the FPRI staff. FPRI has given me many opportunities to speak on and enrich my own knowledge of these topics and the audience for them in and around Philadelphia. Similarly, I wish to thank the Center for European Policy Analysis in DC, Larry Hirsch, Wess Mitchell, Jakub Grygiel, and Peter Doran, for the opportunity to work with you for several years and learn from your perspective and events on Central Europe. In addition, I am indebted to my many friends and colleagues in the DC think tank community, who generously shared their expertise on Russian and East European international affairs. I would particularly like to acknowledge Samuel Charap, Derek Chollet, Daniel Hamilton, John Herbst, Fiona Hill, David J. Kramer, Marc Plattner, Alina Polyakova, Matt Rojansky, Blair Ruble, Steven Stoltenberg, Steve Szabo, Kurt Volker, and all the participants and speakers in the conferences you sponsored and hosted that enhanced my understanding of Russia and Eastern Europe. The United States is lucky to have such a terrific expert community, and I have been lucky to learn so extensively from it. I am also grateful for the opportunity to serve on the board of an EU research project, EU-STRAT: The EU and Eastern Partnership Countries, organized by Professor Tanja Börzel of Free University Berlin and her two terrific former PhD students, Esther Ademmer and Julia Langbein, whose books and articles—as well as those of the many fine participants in this project—have taught me so much about Russian and EU influence on the lands in between.

I would also like to thank my colleagues at the University of Pennsylvania, in particular in the Departments of Russian and East European Studies and Political Science, and the

Philadelphia-area Europeanist network, who have helped me in so many ways through their critical engagement with this work, including Osman Balkan, Richard Deeg, Cristina Dragomir, Kristen Ghodsee, Julia Gray, Orfeo Fioretos, Peter Holquist, Benjamin Katzeff-Silberstein, Ayse Kaya, Dan Kelemen, Julia Lynch, Ben Nathans, Kevin Platt, Mark Pollack, and Peter Steiner. Thanks also to the team at the Perry World House at the University of Pennsylvania, especially William Burke-White, John Gans, LaShawn Jefferson, Lisa Jourdan, Michael Horowitz, and Michael Weisberg, for organizing so many events that have enabled me and the Penn community to stay on top of the issues this book addresses.

Finally, thanks to David McBride at Oxford University Press and his team, including Holly Mitchell, Kayley Gilbert, and Cheryl Merritt at Newgen UK, for helping this book along to publication. It has been a pleasure to work with you. Likewise, I would like to thank Gideon Rose and the young editors at *Foreign Affairs* for working with me to publish a number of short articles on various aspects of the conflict in the region and to my co-authors on some of those articles, Hilary Appel, Bojan Bugarič, Attila Juhász, Dan Kelemen, Péter Krekó, and Kálmán Mizsei. Special thanks also to Dimitar Bechev, Ecaterina Locoman, Elizabeth Sherwood-Randall, Gen. Peter Zwack (ret), and several anonymous reviewers who kindly read drafts of the book prior to publication.

ABBREVIATIONS

AENM	Alliance of European National Movements
BIS	Security Information Service
BRICs	Brazil, Russia, India, and China
CEE	Central and East European
DCFTA	Deep and Comprehensive Free Trade Agreement
EEU	Eurasian Economic Union
EU	European Union
FBI	Federal Bureau of Investigation
FSB	Federal Security Service
GDP	Gross Domestic Product
GRU	Chief Intelligence Directorate
IMF	International Monetary Fund
KGB	Committee for State Security
LNG	liquefied natural gas
MEP	Member of European Parliament
MGIMO	Moscow State Institute of International Relations
NATO	North Atlantic Treaty Organization
NGO	Non-Governmental Organization
RT	Russia Today
UKIP	United Kingdom Independence Party

INTRODUCTION

WHEN RUSSIA BOMBED TARGETS IN Ukraine on February 24, 2022, and sent its troops marching on Kyiv, most Western leaders condemned Russia's actions in stark moral terms. US president Joseph Biden portrayed the war as a "great battle for freedom: a battle between democracy and autocracy, between liberty and repression, between a rules-based order and one governed by brute force."[1] European leaders echoed these sentiments, casting Russia's aggression as an affront to the values of liberal democracy and peaceful coexistence, values embodied in institutions such as the European Union (EU), North Atlantic Treaty Organization (NATO), and Council of Europe. The president of the European Commission, Ursula von der Leyen, portrayed Russia's invasion as a betrayal of the most crucial principle underlying Europe's post-1945 peace. "It cannot be that an autocrat attacks a sovereign country which has the right to the integrity of its territory," she said. Von der Leyen further declared Ukraine "part of our European family," as the European Union moved to offer Ukraine and Moldova candidacy for membership at a Brussels summit on June 23, 2022.[2] British prime minister Boris Johnson also framed the conflict as a battle between autocracy and democracy, between Russian barbarism and Western civilization. Speaking to Ukraine's parliament, he stated, "Putin's mistake was to invade Ukraine, and the carcasses of Russian armour littering your fields and streets are monuments not only to his folly, but to the dangers of autocracy itself." He contrasted Ukraine's "valour, your courage, your sacrifice," to Russia's "barbaric onslaught on your freedoms," "war crimes," and "atrocities."[3]

Yet other European leaders refused to see the war in stark moral terms. Hungary's prime minister, Viktor Orbán, refused to oppose Russia even after its war crimes in Bucha, Ukraine—where unarmed civilians were found shot with their hands tied behind their backs and survivors reported being raped by Russian soldiers. Instead, he defiantly marked out a position in between Russia and the West. While Orbán roundly condemned Russia's invasion of Ukraine, he insisted that Hungary must stand up for its own interests, both security and economic. Orbán supported some EU sanctions against Russia but rejected the most damaging, such as an EU boycott of Russian oil and gas. Orbán also refused to provide military support for Ukraine or to allow other NATO countries' military assistance to traverse Hungarian territory.

"We condemn the aggressor and help the victim of aggression," Orbán said on May 20, 2022,

> but at the same time we know that Ukraine is not defending Hungary. That is a nonsensical idea! Hungary can be defended by NATO and the Hungarian Defense Forces. As a proportion of our population, we have taken in the largest number of refugees, and the Hungarian people are happy to help . . . but they do not want to pay the price of the war, because it is not their war and they will not benefit from it. They know full well that war is accompanied by sanctions, rampant inflation and economic stagnation; they know that war always impoverishes people. . . . Our aim is to restore peace, not to continue the war, because that is what is in our national interest. Hungary First![4]

Hungary's moral prevarication at a time of war angered European leaders, not least Ukrainian president Volodymyr

Zelensky, who stated, "Hungary . . . I want to stop here and be honest. Once and for all. You have to decide for yourself who you are with."[5] But that was exactly the point: Orbán did not want to choose.

Orbán wanted to retain the benefits of being a member of the European Union while not shouldering the costs of cutting his country off from Russian energy, which made up a vast majority of Hungarian supplies. Orbán felt so strongly about this, he was willing to endure the sharp critiques of his EU allies in the midst of a reelection campaign. In March 2022, Orbán stood for a fourth consecutive term as prime minister. When Orbán refused to join EU leaders in condemning Russian war crimes in Bucha and instead criticized Zelensky for intervening in Hungarian politics, European leaders were incensed.

Czech defense minister Jana Černochová refused to attend a meeting of Central European defense ministers in Hungary, stating, "I'm really sorry that cheap Russian oil is more important for Hungarian politicians than Ukrainian blood."[6] Czech prime minister Petr Fiala demanded that Orbán speak out against Russia's war crimes, saying, "We expect an unequivocal and very strong position, from Budapest, condemning the Russian crimes in Ukraine. . . . We cannot close our eyes to what is happening there."[7] Polish deputy prime minister Jarosław Kaczyński added, "When Orbán says that he cannot see what happened in Bucha, he must be advised to see an eye doctor."[8] Yet Orbán won reelection in March 2022 and refused to change his position, stating that Hungary had nothing to do with the war and did not want to stop importing Russian oil and gas. Ultimately, the EU rewarded Hungary with an exemption from EU sanctions on Russian oil imports.[9]

Why do some politicians regard the war in Ukraine as the defining moral issue of our time, a battle of good versus evil, while others insist on playing both sides? Because during all-out conflict, the more polarized politics becomes, the more both sides are willing to pay for allies, and the more cynical power brokers can demand for their loyalty. The most cynical and successful among them seek rewards from both parties to a conflict. This book explores the paradoxical dynamics of hybrid war between Russia and the West, where a stark moral divide both polarizes politics and creates enormous opportunities for arbitrage. It shows that Viktor Orbán's politics of prevarication is far from unique; rather, it is the rule in many countries, including in Western Europe and the United States. In essence, this book makes two main points. First, Russia launched a hybrid war on the West that since 2007 has defined world politics ever since and will continue to do so while Russian president Vladimir Putin remains in power. Second, this hybrid war has had a convoluted impact on the politics of countries affected. On the one hand, it has polarized societies into two camps, supporters of Western liberalism and supporters of Russian illiberalism. On the other hand, it has elevated politicians who seek to profit from both.

A central challenge of analyzing the politics of hybrid war is that many people do not perceive such a conflict to exist. I devote two chapters of this book to simply describing the nature of this hybrid war between Russia and the West: when it started, why Russia launched it, how the West has responded, and how this conflict has been fought in multiple theaters around the world, not just in Ukraine. This lays the groundwork for later chapters, which explore the politics of hybrid war in the lands in between Russia and the West and beyond.

Readers should come away from this book with a clearer understanding not only of the nature of the conflict between Russia and the West but also of its impact on their own country's politics. This book seeks to illuminate the behavior and motivations of some of the most confounding characters in politics today, like Viktor Orbán. Is Orbán a traitor? A Russian agent in the West? Does he seek to destroy the European Union? Play one side off another? Or maximize his own utility by refusing to commit?

THE LANDS IN BETWEEN

When I began to research this book back in 2014, after Russia's initial invasion of Ukraine, I had an intuition that the best place to study the politics of hybrid war was not Moscow or Washington, DC, but in what I call "the lands in between," vulnerable former Soviet states perched precariously between Russia and the European Union. That is where I conducted most of the research and dozens of interviews for this book. Why? Because for a decade and a half, these countries survived on the front lines of a conflict that many in the West perceived only dimly. The lands in between lived through disinformation campaigns, election hacking, military occupation, frozen conflicts, economic sanctions, and cyberattacks long before Western states were forced to confront this reality. Throughout a decade of studying and traveling to these countries, in their capitals and hinterlands, conducting expert interviews, conversing with ordinary people, visiting cultural monuments and history museums, I perceived that these countries were canaries in the coal mine. Their experiences contained vital lessons for the rest of the world. Though these countries are often regarded as backward, both economically and politically, I began to see that their backwardness placed them at the forefront of a new politics of hybrid war, which has broad general relevance.

But where are the lands in between?

For the purposes of this book, I define the "lands in between" as those countries that used to be part of the Soviet Union, and therefore part of Moscow's imagined empire, but seek to develop closer ties with the European Union. These countries constitute what the European Union defines as its "Eastern

Partnership" countries—Ukraine, Belarus, Moldova, Georgia, Azerbaijan, and Armenia—neighbors or near-neighbors of the European Union with which the EU sought deeper integration in terms of trade, governance, and values. Only after Russia's 2022 invasion of Ukraine did the EU open membership negotiations with Ukraine and Moldova and name Georgia a candidate for membership.

Yet these countries' vulnerability to Russian influence creates a complex environment for political and business leaders. They cannot ignore the economic opportunities emanating from the European Union, but they also cannot ignore Russia. Since 2007, when Russia began to sternly oppose these former Soviet republics' integration into Western international organizations, the lands in between have been caught on the horns of a dilemma: how to integrate with the West without angering Russia?

For some politicians and business leaders, the answer is stark and dichotomous: Either support Western integration or align with Russia. Choose whichever side best fits your country's identity and aspirations and pursue that wholeheartedly. Some leaders in the lands in between refer to this as a "civilizational choice" between Western liberalism and Russian illiberalism. Other leaders regard making such a choice as foolish. Just because people want a European future does not mean that Russia will go away. The better strategy, for some politicians, has been not to choose but to maneuver between the two sides. Not choosing enables political and business leaders to maintain flexibility and survive the shifting winds of international politics. For every Maia Sandu, the deeply committed pro-European president of Moldova elected in 2020, the lands in between contain an Aleksander Lukashenko, the oft-wavering, longtime president of Belarus, who, while subdued now by Moscow, has frequently made overtures to the West in the hope of maintaining his country's autonomy.

Why should a Western reader care about the obscure politics of the lands in between? Not only because Ukraine and other lands in between have become strategically important actors in European affairs, but because their politics has become our politics. Hybrid war has polarized politics in the developed West too. Western countries now experience the same contradictory politics of hybrid war, as leading politicians seek to amass power by leveraging divisions between Russia and the West. To understand how and why requires a clear-eyed understanding of the nature of hybrid war—the unwanted war that the lands in between has endured for decades, but which many in the West have preferred to ignore.

DEFINITIONS OF HYBRID WAR

What exactly do we mean by hybrid war? Defining the term can be tricky, since military and civilian analysts have produced competing interpretations of the conflict that defines our world. Military analysts initially used the term "hybrid war" to refer to a type of conflict that appeared to be becoming more frequent, in which standard military modes of battle were combined with non-standard modes or techniques that were asymmetric, ambiguous, and designed to blur distinctions between war and peace. Techniques of hybrid war often sought to act in psychological and cognitive spaces rather than on a traditional battlefield.[10] Defined by their ambiguity, hybrid techniques seem to consist of "hostile actions that are difficult for a state to identify, attribute, or publicly define as a coercive means of force."[11]

In 2009, Frank G. Hoffman raised the alarm about the coming age of hybrid warfare in an important article in *Joint Forces Quarterly*, "Hybrid Warfare and Challenges." He argued that the United States faced new, non-traditional threats and needed to adapt quickly. The problem, as he posed it, was that the

United States held unquestioned conventional military superiority worldwide. However, its adversaries increasingly sought to overcome this advantage by using regular and irregular military actions deployed concurrently to achieve "synergies from the simultaneous application of multiple modes of war." Hoffman predicted that a new era of "hybrid warfare" would produce a "convergence of the physical and psychological, the kinetic and nonkinetic, and combatants and noncombatants." The United States, he argued, was ill-prepared. Using the example of the Peloponnesian War, in which a traditional land power, Sparta, was overcome by a rising sea power, Athens, Hoffman argued that the United States had overinvested in traditional warfare and risked losing a hybrid war. Wielded by weaker adversaries, hybrid warfare could prove superior, "specifically targeting U.S. vulnerabilities."[12] Tactics could range from traditional military measures to psychological operations, criminal actions, smuggling, and terrorism.

When Russia infiltrated "little green men" into Crimea in 2014, the US and NATO militaries began to view Hoffman and other analysts of hybrid war as prescient. Russia succeeded in occupying Crimea by surprise with limited casualties, annexing the territory after an illegal referendum, and raising a "volunteer" army to fight in eastern Ukraine alongside local militias in what was portrayed as a "civil war," supported by "humanitarian convoys" of Russia military. At its 2016 Warsaw summit, NATO defined hybrid warfare as a form of conflict where "a broad, complex, and adaptive combination of conventional and non-conventional means, and overt and covert military, paramilitary, and civilian measures, are employed in a highly integrated design by state and non-state actors to achieve their objectives."[13] NATO believed that its member states faced vulnerabilities to hybrid attacks from Russia, China, and other state and non-state actors that posed a threat to liberal democracy itself. NATO produced a strategy to counter hybrid warfare and even stated that it could decide to invoke Article 5, on collective defense, in response to a hybrid attack.[14] Popular use of the term "hybrid war" spiked.

However, while NATO and military analysts emphasized the military aspects of hybrid war, others began to use the term "hybrid warfare" to refer to "the expansion of the battlefield beyond the traditional military realm." For instance, one analysis by the Norwegian Institute of International Relations in 2016 uses the term "hybrid warfare" to refer to "the full integration of the military and non-military means of state power to achieve political goals, in which the use of force or threat of force plays a central role."[15] Adding the "threat of force" to the definition implies that a state of hybrid war might exist between countries in the absence of a shooting war. Nuclear threats might be enough, for instance, to indicate the existence of a hybrid war. And such a war could be fought largely through non-military means.

Since 2016, when Russia and other powers used disinformation campaigns and cyberattacks to influence the US presidential election, many analysts began to view non-military means as a central feature of hybrid warfare. An adversary could use non-military means such as cyberattacks, threats, and political manipulation to achieve political control of another country without traditional military deployment.[16] Non-military modes of conflict might even replace traditional ones instead of just complementing them.

Yet this blurring of the boundaries between military and non-military means, war and peace, combatants and noncombatants, creates substantial challenges for the definition of hybrid war. Hybrid warfare is meant to be ambiguous. It uses a wide variety of methods simultaneously to confound a stronger opponent by reducing its ability and will to respond. It blurs the battlefield, expanding it beyond the traditional spheres of land, sea, air, and space to include politics, economics, cyber, and information. Hybrid warfare has caused various aspects of modern society, such as information and even migration, to be "weaponized."[17] Hybrid war may pose a particular threat to liberal democracies, since they may be more vulnerable to these sorts of challenges than centralized autocracies.

But if everything—information, discourse, trade, infrastructure—has been "weaponized," does the concept of "warfare" lose all meaning? If hybrid warfare blurs the line between war and peace and can be hard to attribute, how can the average person or politician tell if their country is enmeshed in a hybrid war? What if a country is clearly under attack, but not by traditional military means? For instance, Russia's attack on Estonia in 2007, the first of its kind, combined cyberattacks, disinformation campaigns, disruptive protests by Russian-speaking Estonians, and threats by Russian state actors after Estonia decided to move a Soviet war memorial to a less prominent place in the capital city, Tallinn. Cyberattacks, threats, and protests disrupted Estonian government and banking institutions. This was clearly a hybrid attack. Estonians thought it might be the prelude to a Russian invasion. But an invasion never came. Was this an instance of hybrid war? Today, NATO would define this as a "hybrid action" or "hybrid attack," but not necessarily as a "hybrid war"—even though NATO could declare Article 5 support for a country subjected to a "hybrid attack."[18] So what is the difference?

The very ambiguity of hybrid warfare gets in the way of making a clear distinction between "hybrid war" and a "hybrid attack" or "hybrid activity." It would be useful to know if a hybrid attack often or necessarily leads to a shooting war. In many cases, we have no way of knowing. What if an adversary has no intent to use regular military forces and instead pursues its objectives solely through irregular means? What if the time frame for the use of military force is long and contingent on various factors? What if non-military hybrid activity and threats are designed to topple a government, or exert political control? What if military force is used in one theater of conflict, such as Ukraine, but not in another, such as Germany? Should we consider Ukraine to be at war, but not Germany—even if Germany faces other forms of hybrid attack? Should we even view hybrid war as an interstate conflict between one country and another? Or is the battlefield broader—regional, or even global?

While military analysts tend to distinguish between hybrid "war" or "warfare" and "attacks" or "activities," many Western politicians—and recently Russian politicians as well—have begun to view the conflict between Russia and the West as a global hybrid war. On February 17, 2022, UK foreign secretary Liz Truss stated in Kyiv, "Russia's aggression is not just targeted at Ukraine. Their campaign of hybrid warfare across Europe has brought cyber attacks, attempts to undermine elections, and the use of chemical and radiological weapons on the streets of London and Salisbury. They are supporting destabilising mercenaries across Africa." Russian leaders now also refer to the conflict as a global hybrid war, though in their account it was launched by the West, not Russia. In March 2023, Russian foreign minister Sergei Lavrov accused the United States and NATO of pursuing a global hybrid war against Russia, "to demonize our country in the eyes of the world community, accuse it of all mortal sins," and he emphasized its psychological and informational aspects.[19]

In this book, I build on this broader, popular definition of hybrid war. This definition has several important advantages. First, it focuses attention on the full scope of the conflict between Russia and the West. Second, it emphasizes the existence of a "hybrid" war between Russia and the West that goes well beyond Ukraine, across a multimodal battlefield affecting dozens of countries. Third, it accurately identifies this war as being largely non-traditional, ambiguous, and designed to remain below the threshold of conventional military response. In sum, it highlights the most important features of hybrid war: its existence, its pervasiveness, and its ambiguity.

Russia and the West have been enmeshed in a hybrid war since at least 2007. Russia has used conventional military force in Ukraine and other former Soviet republics. But for the most part, both Russia and the West have chosen to fight through non-military means to prevent direct conflict between nuclear-armed adversaries. I look at five main theaters of conflict—military, economic, cyber, information, and covert— in this book.

Viewing this conflict as a hybrid war is superior to several alternative concepts that have become popular in recent years, such as the notion of a "new Cold War" between Russia and the West, or the idea that we are experiencing the outbreak of World War III. While many highly respected scholars and analysts have argued that we are experiencing the start of a new Cold War in Europe,[20] I have long believed this label to be misleading. First, as the war in Ukraine shows, this war is not cold. Second, a key aspect of the Cold War in Europe was the "Iron Curtain," a clear demarcation between the US and Soviet zones of control. There is no clear line today. Indeed, that is exactly what is at issue in today's hybrid war: control over the lands in between and, to a certain extent, the politics of everywhere else.

While it is certainly possible that we are experiencing the outbreak of World War III,[21] the whole point of hybrid war is to circumvent the need for it. Hybrid war exists to avoid direct military escalation with a great power. By engaging adversaries politically and economically—and, yes, with limited military force, cyberattacks, and covert subversion—both Russia and the West seek to achieve political objectives without triggering a nuclear war. Some suggest we are lucky to have a hybrid war; the alternative is worse.[22] Whatever the case, hybrid war defines our present reality and our politics. I hope the reader of this book will gain a more sophisticated understanding of the nature of hybrid war between Russia and the West and how it affects our politics. Many in the West are still in denial, in part because the West did not choose this hybrid war with Russia. It was thrust upon us by Vladimir Putin and his outsized ambitions. But informed citizens now need to understand this new type of war.

RUSSIA'S HYBRID WAR ON
THE WEST

ON JULY 16, 2009, A group of twenty-two Central and East European (CEE) leaders, mainly former presidents, prime ministers, and liberal intellectuals, penned "An Open Letter to the Obama Administration from Central and Eastern Europe." Václav Havel and Lech Wałęsa, two symbols of the 1989 revolutions that ended communism, were among the signatories. The letter responded to the new US administration's attempt to "reset" relations with Russia. The CEE leaders warned that

> Russia is back as a revisionist power pursuing a 19th-century agenda with 21st-century tactics and methods. At a global level, Russia has become, on most issues, a status-quo power. But at a regional level and vis-a-vis our nations, it increasingly acts as a revisionist one. It challenges our claims to our own historical experiences. It asserts a privileged position in determining our security choices. It uses overt and covert means of economic warfare, ranging from energy blockades and politically motivated investments to bribery and media manipulation in order to advance its interests and to challenge the transatlantic orientation of Central and Eastern Europe.

The signatories called for strengthening NATO and greater US commitment to European affairs.[1]

This appeal appeared to fall on deaf ears.

The Obama administration continued to prioritize improving relations with Russia over CEE security. Even after the Russo-Georgian war of August 2008, the Obama administration and many West European governments believed or hoped that Russia was turning in a liberal direction under President Dmitry Medvedev.[2] The United States thought it could achieve arms control agreements and win Russia's support for its wars in the Middle East by easing tensions with Russia in Europe. On September 17, 2009, President Obama announced that the United States was dropping plans for a missile defense system in Poland and Czechia, in what Republican presidential candidate Mitt Romney later called a "gift to Russia."[3] The timing was unfortunate, as the announcement came on the seventieth anniversary of the Soviet invasion of Poland in 1939. This episode seemed to show that the Obama administration paid little mind to the open letter's warnings and regarded CEE leaders as alarmist.

In fact, the West ignored appeals from CEE leaders at its own peril. Most Western policymakers tended to view East Europeans as a bit paranoid on the topic of Russia. Traumatized by Russia in the past, these countries appeared unusually sensitive to the Russian threat, even obsessed.[4] Yet today, their perspective seems prescient. Being colonized by Russia and/or the Soviet Union in the past made them acutely aware of the Russian threat in the present. They had become canaries in the coal mine for the West, a valuable early warning system that, unfortunately, was not heeded.

By 2009, many CEE leaders believed that Russia had launched an all-out hybrid war on their region, hoping to detach it from the West. Russia pursued this war in a limited and often covert fashion to escape notice. Its methods were largely deniable, such as hacking, media manipulation, and covert funding for political parties. Yet its goals were broad and ambitious. It targeted not only the NATO military alliance, aiming to divide Central Europe from Western Europe and the United States from its European allies, but also the European Union political and economic alliance, by stoking the flames of anti-Europe, xenophobic sentiment. Ultimately, Russia sought to divide Western liberal institutions, promote political extremism, and destabilize Western democracies.[5] This was not a marginal activity for Russia, or a byproduct of various self-interested actions, but a strategy for hybrid war that addressed what Russia saw as an existential threat coming from the West.

For the West, the realization that Russia was serious about its hybrid war came much later. Failure to appreciate it earlier put the West on the back foot in dealing with the Russia challenge. Finally, three events changed the minds of Western policymakers, causing them to understand that the West was under determined attack from Russia. First was the reelection of Vladimir Putin to the Russian presidency in 2012; second, the invasion and annexation of Crimea in 2014; and third, Russian intervention in the US presidential election of 2016. From 2007 to 2012, however, Russia pursued an all-out, mainly covert, political war on the West without much notice or reaction.

Even after the dramatic events of recent years, some in the West still do not believe, or would prefer not to believe, that Western countries are subject to a determined attack from Moscow.[6] The issue became intensely politicized after the US presidential election in 2016 and the impeachment of US president Donald Trump. Therefore, any examination of the effects of Russia's hybrid war on the West needs to start by describing its very nature. What does Russia want? Why did Russia turn against the West in 2007? Why did it begin to wage a hybrid war against Western institutions including not only NATO, but the European Union? What are its methods? And does it really make a difference?

WHY RUSSIA TURNED AGAINST THE WEST

Analysts of Russia's hybrid war with the West have fiercely debated the question of who started it. With so many brilliant analysts taking opposite positions, some blaming the West and others blaming Russia, some looking at current politics and others at deep history, it is hard to know what is true.

Some point to Russian president Vladimir Putin. As opposed to Russia's pro-Western leaders of the late 1980s and 1990s—Mikhail Gorbachev and Boris Yeltsin—who sought closer relations with the West, Putin radically changed Russia's orientation. Putin publicly mourned the loss of Russia's Soviet empire. He personally defended the Soviet Union in its last days, preventing German citizens from ransacking the KGB building in Dresden after the Berlin Wall fell.[7] Later, Putin became enthralled with visions of Russian greatness propounded by Russian fascist thinkers and Eurasianists such as Ivan Ilyin and Alexander Dugin.[8] According to some analysts, Putin always, or eventually, opposed the pro-Western orientation of his predecessors and sought to build a Soviet Union 2.0.[9] This project was bound to generate conflict with the West. As David Satter put it, after the 2013 Maidan revolution in Ukraine "the West was suddenly faced not with a masquerade but with the Russia that had existed all along, that somehow had been overlooked by many Western policy makers and observers." Russia was a kleptocratic, mafia state that was fundamentally disappointed with the collapse of its empire and determined to reconstruct it.[10] This perspective tends to be associated with Russia hawks, who see Putin's Russia as a revisionist power.

My own experiences convinced me of the validity of this perspective. At the very beginning of the Putin era in 2000, I was living in Moscow and working at Moscow State University, reputed to be the leading university in Russia. This gave me a front-row seat to watch the changes he was making. In the first year of the Putin presidency, under a new, Putin-appointed rector, Moscow State University faculty and students began to dispose of their pro-Western orientations and adopt nationalist official rhetoric, as if following a change in the party line. More broadly, we know that Russia's shift from pro-Western partner to geopolitical opponent occurred during the Putin presidency, so it makes sense to blame Putin, who directed this reorientation from the top.[11]

However, drilling a bit deeper, one might consider why Putin made these changes. For instance, did the West push Russia into a corner with NATO expansion and, by creating a sense of insecurity in Moscow, force Russia to respond to a perceived Western threat?[12] In this view, expounded by a number of well-known scholars and analysts, Russia is seen as more of a victim than an aggressor, seeking to protect its own legitimate security interests against a West intent on dominating the world system. In the words of Stephen Walt, "It is lingering fear, rather than relentless ambition, that underpins Russia's response in Ukraine."[13] In the perspective of these scholars, who often describe themselves as "realists," the West must respect Russia's threat perceptions, rather than aggravating them by expanding the anti-Russian NATO alliance into Eastern Europe and admitting former republics of the Soviet Union. By choosing to operate inside Russia's perceived zone of influence, the West generated a predictable, even necessary, reaction.

According to these realists, the conflict between Russia and the West arose not so much from the behavior or characteristics of leaders like Putin, but from what international relations scholars call a "security dilemma." In a classical security dilemma, the security of one country is challenged by the reasonable security precautions of another. So, for instance, when the West acts to prevent a security vacuum in Eastern Europe by admitting vulnerable former Russian satellites into NATO, Russia feels challenged, and when Russia launches military exercises or modernizes its armed forces to confront this challenge, the West feels insecure. When NATO deploys troops in the Baltic states or Poland to deter a Russian invasion, Russia responds by nuclear saber-rattling, and so on.

There is no doubt in my mind that Russia and the West are locked in a security dilemma. And the strong implication of a security dilemma is that both sides are to blame for each other's sense of external threat.[14] Neither side can see the other's actions for what they are, and in that sense, a security dilemma is a kind of tragedy.

Digging deeper still, one might ask why two adversaries fail to understand each other. The answer to that question often raises deeper historical and cultural differences. For this reason, many analysts focus attention on the deep history of the Russian state and explain that Russia is too large, too insecure, too proud, too ambitious in comparison with its means, or with too much of a history of imperial expansion to ever fit in with the West. A break was inevitable from the beginning, and it should be no surprise that Russia has adopted a policy of assertiveness against the West, as it has for many centuries.

Many versions of this type of argument ground Russia's foreign policy behavior in its deep history, rather than in the actions of contemporary leaders like Putin. Some argue that Russia's foreign policy is "honor" based and that slights to its perceived sense of honor can cause radical changes in how Russia treats the West.[15] Others argue that Russia has always been an imperial state and is today either "neoimperial," "postimperial," or "transimperial," still trying to digest the loss of the Soviet empire.[16] In these explanations, Putin is the unsurprising result of Russia's loss of empire after 1991 and the unique linkage between politics and geopolitics in the Russian imagination.

While I would never dare to dismiss these explanations by my academic colleagues, my purpose in this book is to explain why Vladimir Putin launched a hybrid war on the West at a specific point in time. For that purpose, I believe it is necessary to foreground the more proximate causes. While Russia has a distinctive history as a state, and a particular mindset and culture, in 1999, Russia was on the way to closer relations with a West that it emulated in economics and politics, but by 2007, Russia had decided to abandon the pro-Western direction of its foreign policy and launch an all-out political war on the West. Something happened to change Russia's path. Wielding Occam's razor, I would argue that the most obvious change was the elevation of Vladimir Putin to the presidency of the Russian Federation on Christmas Eve 1999. Putin simply had a different perspective than his predecessor, Boris Yeltsin, seeing the West less as an opportunity and more as a threat to Russia's great-power status.

This about-face was surprising to many in the West because, until that time, Russia had followed a policy of progressive integration into Western security and economic structures. Taking Putin out of the equation, I do not see Russia reacting in quite the same way. US president Bill Clinton discussed inviting Russia to join NATO with both Yeltsin and Putin, an idea also floated by Charles Kupchan in *Foreign Affairs* in 2010.[17] Clinton had invited Russia to join the G7 under President Yeltsin, making it the G8, a club of leading democracies and economies, an organization representing the top table of the Western international system. Given their orientation toward integrating Russia into Western institutions, Russia's decision to sharply oppose the West and its international system in 2007 so surprised Western leaders and analysts that, for many years, they failed to believe it was happening. For this reason, it is important to discuss when and why Russia's anti-Western turn happened.

THE TURNING POINT

Russia's turning against the West may not have been sudden, but rather a process that began to unfold from the start of the Putin administration. Analysts disagree when Putin began to oppose the West, but I believe that the most important turning point occurred by 2007.[18]

For in 2007, Vladimir Putin gave an important speech at the Munich Security Conference calling for an end to US unipolar leadership in the world. Putin remarked, "One state and, of course, first and foremost the United States, has overstepped its national borders in every way. This is visible in the economic, political, cultural and educational policies it imposes on other nations. Well, who likes this? Who is happy about this?" Putin advocated instead for a "multipolar" world in which other leading nations would be free to dictate their own foreign policy approach in their own neighborhoods. Putin referred to the dramatic growth of Brazil, Russia, India, and China (the BRICs) and commented, "There is no reason to doubt that the economic potential of the new centres of global economic growth will inevitably be converted into political influence and will strengthen multipolarity."[19] Subsequently, Russia backed up these words with actions. In 2008, Russia stiffly opposed NATO offering Georgia and Ukraine a path toward NATO membership and launched the Russo-Georgian war. In 2009, Russia objected strenuously to the announcement of the European Union's Eastern Partnership program, which sought closer relations with certain former Soviet republics.[20] Russia's relations with the West had been souring for some time. Why was 2007 a turning point?

The most likely answer is Kosovo, a small Muslim country in Europe, a state that barely exists.

In 1999, NATO planes bombed Serbia to help bring the
Yugoslav wars to an end. Russia objected unsuccessfully to
this attack on its historical ally Serbia. As head of the Russian
National Security Council at this time, Vladimir Putin wit-
nessed firsthand Russia's inability to stop Western action. The
bombing campaign ended successfully from a Western perspective, forcing Serbia to the negotiating table and leading to
the Dayton Accords, which forged a tense peace in the Balkans.
Kosovo, a majority-Muslim province of Serbia, remained a
sticking point, however. In 2007, Finnish prime minister Martti
Ahtisaari, acting on behalf of the United Nations, developed a
proposal for "supervised independence" of Kosovo, with the
aim of splitting it from Serbia, seeking to resolve one of the remaining ethnic conflicts in the region. Russia again objected
strenuously, pointing out that the UN mandate gave little basis
for intervening in domestic matters of member states. Russia
insisted that supporting the secession of Kosovo from Serbia
was against international law and would open a can of worms.
Russia threatened to retaliate by recognizing the secession of
pro-Russian ethnic enclaves in several former Soviet states.
Western powers noted Russia's objections, but pushed ahead
regardless, encouraging Kosovo's unilateral declaration of independence in 2008.[21]

Russia made good on its threat by invading neighboring
Georgia in August 2008, just a few months later. After the conclusion of the Russo-Georgian war, Russian president Dmitry
Medvedev wrote an op-ed in the *Financial Times* entitled "Why
I Had to Recognize Georgia's Breakaway Regions."[22] He made
clear that Russia regarded its invasion of Georgia as a tit-for-tat
response to Western recognition of Kosovo's independence. He
wrote, "Ignoring Russia's warnings, western countries rushed
to recognize Kosovo's illegal declaration of independence from
Serbia. We argued consistently that it would be impossible, after
that, to tell the Abkhazians and Ossetians (and dozens of other

groups around the world) that what was good for the Kosovo Albanians was not good for them. In international relations, you cannot have one rule for some and another rule for others."

In retrospect, Russian leaders frequently and publicly warned in 2007 that they had scrapped their pro-Western orientation in foreign policy and were ready to defect from the Western international system. Even so, Western countries— with the United States and Germany in the lead—refused to give up the hope that they could entice Russia to join the Western community of nations. Why?

There were a number of reasons, including the partly covert nature of Russia's assault on Western institutions, but the main reason was a failure by Western leaders to understand or respect Russia's worldview. Western leaders failed to see that Russia was worried not only about the project of NATO expansion, but also about the West's ignorance of Russia's broader security demands, as well as the entire Western project for a "Europe whole and free." Putin demanded that Russia be recognized as a great power in Europe and reframed competition with the West as an existential struggle. Limited in its ability to respond with traditional military means, Russia responded with a different kind of war.

THE WEST IN DISBELIEF

In 2007, while Russia had concluded that it faced an existential struggle with the Western institutions that upheld the unipolar global order, Western leaders did not see it this way. Of course, it was widely recognized that Russia did not like NATO expansion. However, many in the West discounted Russian rhetoric on this point, since the supposed "encirclement" of Russia by NATO had taken place in conjunction with a major drawdown of US troops in Europe—from 300,000 to 30,000[23]—and a dramatic post–Cold War decline in military spending. With US troops leaving Europe in droves and European defense spending falling off a cliff, how could Russia feel threatened? By contrast, most European leaders believed that Europe would never experience a major war again. The Russian threat was gone and no other power seemed to have designs on Europe. With the European Union uniting the continent and security backstopped by NATO commitments from the Americans, Europe was at peace for the foreseeable future. NATO, seeking to justify its existence, took up out-of-area operations, such as in Afghanistan, which Russia supported by allowing US weapons to traverse Russian territory. Western countries had no intention of invading Russia and believed that their force posture showed this clearly. Russia should, therefore, have had no indication of a threat from the West, and concerns about NATO expansion had to be taken with a grain of salt.

What the West failed to realize was that for a Russian government determined to win back the former Soviet empire, the very existence of NATO and its security guarantees to member states constituted a threat. NATO was the embodiment of the unipolar world order that Putin castigated in 2007. Russia had begun to be concerned, not only for its own security, but also by seeing itself locked in competition with NATO for influence over the lands in between—countries formerly part of the Soviet Union, but now independent, that Russia saw as part of its natural sphere of influence. An enlarged NATO alliance threatened Russia's attempts to establish itself as a great power with a legitimate sphere of influence.

In addition, Russia began to perceive a similar threat from the European Union, the other major institution around which European security has been based in the post–World War II period. The EU is a trade bloc with a political purpose: to underpin peace in Europe through mutually advantageous international trade. The EU is so dedicated to the pursuit of peace that in

2012 it was awarded the Nobel Peace Prize for six decades of work helping to transform Europe "from a continent of war to a continent of peace." In his acceptance speech, EU Commission president José Manuel Barroso stated, "It started with six countries and we are now 27, another one is going to join us next year and more want to come. So the EU is the most important project for peace in terms of transnational, supernational cooperation."[24] How could a zone of peace and prosperity ever be perceived as a threat? To Western leaders, it seemed nonsensical. And yet after the Maidan protests in Ukraine in 2013–14, it became clear to all that Russia viewed the EU—and not only NATO—as an existential threat.

THE THREAT OF EUROPE

To explain why, I turn to maps. I have always enjoyed looking at maps, but it was not until recently that I realized that all maps, if you stare at them long enough, reveal the political imagination of their designers. For example, consider figure 2.1. To Western eyes, the map in figure 2.1 looks like something one might encounter in a classroom, a common map of the European Union. Actually, it is an official map of the EU Council. The EU countries stand out, with each one represented by a brightly colored flag. Nothing objectionable here. Or is there? Let's think about this map for a moment from Russian eyes. A Russian might look at this map of Europe and note that Russia is absent. Or nearly absent. While other European countries such as Spain, Germany, and Malta are celebrated with flags and colors, Russia, which occupies one-third of what is geographically recognized as Europe from the Atlantic to the Urals, is represented as a tan mass on the periphery. It does not even justify a label or a border. Russia is presented as a bland background to the

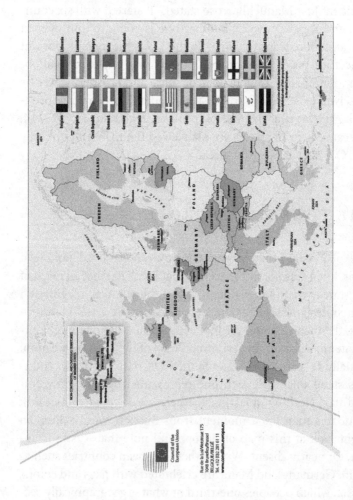

FIGURE 2.1 European Union Official Map. Source: © European Union, 2014. Reproduced with the kind permission of Lovell Johns, Oxford, UK, www.lovelljohns.com. Flag reproduced by Lovell Johns, Oxford, UK and authenticated by The Flag Research Center, Winchester, MA 01890, USA.

European Union's celebration of nations. Russia is barely even part of this vision of Europe.

That must sting. Russia has long identified itself as a great power in Europe. Its cities, its culture, and its history are deeply entwined with Europe. As recently as 1991, Russia controlled an enormous empire in Europe, consisting not only of the European states of the former Soviet Union, but also of Warsaw Pact allies occupied by the Red Army after World War II. Figures 2.2 and 2.3 paint a quite different picture, one in which Russia is a very substantial presence in Europe during the Cold War and in nineteenth-century imperial Europe.

Yet, in today's Europe, Russia occupies a peripheral role. Consider one final map, a map of the new member states of the European Union. Figure 2.4 creates a picture of a tiered Europe. At the top tier are the core member states of the European Union in 1995. A second tier is made up of CEE states that joined the European Union in 2004. A third tier is made up of Southeastern European laggards that joined the EU in 2007. Russia, like Belarus, is relegated to fourth-tier membership in Europe, somewhat behind even stalled, long-term candidate states like Turkey.

These maps speak eloquently to Russia's reasons for wanting to overturn the EU project for Europe. Russia imagines itself to be not a peripheral force in Europe, but a great power. Russia believes that, as a great power, it deserves a sphere of influence in Europe. That sphere of influence is threatened not only by NATO, but also by the EU and its project of creating a European continent dominated by a single trading bloc of democratic nation-states pooling sovereignty in Brussels, its capital.

A Political Threat

In the 2000s, moreover, Russia began to perceive the EU and NATO as threats not only to its geopolitical ambitions, but also

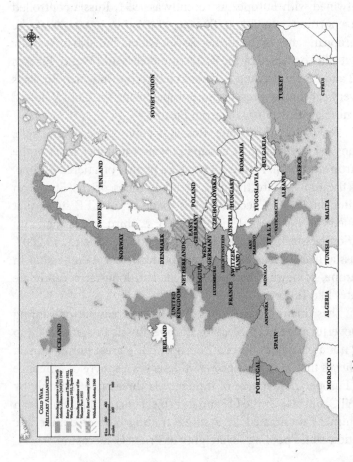

FIGURE 2.2 Cold War Europe

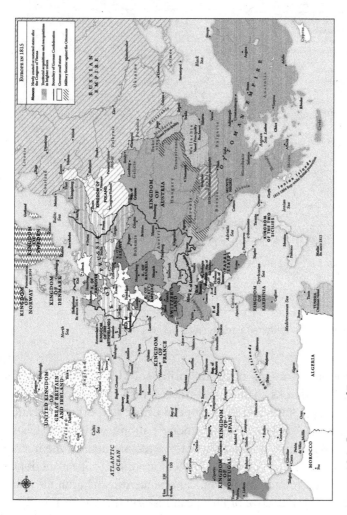

FIGURE 2.3 Concert of Europe, 1815

FIGURE 2.4 A Multitiered Europe. Source: © Nations Online Project.

to the very survival of its authoritarian, kleptocratic political regime,[25] thanks to the West's democracy promotion efforts. The United States and the European Union support democratic governance to foster peace among nations, and the EU has made well-functioning democracy a requirement of membership. Trust in a "democratic peace" among European nations relies on a mountain of political science research, but also on a particular narrative of European history: that the turn to dictatorship in 1930s Germany caused World War II and all its destruction. This showed that dictatorships, lacking respect for individual rights, often use violence at home and abroad.

Democracies, which give multiple groups and individuals a say in decision-making, tend to seek consensus at home and peace abroad. After the end of the Cold War, the United States and EU assiduously promoted democracy in former communist states. They required new member states to create strong democratic political institutions as a condition of gaining access to the enormous EU market. And it worked. According to Milada Vachudova, a leading scholar of EU enlargement, "The European Union . . . may well be presiding over the most successful democracy promotion program ever implemented by an international actor."[26]

Yet there was one problem. Russia, after the color revolutions in Georgia and Ukraine, began to perceive EU democracy promotion in former Soviet states, including in Russia itself, as an existential threat to the Putin regime.

It is easy to see why. Russia itself could be a target of pro-democratic protests and regime change. For while Russia holds periodic elections, it is not a democracy. As one of the leading Russian foreign policy analysts, Dmitri Trenin, puts it, Russia "is clearly authoritarian, despite the formal trappings of democracy."[27] Its elections do not meet the standard of "free and fair," as the playing field in these elections is not level, but rather decisively tipped toward pro-government candidates.[28] Candidates who have a realistic possibility of challenging President Vladimir Putin, the linchpin of Russia's dictatorial system of government, are regularly attacked, poisoned, imprisoned, and denied medical treatment (as in the case of Alexei Navalny), shot (as in the case of Boris Nemtsov), or otherwise excluded, often in creative but ruthless ways.[29] The Kremlin often runs its own pseudo-opposition candidates to soak up votes and create an appearance of freedom, as in the case of Ksenia Sobchak in 2017–18. In addition to using official harassment and even assassination to carefully control who runs, the Kremlin owns or controls most of the media in the country. It regularly blacklists or humiliates opposition politicians, starving them of positive media coverage or plunging them into scandal, especially on television. By contrast, Vladimir Putin is portrayed as a great leader who receives a full complement of positive news coverage on a daily basis. In 2018, state TV channel Rossiya 1 launched a new show devoted entirely to praising Putin, entitled *Moscow. Kremlin. Putin.*[30]

Putin's authoritarian regime resembles a mafia-type organization in which the president is a kind of *capo di capi* controlling the major oligarchs, the politically connected business leaders who own most of the country, as well as chieftains within the state bureaucracy.[31] The regime has many skeletons in the closet, including alleged terrorist attacks against its own people.[32] As a result, the Russian regime would be existentially threatened by the transparency that democratic governance would bring. Since a single electoral defeat would be seen as a sign of weakness and result in a disruption of the entire system, Putin's government cannot countenance democratic elections. Even democratic successes in former Soviet states might give Russians the idea to promote democracy at home. As a result, Russia also feels threatened by democratization in its "near abroad."[33] EU and US support for democratization in countries like Ukraine appears to Russia to threaten the very existence of the regime in Moscow.

The Kremlin further believes that Western powers, specifically the European Union and United States, use pro-democracy movements to undermine the Russian government. It sees pro-democracy street protests as Western-sponsored attempts to launch a coup.[34] Russia also accused the West of supporting a "coup" in Ukraine by unseating elected leader Viktor Yanukovich through street protests, although these protests were an indigenous Ukrainian action. Nonetheless, Russia blames former US secretary of state Hillary Clinton, assistant secretary of state Victoria Nuland, and European leaders for sponsoring the Maidan protests and for Yanukovich's removal from power. The Kremlin often claims that pro-democracy protesters are paid by the West. Putin fears that such protests could break out in Moscow—an existential threat against which he is constantly vigilant. Putin viewed the Bolotnaya protests in Moscow in 2011 as a Western-sponsored "color revolution" and believes that the West deploys such tactics to unseat him.[35] Therefore, it is no exaggeration to say that the Kremlin perceives US and EU democracy promotion activities in former Soviet states to be an existential threat. Where the West sees democracy promotion as a strategy for promoting peace in Europe, Putin sees it as a hostile act against Russia and his regime in particular.[36]

An Economic Threat

Russia also perceives Europe's strategy for building friendly ties between nation-states based on trade, mobility, and investment to be a fundamental threat, since the Russian economy operates in a very different way. The mafia-style political-economic system that Putin has built is incompatible with the law-based system of the EU based on treaties and courts and independent judiciaries. Russia's corrupt economy cannot comply with EU rules. EU laws would effectively undermine the patronage principles that lie at the heart of Russian crony capitalism—and vice versa. For this reason, Russia began to perceive the extension of EU rules as an existential threat. European scholars have found that "any attempts to formalize the EU's interdependence with Russia can only lead to greater friction,"[37] since Russia has such different ideas about what integration and rule of law mean.

Margot Light's study of Russia's attempts at economic integration with the EU found that an accumulation of perceived economic and administrative incompatibilities caused Russia to turn away from the EU in the mid-2000s. After more than a decade of working closely with the EU, she contends, Russia realized that it continually faced difficulties in negotiating agreements with the EU on basic free market treaties such as an open skies agreement. While the EU sought time and again to eliminate overflight tariffs for EU airlines over Russia (and for Russian airlines over EU states), Russia could not see why it should allow free access to its airspace. As a result, the EU canceled a planned aviation summit in Russia in 2007, believing that Russia had limited ability to become part of the European economic space. After a number of similar problems failed to be resolved during the 2000s, Russia turned decisively against the EU. In Professor Light's view, "Russians do not understand how the Brussels bureaucracy works and they complain bitterly about its 'rather woolly decision-making procedure.' A lack of experts in EU negotiations means that Russia is often at the receiving end of EU proposals, rather than making its own proposals, adding to frustration."[38]

Around the same time, Russia also decided that EU efforts to integrate neighboring states constituted a threat. If former Soviet states joined or signed association agreements with the EU, their economies would become incompatible with Russia's too.[39] President Putin complained in December 2021, on the eve of Russia's invasion of Ukraine, that "well before 2014, the U.S. and EU countries systematically and consistently pushed Ukraine to curtail and limit economic cooperation with Russia."[40] When Putin announced the creation of a Eurasian Economic Union (EEU) in 2014, it amounted to a declaration of war against the EU, fought through competition for economic influence in a shared European neighborhood. The Eurasian Economic Union has not been terribly successful, but Russia clearly conceives of it as a Eurasian competitor to the European Union, with one key difference. Since Russia is by far the dominant economy in the post-Soviet space, Russia sees the EEU as an instrument of ever-closer economic and political control over its neighbors. By encouraging its neighbors to join the Eurasian Economic Union rather than the European Union,

Russia seeks to draw a clear demarcation line against EU economic influence in its "near abroad."

A Cultural Threat

Interestingly, Russia has also come to view liberal European values as a threat to its culture, as it promotes conservative values worldwide. Russian media and political figures mockingly label the EU as "Gayropa" and object to expanding rights to homosexuals and transgender people. Opposition to gay rights has become a convenient symbol for Kremlin opposition to Western values of democracy and human rights across the board. Russia has sought to use the Russian Orthodox Church to deliver cultural and political messages throughout the Orthodox world. It has used a stern defense of conservative values to develop alliances with conservatives in Europe and the United States as well. In doing so, Russia plays upon its long-standing claim that Moscow is the "third Rome" within Christianity, after the fall of Rome and Constantinople, and a tough defender of the traditional nuclear family, religious practice, a subordinate role for women, and opposition to sexual and gender minorities.[41]

Russia also plays on fears of Muslim immigration in Europe, making common cause with xenophobic and anti-immigrant governments and parties.[42] It supports European states like Hungary in their attempts to preserve a conservative national culture through opposition to immigration,[43] though this is a touchy issue in Russia itself, with its large, multiethnic population and sizable immigration from Central Asia. Regardless, as Russia attempts to build a strong nation-state led by Russians, it perceives, or at least purports to perceive, EU values of multiculturalism and tolerance as a fundamental threat.[44] By contrast, Western institutions see individual and minority rights as key aspects of their democratic peace project and seek to promote these values worldwide.

A Zero-Sum Game

At least since the mid-2000s, Russia has felt threatened by Western democracy promotion, economic integration, and culture. While Western leaders regard all three elements as building blocks of peace and prosperity in Europe, Russia sees them as attempts to expand the EU's zone of influence and as existential threats. It wasn't always this way. While Russia was always concerned about NATO enlargement, especially the placement of nuclear weapons closer to Moscow, or missile shields that might enable nuclear first strikes, EU enlargement was seen as relatively innocuous or even as an opportunity. Since the EU has negligible armed forces and a complex decision-making structure, Russia tended to view the European Union as a sideshow or a vehicle of the European great powers: Germany, France, and Britain. However, with the enlargement of the EU in the 2000s, Russia began to view the EU as a competitor for influence in its "near abroad." The Kremlin observed that no CEE country joined the EU without joining NATO first. Therefore, to accede to EU membership was akin to agreeing to join NATO. By 2007, Russia had decided to oppose EU membership—and even visa-free travel to the EU—for former Soviet states.[45] The Western project of a "Europe whole and free" poses an existential threat to the Putin regime. Russia regards the battle for influence in the lands in between as a zero-sum game, to be won or lost, not as a potential win-win.

RUSSIA'S HYBRID WAR

Russia, perceiving an existential threat from the West, responded in 2007 by launching a hybrid war. Russia did not use that term much, however, until 2022, when Foreign Minister Sergei Lavrov accused the West of launching a hybrid war against Russia. On May 14, 2022, he stated, "The collective West has declared a total hybrid war on us and it is difficult to predict how long all this will last, but it is clear that the consequences will be felt by all."[46] Prior to that point, Russian and Western analysts and officials used a wide variety of terms to refer to the various modes of warfare Russia deployed. Some analysts referred to Russia's strategy as the "Gerasimov doctrine," after a now famous article by a Russian general on the future of warfare that emphasized the "role of nonmilitary means of achieving political and strategic goals."[47] However, the analyst who coined that term, Mark Galeotti, later disavowed it, stating that the "Gerasimov doctrine" never existed as a Russian military doctrine. He instead entitled his 2019 book *Russian Political War*.[48] Other analysts point out that Russian military thinkers more often refer to "strategic deterrence," "reflexive control," or "new generation warfare" in their military strategy documents, rather than "hybrid war."[49]

Yet, as argued in the previous chapter, "hybrid war" remains the most relevant and descriptive term. Why? First, policymakers and officials in Russia and the West now see the conflict they are engaged in as a "hybrid war." Using this term enables analysts to connect with public debate. But "hybrid war" not only is a convenient label, but focuses attention on certain realities of this conflict. It showcases the fact that this conflict is fought not primarily through military means. Instead, it combines nuclear threats and traditional warfare, as in Ukraine, with a wide variety of non-military methods, such as information, cyber, economic, and covert warfare, that touch many more countries. By broadening the definition of the battlefield, the term "hybrid war" emphasizes the pervasiveness of this conflict, not restricted to one battleground or country, but engaging dozens of countries worldwide through economic sanctions, disinformation campaigns, cyberattacks, and covert activity.

Russia's objectives in this hybrid war are ambitious, perhaps more ambitious than in a traditional war. Russia seeks to polarize, disable, and ultimately destroy the European Union and NATO without incurring too great a reaction from the West, and ideally to create a new European and international security system. Angela Stent, former US national intelligence officer for Russia and Eurasia, stated that Putin wants to "revise the current Euro-Atlantic security system and recreate a sphere of influence in the states of the former Warsaw Pact."[50] Since 2008, Russia has pushed for a "new security architecture" in Europe that would "redefine Europe in ways that are more inclusive of Russia and its interests" and legitimize its indirect control over former Soviet states.[51] Destroying, or even substantially weakening, the EU and NATO would halt Western attempts to integrate former Soviet republics and strengthen Russia's hand with its former imperial subjects. On the eve of Russia's 2022 invasion of Ukraine, Russia asked for legally binding security guarantees that would prevent Ukraine from ever joining NATO and return NATO's force posture to the position of 1997, before NATO expansion to CEE. Likewise, Russia wishes to weaken Europe's ties with the United States. The United States sees EU enlargement as a way of extending a zone of peace and prosperity on the European continent. Russia wants to limit US involvement and make EU states more reliant on Russia.

Russia's secondary objective has been to secure its position as Europe's preeminent supplier of oil and natural gas and its growing presence in nuclear power generation, using those to render Europe geopolitically dependent upon Russia. The events of 2022 revealed that Russia intended to use pipeline projects like Nord Stream 1 and 2 to drive a wedge between European countries. The plan was to make Western Europe dependent on Russian supplies, while bypassing East European transit countries. This would enable Russia to invade Ukraine or other states without interrupting gas supplies to the

European Union, weakening the will of Western countries to resist. Russia has long been one of Europe's largest sources of hydrocarbons, but it faces competition from Norway, the Gulf States, North Africa, and the United States. Since 2022, Russia has also faced growing EU sanctions. By 2024, Russia's strategy of energy blackmail in Europe had clearly failed. Soon after Russia's 2022 invasion of Ukraine, the EU slashed Russian imports and accelerated its transition toward renewable energy in order to lessen reliance on Russia. Unattributed explosions ripped through the Nord Stream pipelines in October 2022, disabling all but one of the pipes.[52] This put an end to Russia's attempt to use Europe's dependence on Russian energy to further its geopolitical goals.

In sum, Russia's hybrid war has been defined more by its methods than by its objectives. It deploys a wide array of military and non-military methods designed to prevent retaliation by keeping its aggression limited, ambiguous, and deniable. Russia pursues its hybrid war across five main theaters: military, economic, cyber, information, and covert. Russia seeks to achieve core objectives while avoiding escalation as it confronts a stronger West. Russia's February 2022 attack on Ukraine could be seen as an exception to this approach, a bold gamble President Putin made to prevent Ukraine from integrating further with the West. Still, Russia's original plan to capture Kyiv in three days and install a friendly leader suggests that Russia hoped to win before the international community had time to react, forcing acceptance of a fait accompli. Russia values avoidance of escalation because the United States and its European allies have unquestioned superiority over Russia in conventional arms.[53] Neither do the United States, the United Kingdom, France, nor Russia wish to use nuclear weapons, though Russia frequently reminds the West of its nuclear capacity.[54] Russia continues to deploy hybrid war techniques to expand its sphere of influence while avoiding setting off World War III. The following sections provide a brief overview of the techniques Russia has used in its war on the West.[55]

Covert Action

The first thing to know about Russia's hybrid war on Europe and the United States is that it is largely covert. While Russia sometimes uses direct military force, as in Ukraine or the Russo-Georgia war, it has more often masked its actions and intentions through covert action, computer hacking, and use of proxies and state-run entities to achieve plausible deniability and keep its opponents confused and off guard. In 2009, Janusz Bugajski observed that "Russia is operationally stealthier than the Soviet regime was prior to its collapse. Without declaring any ideologically motivated global mission and by claiming that it is pursuing pragmatic national interests, the Kremlin engages in asymmetrical offensives by interjecting itself in its neighbor's affairs, capturing important sectors of local econ-omies, subverting vulnerable political systems, corrupting or discrediting national leaders, and systematically undermining Western unity."[56]

Because Russia uses stealth methods, uncovering the full range of Russian actions in its hybrid war with the West has taken time, and even now, the full extent may not be known. I rely almost entirely on what the intelligence community would call "open-source intelligence," meaning publicly available information, supplemented by interviews. While the public has access to a very rich array of information about Russian strategy, tools, and tactics, many in the West still ignore this information—as in 2009—or prefer not to look at or believe it.[57] In 2022, Alexey Kovalev, an investigative editor with Meduza, the prominent Russian opposition news site, observed, "There are still plenty of Western intellectuals, politicians, journalists, and activists willfully ignoring what Russia is telling them again and again, loud and clear."[58]

Western intelligence agencies have been sounding the alarm about Russia's hybrid war for over a decade. According to Belgian intelligence chief Alain Winants, Brussels, the capital of the European Union, where the EU institutions and NATO are based, has become "one of the big spy capitals of the world," a major target of Russian intelligence and influence operations.[59] Winants reports that "in Belgium, espionage, Russian espionage and from other countries, like the Chinese, but also others, [is] at the same level as the Cold War. . . . We are a country with an enormous concentration of diplomats, businessmen, international institutions—NATO, European institutions. So for an intelligence officer, for a spy, this is a kindergarten. It's the place to be."

Beyond reports carefully redacted and made public by European spy agencies, it is very difficult to know exactly what this spying consists of. However, my own discussions with EU officials over the years make clear that many of them believe Russia hears everything that goes on in Brussels—even in closed meetings of top EU councils. There are no secrets. While some of this may be due to wiretaps and other signals intelligence, much of the information is generated by EU officials themselves, who freely communicate with Russian intelligence agencies and their surrogates, such as the Belarusian authorities, often on an informal basis. Many EU officials believe that the Russians should be informed of EU actions and discussions to prevent misunderstandings—or that they are potential allies. EU ambassadors frequently use insecure forms of communication, such as cellphones. So the EU bureaucracy is enormously leaky. Russians have ears everywhere.

After Russia's invasion of Ukraine in 2022, European institutions finally got serious about countering Russian spying. "In

March 2022, The Special Committee on Foreign Interference at the European Parliament specifically asked Belgian authorities to boost counterintelligence operations, to prevent infiltrations within the EU-institutions," according to a report by Egmont, the Belgian Royal Institute for International Relations.[60] NATO expelled from NATO headquarters in Brussels eight undeclared Russian intelligence officers posing as diplomats. On March 29, 2022, the Belgian government expelled another twenty-one diplomats believed to be involved in espionage. However, the Egmont report suggests that Russia has hundreds of operatives in Brussels working under official cover as well as illegals "posing as businessmen, academics, or journalists." Russia not only gathers information, but also sometimes deploys it to discredit, mislead, or divide EU, US, and NATO officials—for instance, by recording and leaking a 2014 conversation between two US diplomats that disparaged the EU.[61] In 2024, the European Union Parliament opened an investigation into a Latvian member of the European Parliament (MEP), Tatjana Ždanoka, after a Russian newspaper accused her of acting as an agent of the Russian Federal Security Service (FSB). Other members of the Latvian delegation stated, "There are other MEPs . . . knowingly serving Russia's interests."[62]

One of the most successful operations to mislead Western officials was the election of Dmitry Medvedev as Putin's successor as president in 2008. Serving one term from 2008 to 2012, Medvedev portrayed himself as a Western-leaning leader. Medvedev seduced EU and member state officials with his plans for economic modernization; one example is Western participation in building a Russian high-tech center in Skolkovo, near Moscow. The US Federal Bureau of Investigation (FBI) warned that Skolkovo was most likely designed to deceive Westerners into turning over vital technology.[63] Yet many European and US officials trusted Medvedev, failing to recognize that he was only a convenient front for Vladimir Putin, who had exceeded the term limits specified in Russia's constitution and had to step aside. Yet after a constitutional change that Medvedev pushed through, Putin returned to the presidency in 2012 for three additional six-year terms. This ruse should have been evident to observers. Indeed, some saw through it. Top UK scholar and analyst Andrew Wilson warned in 2008 that "Medvedev may indeed be business friendly and a relative liberal for Russia, but EU leaders should not race against each other to be his new best friend," noting his long history as Putin's henchman.[64] But others preferred to believe that Medvedev indicated a decisive shift in Russia towards modernization and liberalization. Belief in Medvedev disarmed the West for years as Russia pursued its hybrid war. He was, in many senses, a modern false Dmitry, pretender to the Russian throne.[65] The success of Medvedev's deception can be seen by the fact that it took until 2022 for the Massachusetts Institute of Technology to sever its ties to the Skolkovo Institute of Science and Technology, despite FBI warnings and espionage fears.[66]

In addition to intelligence-gathering and information operations, Russia also deploys "agents of influence" against the West. These are people who not only trade in information, but also take actions on behalf of Russian spy services to undermine Western institutions. I reported with Hungarian analyst Péter Krekó on one such case in 2014 in *Foreign Affairs*: the case of KGBéla. Béla Kovács was a member of the European Parliament from Hungary from 2010 to 2019 and a representative of the far-right Jobbik Party until 2016. He was investigated by the Hungarian parliament in 2014 and had his parliamentary immunity lifted by the European Parliament in 2015, which investigated him for spying for Russia.

Kovács grew up in Japan, where his foster father worked in the Hungarian embassy as a building superintendent and his foster mother as a cook. He apparently was recruited into the KGB, spent years working in business in Russia, and then returned, wealthy, to Hungary to become the treasurer of the Jobbik Party. Jobbik enjoyed a sudden rise in Hungarian politics with extensive new financial resources. Simultaneously, the party adopted a pro-Russian and pro-Iranian foreign policy stance, positions not typical of the Hungarian far right. After winning election to the European Parliament, Kovács became treasurer of a small far-right European faction in 2010. The Alliance of European National Movements (AENM) brought together extremist parties including France's National Front, Italy's Tricolor Flame, Sweden's National Democrats, and Belgium's National Front. Kovács was photographed in regular meetings with Russian intelligence services and frequently visited Moscow. His wife was revealed to have several other husbands, including a Japanese nuclear scientist and an Austrian mafia boss, and to have worked as a courier for Russian intelligence.[67] In 2022, the Hungarian Supreme Court, the Curia, finally convicted Kovács of spying for Russia and sentenced him to five years in prison. Yet by then, Kovács had fled to Russia, where he taught at Moscow State Institute for International Relations (MGIMO).[68]

As with Jobbik in Hungary, it became clear in recent years that Russia has funded and promoted far-right and far-left parties throughout the EU whose programs seek to undermine, destroy, or pull their countries out of the Union.[69] Russia-supported parties in the EU have two things in common: they oppose the European Union and they offer explicit support for the Russian annexation of Crimea and other controversial Russian foreign policy positions. One study of France's National Front (now National Rally), Italy's Lega Nord (now Lega), the UK Independence Party (UKIP), and The Left (Die Linke) found that "all have prominent party leaders who express favorable views of Russia, received financial support, or have attended Kremlin-sponsored conferences." Voters for these parties were found to develop more confidence in Vladimir Putin over time.[70]

Consider the case of Marine Le Pen's National Front (now National Rally). In 2014, it was widely reported that her presidential election campaign was financed by a Kremlin-connected Russian bank. During the last stages of her election campaign, she made a prominent state visit to Russia and met with Vladimir Putin. She also voiced her support for Russia's annexation of Crimea.[71] It is not clear how supporting the annexation of Crimea helped her in her bid for the French presidency. Articulating support for controversial Russian foreign policy positions may have helped her, however, to obtain financing from a Russian bank. Numerous other far-right and far-left parties in Europe have vocally come out in support of Russia's annexation of Crimea, even sending observers to validate the Crimean annexation referendum in 2015. Parties that sent observers to validate the Crimea referendum include the Austrian Freedom Party, Alternative for Germany, Ataka (Bulgaria), Change (Poland), Italy's Lega Nord, the Serbian Radical Party, the Czech Freedom and Direct Democracy Party, and the UK Independence Party.[72]

Given UKIP's close ties to Russia, some have wondered what role Russia may have had in financing and supporting the Brexit campaign, which seriously disrupted the European Union. A UK parliamentary report criticized the UK government for failing to investigate Russia's involvement in the Brexit referendum, arguing that "it is important to establish whether a hostile state took deliberate action with the aim of influencing a UK democratic process, irrespective of whether it was successful or not." Parliament's calls for further intelligence community investigation and publication of a summary report went unheeded, however.[73] UK investigators did find substantial Russian-sourced donations in the 2019 parliamentary election.[74] And the House of Commons published a 2022 report, "Countering Russian Influence in the UK," calling on the government to "bring forward long-awaited proposals on countering foreign influence," including addressing election finance by Russian oligarchs.[75]

Russia also seeks to subvert EU institutions by developing relations with "Trojan horse" governments inside the EU, which can act as agents of influence.[76] For instance, Russia has forged a strong partnership with the government of Viktor Orbán in Hungary. The relationship is cemented by an energy partnership that includes promises to make Hungary a key distribution point for Russian pipeline projects and Russian financing and construction of a new nuclear power station in Hungary. It is further underpinned by Orbán's pro-Russia foreign policy—for instance, his support of Hungarian irredentist groups in Ukraine during the 2014 war—as well as similarities between Orbán's authoritarian style of government and that of Putin, both examples of what Bálint Magyar has called a "post-communist mafia state."[77]

Russia seeks to use Trojan horse governments to break European unity on policy toward Russia, particularly the sanctions regime or funding for Ukraine. Hungarian and Greek leaders, for instance, have frequently spoken out against EU sanctions on Russia. In May 2016, Greek prime minister Alexis Tsipras told reporters, "We have repeatedly said that the vicious circle of militarization, of Cold War rhetoric and of sanctions is not productive. The solution is dialogue."[78] Nonetheless, Russia's Trojan horses within the EU have consistently voted in favor of sanctions within the EU Council. The reason is simple: although EU voting in many instances is formally based on unanimity, a lot of horse-trading occurs. For smaller states reliant on EU financing, it can be very costly and painful to vote against a large majority. It could mean the loss of EU funds that countries like Hungary or Greece rely upon. Smaller countries can still be used by Russia to articulate its foreign policy positions within the EU. However, Russia has learned that to subvert EU institutions from within requires more powerful Trojan horses. This may explain why, in 2017, Russia targeted election campaigns in France and Germany. These powerful states might have the capacity to shift EU policy on vital foreign policy matters.[79]

So, in addition to support for far-right fringe parties and paramilitary organizations, Russia relies on relationships with top government leaders from mainstream parties, such as former Czech president Miloš Zeman, to provide multiple, reinforcing levers with which to influence national politics. As one think tank report put it in the case of Czechia, "While these actors have little political significance on their own, together they amount to a loud pro-Russian lobby demanding Czechia's secession from the EU and NATO and the recognition of the unlawful secession of Crimea."[80]

Propaganda and Disinformation

Russia's disinformation became famous after its massive and widely investigated intervention in the US presidential election in 2016. Yet Russia had launched similar campaigns previously in many European countries. Within Russia itself, state media consists of a powerful propaganda machine, combining high-quality entertainment television and pro-Kremlin messaging. Many people watch Russia's state-owned channels primarily for the entertainment and imbibe political messages along the way.

It is hard to understand Russian propaganda without first getting a taste for how it works in Russia, where international news stories often are turned on their heads and fantastical, made-up news regularly dominates the airwaves. For instance, Russian state media creatively reported the downing of Malaysia Airlines MH-17 in July 2014, which Dutch investigators found was shot down by a Russian missile in territory controlled by Russian-supported rebels in Ukraine.[81] Russian news channels spread a variety of inconsistent conspiracy theories about it, including that a Ukrainian government missile shot down the plane after radar operators mistook it for Putin's own plane, that the Dutch government loaded the plane with corpses and downed it intentionally in Russian territory, and that a Ukrainian jet shot it down in a "false flag" operation to pin blame on Russia.[82] Russian propaganda extends beyond Russia itself since Russian-speakers in countries of the former Soviet Union often watch Russian state TV and imbibe the same propaganda. Agnia Grigas writes of Russian influence in the Baltic states, "Russia has been particularly successful in creating a virtual community involving not only the Russian diaspora but also a segment of the Baltic population that remains linked culturally, linguistically and ideologically to Moscow."[83] Timothy Snyder writes that Russian media intentionally lies to create a fictitious world for a malleable audience willing to be lied to and enthralled with Kremlin power. Russia's information war is "designed to undermine factuality while insisting on [Russian] innocence."[84] Russia must always be the innocent victim in this narrative, to justify as self-defense any aggressive action Russia might take.

Russia has also invested in foreign-language broadcasters, which offer a digestible version of the same messages for foreign audiences. Russia Today (RT) has been the seemingly respectable flagship of Russian foreign-language TV propaganda, available in more than one hundred countries in Arabic, English, Spanish, Russian, German, and French. It is accompanied by the less respectable Sputnik radio, which peddles a *National Enquirer* brand of trash journalism on the internet. Both outlets mix propaganda with reasonable reporting on social issues in the West, designed to win readers and get them to trust the more fantastical fare. RT and Sputnik often manufacture stories out of whole cloth. A US intelligence report on the 2016 US presidential elections found that RT published sensationalist stories including "an exclusive interview with Julian Assange entitled 'Clinton and ISIS Funded by the Same Money.' RT's most popular video on Secretary Clinton, 'How 100% of the Clintons' "Charity" Went to . . . Themselves,' had more than 9 million views on social media platforms. RT's most popular English-language video, called 'Trump Will Not Be Permitted to Win,' featured Assange and had 2.2 million views."[85]

As the US director of national intelligence found, the impact of these fake news stories was magnified by a network of right-wing news sources in all Western countries that broadcast Russian disinformation to a much larger audience. Russian propaganda messages also are "amplified on social media, sometimes by computer 'bots' that send out thousands of Facebook and Twitter messages." Russia has famously used Twitter bots to disseminate defamatory information about political candidates, as well as an army of trolls who seek to influence debates in a variety of social media settings. Trolls make harsh and negative comments to discredit views they do not like. Moscow employed hundreds of trolls at a "troll factory" in St. Petersburg, Russia.[86] According to the CEO of the US Broadcasting Board of Governors, John Lansing, Kremlin messaging is "really almost beyond a false narrative. It's more of a strategy to establish that there is no such thing as an empirical fact. Facts are really what [is] being challenged around the world."[87]

Foreign Policy Research Institute fellow Clint Watts showed that during the 2016 US presidential election campaign, Russian "active measures" propaganda and disinformation were distributed and amplified by candidate Donald Trump and his campaign team. "Part of the reason active measures have worked in this US election is because the commander in chief has used Russian active measures at times against his opponents," Watts, a former FBI agent, testified to the US Senate Intelligence Committee. Watts cited several instances in which the Trump campaign deployed false Kremlin propaganda stories to attack opponents, including false reports of a terror attack on a NATO base in Turkey and false claims of pervasive election fraud.[88]

Despite their limited audience ratings, Russian news channels provide a useful outlet for extremist politicians in many countries.[89] Since extremists often do not get much media coverage at home, the publicity that Russian channels provide can mean a lot. For instance, before the UK Independence Party was taken seriously in Britain, its leader, Nigel Farage, appeared repeatedly on Russia Today, and became a regular, paid commentator for the station, effectively an employee of the Russian state.[90] In the United States, Russia Today broadcast the Green Party presidential debate in 2012 and 2016. The 2016 Green Party candidate Jill Stein visited Moscow during the presidential election campaign for an RT event and made glowing statements about Russian foreign policy. RT has sought to defend Stein from a supposed "smear campaign" examining the Russia ties of her campaign.[91] Russian intelligence knows that fringe parties can have a real impact on elections by drawing away support from mainstream parties and, in the case of the US elections, tipping the Electoral College in certain key states.

One of the key objectives of Russian disinformation in Europe has been to spread fear of Muslim immigration, which peaked in 2015–16. Former Hungarian counterintelligence officer Ferenc Katrein accused Russian intelligence of aggravating a perceived migration crisis by spreading false stories or exaggerating real ones, such as the sexual assaults of young women at a New Year's party in Cologne, where the offenders were described as recent migrants.[92] By exacerbating the immigration crisis and shaping negative perceptions of it, Russia has hoped to destabilize European governments, raise awareness of Russia's position as a defender of European values, and undermine support for democratic institutions and the EU. The "Lisa" case in Germany is another instance: Russian news outlets spread the false story of a young girl who was supposedly gang-raped by Muslims. Russia even organized protests in Germany by Germans of Russian origin against supposed German government inaction over this fake event.[93] Such attacks have a direct impact on the domestic politics of affected countries, furthering discontent and political polarization.

Cyberattacks

In addition to propaganda and disinformation campaigns using TV and social media, Russia has deployed cyberattacks against opponents in Europe and the United States. Some of the worst have been unleashed against Ukraine. These encompass both computer hacking designed to gather and release damaging information about political figures and attacks designed to disrupt public infrastructure, such as shutting down the electric grid.[94] One of the most disruptive incidents occurred during the tabulation of votes during the 2004 presidential election in Ukraine, when Russian hackers gained access to the Central Election Commission and changed the vote in favor of Viktor Yanukovich.[95] This led to a massive protest—the Orange Revolution—requiring international intermediation, which resulted in a decision to rerun the election. In the rerun, opposition figure Viktor Yushchenko defeated Yanukovich. Other attempts have occurred in the European Union, where Russian hackers connected with various intelligence agencies accessed the accounts of the Christian Democratic Party in Germany, temporarily took over the French television channel TV5,[96] and stole the emails of French president Emmanuel Macron, among other disruptive feats. Often, Russia has chosen to release hacked information through WikiLeaks, an organization funded by RT, according to a 2020 US Senate Intelligence Committee report.[97] In 2018, the *Guardian* reported that Russian diplomats offered to spirit WikiLeaks founder Julian Assange out of the United

Kingdom, where he faced sex crimes prosecution and was holed up in the Ecuadorian embassy.[98]

In 2014, Russian hackers attempted to breach Ukraine's election computers to declare victory for a marginal right-wing candidate Dmytro Yarosh, who received 1 percent of the vote. Yarosh's "victory" was reported on Russian TV. As Peter Ordeshook, a California Institute of Technology political scientist, told the *Christian Science Monitor*, "We've seen vote fraud before in Ukraine, including a rigged computer system in 2004. But this wasn't an effort to steal the election outcome, so much as to steal the election itself—by entirely discrediting it in the eyes of key segments of the population in Ukraine and in Russia, too." The attack was narrowly averted by Ukrainian cybercrime investigators.[99] In 2016, Russian hackers—for the second time—shut down Ukrainian power plants, proving that they could use malware to disable critical infrastructure. Ukrainian president Petro Poroshenko stated that these attacks were performed with "direct or indirect involvement of secret services of Russia, which have unleashed a cyberwar against our country."[100] Russia also deployed cyberattacks to further its 2022 invasion of Ukraine, "to disrupt or degrade Ukrainian government and military functions and undermine the public's trust in those same institutions."[101] While Russia has used Ukraine as a testing ground for its cyberwarfare capabilities, it has the capacity to attack Western countries as well. In September 2017, a Russian attack penetrated the US power grid, demonstrating the possibility that hackers could produce blackouts in the United States.[102] In a separate attack in 2017, suspected Russian hackers targeted nuclear power plants and manufacturing facilities in the United States, trying to gain access to control systems. In March 2022, US president Joseph Biden "warned about the potential that Russia could conduct malicious cyber activity against the United States, including as a response to the unprecedented economic costs we've imposed on Russia alongside our allies and partners. It's part of Russia's playbook."[103]

Energy Blackmail

Russia has also deployed energy diplomacy and threats of gas cutoffs to exert control over European countries. In 2006 and again in 2009, Russia cut off gas supplies to Europe during a payment dispute with Ukraine. These gas cutoffs forced the European Union to question whether Russia was a reliable supplier. Since that time, Russia viewed Ukraine as an unreliable transit country and sought to build pipelines that avoid Ukraine. These include the Nord Stream pipeline that directly connected Russia and Germany under the Baltic Sea; Nord Stream 2, which added capacity along this route; and South Stream, now TurkStream, which sought to enhance Russian dominance of supply routes for Caspian and Central Asian gas to Europe. European Union states' participation in the construction of some of these pipelines angered CEE transit states such as Poland, Belarus, and Ukraine, making them vulnerable to Russian gas cutoffs, blackmail, and a reduction in revenue from transit fees.[104] Russia uses pipelines and other energy projects to create networks of high-level business and political allies within the countries in which it operates.[105] However, Russia's attempts to blackmail European countries into relinquishing support for Ukraine backfired in 2022, when the EU imposed harsh sanctions on Russian hydrocarbons and accelerated its reliance on renewable sources of energy.[106]

Military Threats and Invasions

Russia's invasion of Ukraine on February 24, 2022, brought home the fact that hybrid war can and does encompass traditional modes of conflict, not just "political war." Russia may prefer to use other techniques that more easily avoid Western reactions, but it also invades countries to achieve its objectives. Russia tends to attack neighboring countries that it believes it can subdue quickly. Russia appears to have intended its 2022 war in Ukraine to be over in a few days by capturing the capital city, Kyiv, and putting in place a pro-Russian government. It may have sought to limit Western reactions by deploying a lightning strike modeled on its capture of Crimea in 2014, where Russia used the element of surprise and deployed unmarked forces (called "little green men"), combined with local political leaders, to take control of the territory with little violence. Russia's invasion of Georgia in 2008 also produced a quick Russian victory. Though limited in scope, Russia does deploy military power, particularly in the lands in between.

Russia has sought to limit Western reactions through a range of techniques. For one, Russia has never invaded a NATO state, which would trigger a declaration of war by all NATO countries. Second, in Donetsk and Luhansk, Russia created and supported local militias in Ukraine to rebel against the government in Kyiv after President Yanukovich fled the country in 2014. Russia recruited volunteers to fight in Ukraine, rather than send the regular army, and only deployed its own troops to prop up the Donetsk and Luhansk republics when they looked like they might be defeated by the Ukrainian national government in 2014. Russia provided direction and leadership for these movements, appointing and dismissing or killing their leaders at will.[107] These techniques, aimed at creating the optics of a civil war, masked Russia's true involvement for both foreign and domestic audiences. As a result of its careful masking of its true intentions and actions, Russia's full-scale invasion of Ukraine came as a shock to many Russian citizens, who believed that Russia had never invaded another country unprovoked.[108]

While Russia's military interventions in Georgia and Ukraine are well known, its funding for paramilitary organizations in

Central and Eastern Europe—and in the West itself—has more often been ignored. These paramilitary organizations seek to subvert established governments, create a chaotic security environment, and give Russia some cards to play in Europe's internal security. Russia provides direct assistance to paramilitary organizations in EU member states and places its spies within these organizations, giving Russia an armed base of operations within Europe. In Hungary, Russian embassy officials provided military training to the Hungarian National Front, a neofascist organization, participating in airsoft drills. This came to light after Hungarian National Front leader István Györkös shot and killed a police officer who was trying to exercise a search warrant on his house. The Hungarian National Front disseminated Russian disinformation during the 2014 Ukraine war, alleging incorrectly that Hungary, a NATO ally, had been sending tanks to Ukraine.[109]

Russian-funded and trained paramilitaries exist throughout Central and Eastern Europe. The Hungarian liberal think tank Political Capital issued a series of reports showing that Russia has supported far-right and paramilitary organizations in Czechia, Slovakia, and other EU countries. From 2013 to 2015, far-right paramilitary organizations were founded in Czechia with pro-Russia foreign policy stances and Facebook pages, including the Czechoslovak Soldiers in Reserve and National Home Guard, whose leaders visited the Donetsk People's Republic. Starting in 2010, a number of Slovak paramilitary organizations began to align themselves with Russia, and new organizations were founded. One of their main activities has been to spread Russian propaganda and disinformation through their websites and Facebook pages. Poland's minister of defense Antoni Macierewicz, of the Law and Justice Party, who supported the development of nationalist paramilitary organizations in Poland, was accused of ties to Russia before being dismissed in a government reshuffle in 2018.[110]

Russia also maintains troops in Transnistria, a breakaway republic of Moldova where Russia prevented Moldova from exerting control in a short war in 1991, as well as in Belarus and Armenia. Russia used Belarus as a staging ground for its 2022 invasion of Ukraine. Armenia welcomes Russian troop presence to deter conflict with Azerbaijan, though this proved of limited use when Azerbaijan took back Nagorno-Karabakh in 2023.

Russia occasionally uses limited force against the United States and United Kingdom as well, though it does not engage in anything like its military invasions of Ukraine or Georgia. Russia deployed its GRU military intelligence agency to launch a nerve agent attack on a former spy, Sergei Skripal, in the United Kingdom in 2018, a highly unusual deployment of chemical weapons in Europe. The United States announced it has evidence that Russia launched a sonic or microwave attack on its embassy staff and their families in Cuba and China that resulted in brain damage.[111] Such attacks are meant to warn and frighten Western states while maintaining a façade of deniability.

TOOLS OF HYBRID WAR

In summary, Russia has developed a wide range of tools, from covert operations to media influence campaigns, cyberwarfare, energy blackmail, and military action, to undermine the European Union and NATO, to deter these institutions from exerting influence in lands in between, and to divide Europe from the United States. Starting in the mid-2000s with the gas cutoffs to Ukraine and the Russo-Georgian war, and particularly after Russia's covert invasion of Ukraine in 2014, people in the West have become more aware of the tools and techniques of Russian influence. At the same time, Russia's hybrid war has been designed to create a façade of plausible deniability. For instance, when Russia is accused of fostering violent extremism in the West, it can claim that it did not create populism or xenophobic nationalism in the West, anti-immigrant sentiment, or resentments between Hungarians and Ukrainians. It simply inflamed these divisions in Europe and North America, using a variety of techniques. This leads many to doubt whether Russian influence or intervention exists or matters very much. Still, Russia's hybrid war has helped to polarize politics in the West along a number of fault lines, to destabilize, to warn, and to control.

Knowing what we know now about Russia's hybrid war, it is hard to regard it as anything but an all-out assault on Western institutions, conducted largely by covert methods to escape notice and avoid provoking a strong response. As Mark Galeotti writes, "Russia is indeed waging an essentially political struggle against the West through political subversion, economic penetration, espionage, and disinformation."[112] While Russian efforts to undermine the West are often decentralized and give off a somewhat disorganized air, Galeotti concludes that they are in fact centrally coordinated, most likely by President Putin himself. A wide array of Russian agencies participates, with limited central control and a lot of room for experimentation, competing with one another to please the boss. They pursue different objectives and priorities in different countries. Yet Galeotti writes that, "insofar as there is a command-and-control node, it is within the Presidential Administration, which is perhaps the most important single organ within Russia's highly de-institutionalised state."[113]

Still today, the West still struggles to understand and address the determined Russian assault on our institutions of government and international relations through this hybrid war. In the next chapter, I will show why the West responded so slowly after 2007, but also show that, once the danger became known, Western institutions did respond vigorously, presenting a remarkably united front in the face of newly perceived Russian threats. The EU and NATO have been no passive victims of Russia's hybrid attacks but have retaliated in ways that have been painful for Russia, even taking some pages from Russia's playbook.

THE WEST'S BELATED

RESPONSE

THE WEST'S RESPONSE TO RUSSIA'S hybrid war was slow in coming. While the Russian invasion of Georgia in 2008 gave ample warning that Russia would oppose, by military force if necessary, Western attempts to integrate countries in its near abroad, it was not until 2012 that Western leaders began to realize that Russia had launched a major political assault on Western institutions. During the Medvedev presidency, from 2008 to 2012, many Western leaders believed that Russia was moving in a liberal direction.[1] The covert nature and plausible deniability of Russian attacks enabled this perception, playing into the West's unwillingness to come to terms with an unpleasant reality. However, when Putin returned to power in 2012,[2] and particularly after Russia's invasion of Crimea in 2014, things changed. A powerful Western multilateral response finally began to materialize. The West deployed its vast economic superiority, as the United States and European Union coordinated economic sanctions on Russia and the EU pushed for energy diversification in Europe. NATO deployed rapid response battalions in Central and Eastern Europe to signal that it would mobilize to prevent another invasion.[3] And in terms of values and objectives, the West never gave up on its vision of a Europe "whole and free." The result of its relatively decisive action, however, has been not to scare Russia off, but rather to deepen a geopolitical divide in Europe and intensify a game of tug-of-war between Russia and the West over the lands in between. Some argue that it was not enough and that only arming Ukraine would have worked.[4] But the West preferred to use economic tools in the hope of avoiding a direct military confrontation with Russia.

DELAYED REACTION

The most striking success of Russia's hybrid war on the West has been the failure of Western leaders to recognize it from 2008 to 2012. The West "missed the warning signs" that it was facing an all-out political offensive from Russia.[5] It ignored evidence that Russia was pulling back from economic integration with the EU.[6] The George W. Bush administration ignored Russia's cyberattack on Estonia in 2007.[7] Western leaders surely noticed the gas cutoffs to Ukraine in 2006 and 2009 that limited supplies to some home markets. They heard President Vladimir Putin's speech at the Munich Security Conference in 2007 that railed against a unipolar world led by the United States.[8] And they experienced the Russo-Georgian war of 2008. Yet, in the face of these realities, many Western leaders continued to believe that Russia remained on a path toward political and economic modernization. Germany in particular, whose leaders suffered from a deep sense of guilt toward Russia for the crimes their country committed against Russia during World War II, continued to feel that the best way to deal with Russia was to invest in a "modernization partnership." Over time, they believed, economic partnership would win out as Russia modernized its resource-dependent economy,[9] liberalized its politics, and sought peaceful coexistence with the West. This was reflected in the EU's approach to the Russo-Georgian war, which was to accept Russia's annexation of Georgian territory while offering ineffectual EU peacekeepers, papering over the conflict after a visit from French president Nicolas Sarkozy. Many Western leaders did not want to rock the boat, did not understand the stakes, and assumed that the long-term trajectory was positive.

Why did it take so long for the West to realize that Russia had launched an offensive against the Western international system?

It is possible that Western leaders suffered from "end of history" thinking, a perception that the forward progress of Western capitalism and liberal democracy was inevitable.[10] Many in the West did not believe that Russia would reject the Western orientation of Mikhail Gorbachev and Boris Yeltsin and revert to a former Soviet outlook. Few took Putin literally when he said that the collapse of the Soviet Union was the greatest geopolitical catastrophe of the twentieth century. Fewer still thought that he wanted to create Soviet Union 2.0. "The West found it easier at the time to disregard [warning signs] and indulge in the fantasy that Russia was progressing toward a liberal-democratic model with which the West felt comfortable."[11] From a business perspective, it certainly seemed as if Russia remained Western-oriented. Western companies flooded Russia with investment in the period 2010–14, never imagining that they were feeding an enemy determined to destroy the West. In one extreme example, German security firm Rheinmetall built a $140 million combat simulation training center in Russia in 2011 to train Russian special forces, never thinking that these forces would be used to annex Crimea or fight against Western interests in Syria. Germany pulled out of this relationship only in 2014, as its "modernization partnership" backfired spectacularly.[12]

A second factor was Western leaders' failure to see through the misleading optics of the Medvedev presidency from 2008 to 2012, discussed earlier. Medvedev was a smooth operator with good language skills; he knew how to talk to Western leaders and was welcomed warmly in the West. Although Western

governments realized that Putin wielded power from the side-
lines, US president Barack Obama, German chancellor Angela
Merkel, and other Western leaders treated Medvedev as the real
president of Russia, in the hope that he would one day sideline
Putin and encourage Russia to progress in a more liberal direction. Yet Putin remained firmly in charge. Medvedev got his
start as Putin's assistant,[13] and his assistant he remained.

A third factor in the West's failure to perceive Russia's hybrid war has been the plausible deniability created by Russia's
use of disinformation and covert methods. Many in the West
believed Russia's contention that it had invaded Georgia in a
defensive operation designed to protect the South Ossetians.
In fact, Russia intentionally provoked the war by using South
Ossetian militias to bomb Georgian towns. Georgia unwisely
responded to this provocation, and Russia invaded as planned.[14]
Yet after the war, Russia managed to convince French president
Nicholas Sarkozy, representing the European Union, to support Russia's peace plan for the region. Similar disinformation
tactics were used in the Crimea invasion in 2014, which was
conducted by "little green men"—soldiers wearing uniforms
with no insignia—who were not readily identifiable as Russian
military until after they had gained control of the peninsula.
As one Dutch think tank report put it, "The Georgia War was
not a one-time exception. It turned out to be just a step in
President Putin's campaign to restore the international gran-
deur of Russia."[15] Western leaders did not fully appreciate this
early enough.

Finally, there is the question of self-interest. Western
countries faced powerful economic incentives to improve and
deepen relations with Putin's Russia. Few in the West wanted
to acknowledge the existence of a hybrid war that would disrupt business relations and force countries to increase military
expenditures. Many Western companies piled into Russia, a
fast-growing, emerging economy, just as Russia was ramping

up its hybrid war on the West. Inward investment into Russia boomed in the 2000s.[16] Russia used Western eagerness to participate in Russian growth to raise money for its companies through minority stock offerings and to develop close relations with powerful businesspeople and interest groups in the West. Russia created business councils in Germany, France, and many other Western countries that Russia could deploy to spread pro-Russia sentiments within Europe and bolster anti-Americanism.[17] Russia's strong links with European energy companies effectively turned executives into "lobbyists for the Kremlin, leaning on their governments to put their national interests above a unified European energy strategy."[18] Russia used a cresting wave of foreign investment to fund its ambitious foreign policy agenda—with Western support.

For a variety of reasons, Western leaders fooled themselves about Russian intentions, ignored experts and analysts ringing alarm bells about Russia's political war on the West, and remained bullish on Russia and its prospects of integration with the West until 2012.[19] President Obama launched a hopeful "reset" of relations with Russia from 2009 to 2011, despite overwhelming evidence that Russia had abandoned the West and embarked on a Eurasian adventure.[20] German chancellor Angela Merkel remained committed to the modernization partnership with Russia until 2012.[21]

THE END OF PARTNERSHIP

This changed when Vladimir Putin returned to the presidency in 2012. After Russian parliamentary elections in 2011 that gave the appearance of being rigged, thousands of protesters appeared on the streets in Moscow and St. Petersburg demanding fair elections and calling for an end to the Putin regime.[22] Putin reacted by tightening control and working harder to rig the

2012 presidential election. He developed a deep resentment toward US Secretary of State Hillary Clinton, whom he accused of organizing and supporting the protests.[23] For Western leaders who had embraced the view that Medvedev represented a more liberal future for Russia, Putin's "return" to power came as a shock. In May 2012, *Der Spiegel*, the leading German magazine, wrote that Chancellor Angela Merkel "felt hoodwinked. She was forced to realize that the man she had placed such great hopes in [Medvedev] was merely a Putin puppet."[24] Led by Germany, the EU began to reassess its approach toward Russia.

Even then, few in the West were prepared to believe the outlandish claim that a relatively poor, weak Russia was attempting to destroy the European Union and NATO and divide the United States from its European allies. During the 2012 US presidential election campaign, President Obama mocked his Republican opponent, Mitt Romney, for labeling Russia America's greatest strategic enemy. During the third presidential debate in 2012, President Obama jested that "the 1980s are now calling to ask for their foreign policy back because the Cold War's been over for 20 years."[25] Obama won reelection on a policy of not worrying too much about Russia. Though he imposed sanctions on Russia after the 2014 invasion of Crimea, the Obama administration underestimated the Russian threat throughout the 2016 election campaign, despite evidence of a massive influence operation waged by Russian intelligence.[26]

It was only after the Maidan protests in Ukraine in late 2013 and the Russian invasion of Crimea and the Donbas in 2014 that most European Union leaders began to see Russia as a "strategic problem" rather than a "strategic partner," in the words of EU Council president Donald Tusk, a former Polish prime minister.[27]

The troubles began in 2013, when Russia pressured Ukraine's president, Viktor Yanukovich, not to sign a Deep and Comprehensive Free Trade Agreement (DCFTA) with the EU at a summit in Vilnius. Yanukovich's government had pains-takingly negotiated this agreement over a two-year period and gave every appearance of being ready to sign, ushering Ukraine into a new era of prosperity with greater access to EU markets and investment. Yet, having vetoed Ukraine's progress toward NATO membership in 2008, Putin wished to veto Ukraine's economic integration into the EU as well. Shortly before the summit, Yanukovich was summoned to Moscow and prom-ised $15 billion in emergency economic assistance as well as lower gas prices if Ukraine canceled its participation in the Vilnius summit where the EU free trade agreement was to be signed.[28] Yanukovich agreed, setting off street protests in Kyiv's Maidan Square to demand that the government keep Ukraine on a path to European integration. During the protests, called "Euromaidan," protesters waved EU flags, exhibiting a stun-ning belief in the economic benefits of EU integration at a time when the EU suffered from a sovereign debt and internal crisis of confidence.

After repeated attempts over several months to disperse protesters and tear down their fiercely defended barricades, spawning street battles that captured international media at-tention, the Yanukovich government decided to fire on pro-testers on February 18, 2014, in a botched attempt to use overwhelming force. At the same time, armed opposition to the government grew, and EU leaders stepped in to nego-tiate and prevent an emerging civil war. The French, German, and Polish foreign ministers brokered a deal on February 21, 2014, for President Yanukovich to resign after six months and make way for a transitional government and new elections.[29] However, this deal collapsed soon after it was inked, when President Yanukovich fled to Russia, worried for his personal safety and no longer commanding the allegiance of the armed forces.[30] Russia declared that Yanukovich had been removed in a "coup" and decided to invade Crimea a few days later, right after the closing ceremony of the Sochi Olympics, when President Putin returned to Moscow.[31] As "little green men" appeared on the streets of Crimea, Russia used its Sevastopol naval base, home of Russia's Black Sea fleet under a long-term lease agreement with Ukraine, to take over the peninsula in a rapid and well-planned military operation. Western leaders, shocked by the invasion—and then annexation—of part of a sovereign European state, began to see the Russian threat for what it was and respond in kind.

THE WEST PUSHES BACK

In 2014, most Western leaders finally acknowledged that something had changed in Russia and began to push back. Russia, which had not met much resistance before then, was taken aback, particularly by the German reaction. Germany had long been an advocate of treating Russia as a partner. According to one 2015 report published by a Russian government think tank, the Russian International Affairs Council, "Germany's position with respect to Russia's policy proved to be much tougher than expected," and, as a result, Europe achieved an unexpected level of unity on sanctions against Russia.[32] Why did the West respond so much more vigorously to an annexation of part of Ukraine than to a similar de facto annexation of parts of Georgia in 2008? Perhaps because Ukraine was a large state, more centrally located in Europe. Perhaps because of the extensive media coverage of the Maidan protests, which reminded viewers of the revolutions of 1989. Perhaps because this was Putin's war, not Medvedev's. Whatever the reason, something broke in Russia's relations with the West in 2014. And the divide only worsened after revelations of Russian intervention in elections in France, Germany, and the United States in 2016.

A growing chorus of Western leaders began to argue that Russia was fighting a hybrid war on Western political and international institutions to debilitate the West from the inside, causing usage of the term "hybrid war" to spike.[33] US, EU, and allied economic sanctions seriously jolted the Russian economy. In total, thirty-seven countries representing 55 percent of world GDP imposed sanctions on Russia, starting in March 2014.[34] EU energy regulations (see below) began to bite as the EU sued Gazprom, Russia's state-owned gas company, to enforce market rules that would ensure supplies without disruption.[35] A reenergized NATO took measures to shore up its defensive posture in the Baltic states and Central Europe, creating a Very High Readiness Joint Task Force and increasing the size of its NATO Response Force from 19,000 to 40,000 troops.[36] And the West continued to support democratization and Western integration for the lands in between.

Meanwhile, Russia continued to intensify its own efforts, leading to a sharpening of geopolitical conflict after 2014.[37] Thus began a battle to the finish. Either Western institutions would collapse, giving a victory to Putin's Russia, or they would outlast his regime. The pressure building up between the two sides was felt most acutely in the lands in between Russia and the West, small, vulnerable states of the former Soviet Union that were caught between two worlds enmeshed in a hybrid war.

Sanctions

By far the most important element of the Western response to Russia's hybrid war has been economic sanctions. Since the West controls a far greater share of world gross domestic product (GDP) than Russia, approximately twenty-five times more,[38] it can impose serious costs on Russia without much worry of retaliation. By fighting Russia through sanctions, the West sought to avoid military engagement due to Russia's status as a nuclear power. In March 2014, Western countries imposed a first wave of sanctions on Russia in response to its annexation of Crimea. Since that time, scholars and analysts have debated how effective economic sanctions have been and whether they have worked to deter Russia. This is a complicated debate, with many aspects to consider, but in brief, the evidence suggests that sanctions have had a significant impact on the Russian economy.[39] Sanctions sent a strong signal to Russia of Western resolve. But they have not persuaded Russia to back down. To the contrary, painful sanctions only intensified Russia's urgency to undermine Western institutions. Russian analyst Ilya Matveev's study of the sanctions imposed after Russia's 2022 invasion of Ukraine concludes that

> sanctions against Russia represent an unprecedented weaponization of economic ties. In their scale and significance, they are comparable to the Russo-Ukrainian war itself, which is the biggest military conflict in Europe since the Second World War. The long-term impact of sanctions on the Russian economy will be devastating, even though they have not—and probably cannot— end the war or trigger regime change in Russia.[40]

Western sanctions against Russia can be divided into three types: sanctions that punish specific individuals thought to be involved in Russian aggression, sectoral sanctions that target specific sectors of the Russian economy, and economy-wide sanctions that seek to isolate Russia from the international economy. Targeted individual sanctions punish high-level decision-makers, freezing their assets in the West and imposing travel bans, without much collateral damage to average Russian citizens. Sectoral sanctions force the general population to reckon with the costs of aggression by cutting off vital economic sectors, such as energy or finance, from the global economy. Economy-wide sanctions target the entire economy, imposing a maximal cost, seeking to render Russia a pariah state.

For the most part, the Crimea sanctions in 2014 were of the first type. A long list of Western countries (plus Japan), led by the United States and European Union, imposed sanctions on a list of Russian officials connected to the Crimea invasion, freezing their assets and banning them from travel to the West. Additionally, the Crimea sanctions banned Western companies from doing business in occupied Crimea and stopped cruise ships from docking at Crimean ports. Visa and Mastercard, among other companies, withdrew from Crimea.

When these sanctions failed to prevent Russia's invasion of eastern Ukraine in 2014, Western countries coordinated to impose sanctions on specific sectors of the Russian economy, helping to send the Russian economy into recession in 2015–16. These sectoral sanctions banned leading Russian banks from accessing international markets, limited Western companies' investment in Russian oil and gas exploration, and banned trade and investment in military equipment and services. These sectoral sanctions caused a sharp decline in Western investment and business activity in Russia. Inward investment into Russia declined precipitously from $53 billion in 2013 to $12 billion in 2015.[41]

When existing sanctions failed to deter Russia's 2022 full-scale invasion of Ukraine, Western and allied Asian (Japan, Korea, Taiwan) countries imposed much more severe sanctions on the Russian economy. According to one analyst,[42] "Never before has an economy of this size been subjected to such a sweeping blockade." A centerpiece was cutting off the Russian central bank from international banking systems and freezing the $300–400 billion of Russia's foreign currency reserves held in sanctioning countries. The sanctions were "limited only by the capacity of their own economies to cut off ties with Russia, primarily in terms of energy imports." European countries closed their airspace to Russian planes and their ports to Russian ships. More than a thousand Western companies stopped doing business in Russia. These sanctions severely damaged the Russian economy, sending it into a deep recession. Almost all car plants in the country stopped working since they relied on imports of foreign parts. Hundreds of thousands of skilled professionals left the country. EU countries restricted tourist visas for Russian citizens and debated an outright ban.

While sanctions punished the Russian economy, they did little to deter Russian aggression. Therefore, should we regard this economic warfare as a failure? I think not. First, economic sanctions sent a strong signal of Western unity. In 2014, Russia had not anticipated that Western sanctions would be as severe as they were, as coordinated, or as long-lived.[43] After all, the EU had dropped the idea of imposing sanctions after the 2008 Russo-Georgian war when Russia threatened to cut energy supplies.[44] Russia expected a similarly frail response in 2014, believing that the European Union—Russia's largest trade and investment partner—would not be able to maintain coordinated sanctions on Russia for any substantial length of time, especially since all twenty-eight (now twenty-seven) member states had to vote to renew sanctions every six months, and it was widely known that several EU countries had become Russia's "Trojan horses" within the EU, openly opposing the sanctions regime.[45] Yet sanctions endured for years, with US support and encouragement, and in the face of Russian war atrocities.

Europe's sanctions endured because smaller states that opposed sanctions deferred to the Big Three powers in the European Union—Germany, France, and the UK (at that time, the UK was still a member)—on foreign policy matters. The Big Three had begun to recognize the seriousness of the Russian threat by 2014. Britain had long accused the Putin regime of assassinating émigrés in London, such as Alexander Litvinenko, who was poisoned in November 2006 by the radioactive isotope polonium-210. Its radioactive trail was traced back to Moscow.[46] As a result of this and other issues, Britain had long had a poor relationship with Russia and was skeptical of the Putin regime. France and Germany had taken a softer line toward Moscow prior to 2012, but Chancellor Angela Merkel and other German leaders grew increasingly concerned with Russia's return to authoritarian rule. German leaders objected strenuously to Russia's crackdown on human rights, anti-gay legislation, and harsh imprisonment of members of the Russian protest rock group Pussy Riot. After the annexation of Crimea, Germany made clear that "no partnership can work without a core set of shared values."[47] Merkel was disillusioned that President Putin, with whom she had frequent phone conversations, had lied about key facts, including whether Russia had troops in Crimea. She told President Obama that Putin appeared to have lost his grip on reality and was living "in another world."[48] In 2014, Germany rallied European support for economic sanctions. French president François Hollande also condemned Russia's annexation of Crimea in March 2014 and promised a "strong and coordinated" EU response.[49]

Leaders of other EU states followed, either because they agreed, did not want to be seen as spoilers of a common European foreign policy, or were subject to pressure and logrolling by the Big Three. Greece is a case in point. Despite Greek prime minister Alexis Tsipras holding a press conference in Athens with President Putin on May 28, 2016, and calling sanctions "not productive," Tsipras's government voted to renew sanctions on Russia a few days later, under threat of losing a vital EU rescue package for Greece's ailing economy. In 2018, a far-right Italian government came to power criticizing Russia sanctions. In October 2018, Italian prime minister Giuseppe Conte labeled Russia a "strategic partner," invited Putin to Italy, and called for "dialogue" to replace EU sanctions.[50] But ultimately, Conte's government continued to vote in favor of EU sanctions every six months, though at a press conference with his Russian counterparts, Conte said that it made him "sad."[51]

Russian atrocities also generated European support for sanctions, especially the downing of Malaysia Airlines flight MH-17 on July 17, 2014. En route from Amsterdam to Kuala Lumpur, MH-17 was shot down over rebel-held territory in eastern Ukraine by a Russian-made BUK missile. The death toll of 298 mainly Dutch passengers and crew members included many top scientists traveling to an international AIDS conference in Melbourne, Australia.[52] MH-17 brought home to Europeans that there was a war raging in Europe that could not be ignored. It cast Russian-supported rebels as the bad guys. Footage of rebels sifting through passengers' personal effects in the debris while failing to secure the crash site or allow access to investigators left a very bad impression in the West, as did President Putin's denial of responsibility for deploying the BUK missile that brought down the plane.[53] More than anything before, this episode severed trust between Russian and European leaders.

The downing of MH-17 had a particular effect on the Netherlands, Russia's largest trading partner in the EU. Much of Russia's oil was refined in Rotterdam and shipped from there to the world. Although the Netherlands had been very reluctant to support a hard line against Russia in the past due to its strong business interests with Russia, the MH-17 incident forced the Dutch to support the call for sanctions. As Dutch foreign minister Frans Timmermans blamed Russia for the BUK missile attack and made an emotional appeal for justice at the United Nations,[54] the European Union joined the United States and other nations in imposing sanctions targeting key Russian enterprises in the financial and energy sectors. They banned the export of arms and dual-use technologies to Russia, restricted the issuance of financial instruments on behalf of Russian companies, and placed controls on oil-drilling technology exports to Russia. The Western community of nations displayed a common front, something Russia had not anticipated.

Beyond a display of unity, Western sanctions imposed a substantial cost on Russia's economy. After the second round of sectoral sanctions in July 2017, Russia's previously fast-growing economy sank into a sustained recession. Following years of dynamic economic growth, the Russian economy grew by only 0.7 percent in 2014 before shrinking by 2.8 percent in 2015 and 0.2 percent in 2016. Capital flowed out of the country. Net outflows totaled $152 billion in 2014, $59 billion in 2015, and $15 billion in 2016, exceeding the amount of capital that flew out of Russia during the global financial crisis in 2009. The Russian ruble devalued by 50 percent versus the US dollar in 2015, and inflation jumped from 6.8 percent in 2013 to 15.5 percent. Russia's government budget deficit widened from 0.9 percent in 2013 to 3.2 percent in 2015, forcing it to tap international reserve funds, which dropped from almost $500 billion at the start of 2014 to $368 billion at the end of 2015. Overall, the 2014–16 recession had a more enduring impact on Russia than the global financial crisis of 2009. The sanctions regime forced analysts, investors, and Russian officials to question whether high growth would return.[55]

Russia responded to the West's 2014 sanctions with countersanctions of its own.[56] Unable or unwilling to retaliate against its major customer, the European Union, with an oil and gas cutoff, Russia instead retaliated with a ban on the import of food and agricultural products. The worst-affected states were neighboring countries that exported a high proportion of their agricultural products to Russia. Polish apple farmers, Danish and Latvian dairy farmers, and Norwegian fisheries were badly hit.[57] Products such as French cheese, Norwegian salmon, and Hungarian salami quickly disappeared from Russian shops, to be replaced with Belarusian or Russian substitutes. Russia undertook dramatic enforcement actions against smuggling, destroying tons of imported food that made their way into Russia after the sanctions were imposed. President Putin stated that the sanctions would be good for Russian domestic producers, helping to build local industry. He later invested in import substitution projects throughout the economy.[58]

However, Russian countersanctions also had a devastating impact on Russian household budgets. According to one group of Russian academic researchers, food prices rose dramatically in 2014 and 2015, and "household spending associated with the acquisition of food and non-food products, transport, medical care, [and] housing services have risen sharply." As a result, consumers focused their spending on essential items and saved any additional funds.[59] While inflation in Russia peaked at 15.5 percent in 2015,[60] prices for some food items rose much more dramatically. Overall, food inflation reached an average of 21 percent in 2015.[61] As a result, discretionary spending plummeted. The number of Russians in poverty rose by 3.1 million to 19.2 million in 2015, a total of 13.4 percent of the population.[62]

Western sanctions hit Russia at the same time as oil prices dropped sharply after Saudi Arabia decided to punish Russia for failing to reach an agreement on limiting oil production. The Saudis flooded world markets in an attempt to win market share. Oil prices plummeted from approximately $100 per barrel in July 2014 to $40 per barrel in February 2016. These simultaneous shocks damaged the Russian economy. Economists have estimated that approximately two-thirds of the damage was done by oil price drops and one-third by sanctions. The International Monetary Fund (IMF) estimated that sanctions were costing the Russian economy about 1.0–1.5 percent of GDP per year, or a total of 9.0 percent over the medium term, approximately $123 billion.[63] President Putin stated in November 2016 that the sanctions are "severely harming Russia" in terms of access to international financial markets, although the impact was not as severe as the decline in energy prices.[64]

Russia's intervention in the US presidential election in 2016 led to a third round of sanctions from the United States alone. In 2017, the US Congress passed tough new sanctions on Russia, Iran, and North Korea. New legislation gave the US president sweeping powers to sanction any company worldwide doing business with a sanctioned Russian company. Among other things, the law enabled the president to sanction companies involved in new gas pipeline deals with Russia. Europeans opposed these sanctions, worrying about their effect on the vital energy trade with Russia and, in particular, the Nord Stream 2 pipeline project. In 2018, the United States added Putin-connected oligarchs and their companies to the list of sanctioned entities, including Oleg Deripaska and his company Rusal, the dominant force in Russia's aluminum industry and exports. This extension of the sanctions regime to Putin-connected oligarchs and their companies further damaged Russia's reputation and changed perceptions about whether Russia's economic ties with the West would recover. A leading Putin aide, Vladislav Surkov, wrote that "Russia's epic journey toward the West" was over, marking an end to its "repeated fruitless attempts to become a part of Western civilization" over four centuries.[65] As discussed above, the economic impact of sanctions imposed after Russia's 2022 invasion of Ukraine was greater still.

Despite the surprising unity shown by Western states, many analysts have questioned whether sanctions effectively altered Russia's behavior. Russia's 2022 invasion of Ukraine showed that the answer is obviously not. Sanctions did not cause Russia to reevaluate its hybrid war on the West. In fact, Russia appeared to accelerate and intensify its interventions in democratic elections in Western countries after 2014. Sanctions did not deter President Putin from invading Ukraine in 2022 or denying Ukrainian independence and sovereignty in his July 2021 article "On the Historical Unity of Russians and Ukrainians."[66] Sanctions only imposed a cost for undertaking such actions, a cost that Russia anticipated and prepared for. Some argued that sanctions merely hurt innocent Russian civilians and blocked opportunities for trade and investment that would benefit the West.[67] Others contended that only a military response would have been effective.[68] But there remains another possibility: that nothing would have deterred Russia from invading Ukraine. Sanctions may not have achieved their desired goals, but they remain an important signal of unified opposition and an effective means of imposing costs on an aggressor. The alternative—no response—might have produced worse results.

Sanctions imposed in 2022 by leading economies to punish Russia for its full-scale invasion of Ukraine have incited similar controversies. These sanctions are truly debilitating, making it nearly impossible for Russian companies to access Western capital markets or trade. Yet Russia has succeeded in redirecting its trade to countries like China and India and evading Western sanctions using third-country intermediaries. Some analysts again suggest that sanctions are not working, since the wartime Russian economy continues to grow. Yet the value of the Russian ruble remains between a half and a third of what it was in 2014. And while wartime production can stimulate an economy, EU High Representative for Foreign and Security Policy Josep Borrell contends that EU sanctions have "limited Moscow's political and economic options, causing financial strain, cutting the country from key markets, increasing the costs of trading and significantly degrading Russia's industrial capacity."[69]

While the debate on sanctions rages in the West, it must be noted that sanctions are not the only measure Western governments and institutions have taken to respond to Russia's hybrid war on the West. One of the most important EU countermeasures escaped notice until recently: Europe's push to unify its energy markets and ensure the security of its energy supplies.

Energy Union

The great irony of Russia's assault on the EU and NATO is that Russia has relied heavily on Europe for its foreign trade revenues. Prior to 2022, Europe was by far Russia's largest market for hydrocarbons, particularly for natural gas, distributed primarily through pipelines to contiguous territories. Nearly 80 percent of Russian gas was sold in the EU, with most of the rest going to Turkey and the lands in between. Russia also depended on the EU for its crude oil exports, much of which was refined in the Dutch port of Rotterdam before being exported to the world.[70] In 2014, Russia supplied more than 30 percent of the EU's crude oil and natural gas; it was Europe's largest energy supplier.[71] Russia's dependency on the EU for refineries and trade complicated its ability to project power over EU states through energy geopolitics.[72]

Russia's strategy to address its dependence on European markets was to divide and rule. Russia understood that if the EU ever banded together in a buyers' consortium, it would have tremendous pricing power. Therefore, Russia preferred to make special deals with individual countries, bypassing common EU regulation. Russia realized that "a common EU policy would foster diversification of sources and unbundle national utilities, in the process cutting profit margins and reducing Gazprom's incentives to buy European companies. It would also weaken bilateral special relationships with Russia."[73] Some European countries were more dependent on Russian gas than others. Finland and some East European countries depended almost entirely on Russian gas for home heating; Russia used its power in these markets to charge higher prices. Until recently, European countries paid very different prices for Russian gas, based on their specific relationship with the Kremlin and other political criteria.[74]

However, Russia's gas disputes with Ukraine in the 2000s caused alarm bells to ring in Europe and pushed EU policy-makers to take steps toward an EU-wide energy market. In 2006 and 2009, Russia cut off gas supplies to Ukraine in a dispute over back payments. Since most of Europe's pipeline gas traveled through Ukraine, these cutoffs threatened the energy security of the European Union, one of the largest economies in the world. Several EU member states faced supply disruptions and some were forced to tap reserves or ration gas. To the corporate captains of EU industry, this was an intolerable situation. EU leaders realized they needed to protect their economies from excessive reliance on Russian gas.[75]

Russia's gas cutoffs to Ukraine led to the passage of an EU "third energy package" in 2009, followed by an Energy Union in 2015.[76] The third energy package mostly consisted of measures that had previously been proposed in Brussels, but had met with stiff opposition from German and French energy companies that wanted to protect dominant positions in their home markets. Russia's gas geopolitics, however, generated a consensus long lacking in Europe to further integrate EU energy markets to limit price differentials and ensure energy security.

The third energy package—and the later Energy Union—employed two basic methods to respond to Russia's attempts to divide and rule European energy markets: first, connecting European energy grids and gas pipeline networks to enable resource sharing across national boundaries, and second, developing alternative supplies and ensuring that no country is dependent on any individual supplier. In a 2014 statement, EU energy commissioner Günther Oettinger declared, "We want a uniform gas price in the European common market. The game of 'divide et impera' (divide and rule), or a game of this type proposed by Moscow cannot be and will not be accepted by EU member states."[77]

Interconnectors were relatively inexpensive to build but had a massive impact on countries that previously relied on a single source of gas or electricity, such as Finland and many CEE countries. Overreliance on one supplier was potentially disastrous in a crisis and opened countries to energy blackmail. Russia's 2009 gas cutoff to Ukraine had forced Bulgaria, an EU member state, to cut off gas supplies to industrial users. Under the third energy package, Bulgaria sought to enable reverse flows at the Greek border and build an interconnector with Romania under the Danube River. After delays in construction, the project was taken over by an Austrian company in 2016 and completed in 2022.[78] In contrast, Czechia quickly built interconnectors that enabled it to survive the 2009 cutoff and reduce prices dramatically. In 2014, gas prices at Czechia's main hub were 30 percent higher than in the Netherlands. By 2017, prices had converged. A similar process took place across the EU. Now, nearly all EU pipelines, as well as those running through Ukraine, can handle reverse flows. Building interconnectors "changed the status quo forever." Increasingly, pipeline gas in Europe is priced in connection with spot markets, not long-term contracts.[79] One study showed that the variance of gas prices between EU countries in 2017 dropped to one-quarter of 2014 levels.[80] Russia's ability to punish or reward countries with higher or lower gas prices was greatly diminished, eliminating a key tool of Russian geopolitical strategy.

A second feature of the third energy package and Energy Union was to diversify supplies by constructing new pipelines and liquefied natural gas (LNG) terminals at strategic points around the continent. Liquification enables natural gas to be loaded into tanker ships and transported from Qatar, North Africa, the United States, and elsewhere to Europe. While Spain and other southern European countries already had LNG terminals, countries reliant on cheaper Russian pipeline gas initially had none. LNG is more expensive than pipeline gas thanks to the high costs of compressing gas at super-cold temperatures and transporting it in special tanker ships. However, an LNG terminal ensures continuity of supply, which can be invaluable. Lithuania and Poland were the first East European countries to build new LNG terminals after 2009 with EU support. Lithuania pointedly named its terminal "Independence." Finland, also reliant on Russian gas, developed plans for several terminals.[81] Russia's 2022 invasion of Ukraine further accelerated the construction of new LNG terminals, with Germany building a floating terminal at Wilhelmshaven within ten months of the invasion.[82] As EU gas networks became increasingly interconnected, these terminals served neighboring countries as well. Building LNG terminals reinforced the trend away from long-term contracts and toward spot markets, dramatically reducing suppliers' ability to control prices.

In addition to interconnecting networks and diversifying supplies, the EU passed powerful anti-monopoly regulations. The third energy package required companies to "unbundle" electricity and natural gas production from supply and distribution. Russia perceived this as a direct assault on Gazprom's strategy of vertical integration. Gazprom had bought up pipeline networks and distribution companies throughout Europe to control the entire business from gas extraction to supplying the end user. As a result, when the EU's third energy package was announced in 2009 and implemented in 2011, Russia launched an open campaign against it.[83] As Ukrainian Opposition Bloc lawmaker Yuliya Lovochkina put it in 2017, "The third energy package is seen as a threat to Russia."[84] It also invalidated clauses in existing contracts that prevented recipient countries from reexporting gas.

Russia raised several objections. First, Russia felt that, as a non-member of the EU, its companies and pipelines should not be bound by EU rules. Second, it argued that unbundling supply, transit, and distribution companies discriminated against Gazprom. Third, Russia insisted that it had long-term contracts with gas consumers that should be enforced and that the prices specified in them were legal. Fourth, it insisted that Russia, as a large supplier, needed preferential access to pipelines to uphold its own contract commitments. Therefore, Russia could not abide by the letter of open-access laws.[85]

The first test of the anti-monopoly provisions of the third energy package came when Lithuania took Gazprom to court to force it to sell its Lithuanian pipeline network as part of "unbundling." Lithuania had suffered from politically motivated Russian gas cutoffs in the past.[86] Though Gazprom protested, it ultimately agreed to sell its Lithuanian assets, not wanting to fall afoul of EU regulations and jeopardize access to its biggest market. This is something that Lithuania could never have achieved on its own. EU regulations hit Russia even harder in 2014 when the EU forced Bulgaria to cancel construction of Russia's South Stream gas pipeline. Russia launched a countersuit with the World Trade Organization. However, ultimately, Gazprom decided that it made more sense to follow EU law than to become a pariah in its largest market. There is little doubt that this shift harmed Gazprom's profitability, which dropped sharply after a decline in world oil prices and the conclusion of the Iraq War.[87]

After starting to divest Gazprom of its European pipeline assets, the EU announced that it would sue Gazprom in 2013 over price gouging in gas contracts with Lithuania and other CEE markets that relied on Russia as their primary supplier.[88] The priciest gas was found in countries where Gazprom dominated the market and Russia had political disagreements with ruling parties. The EU-Gazprom case dragged on for several years but was ultimately settled in May 2018 after Gazprom agreed to drop discriminatory pricing in Europe and eliminate clauses that banned the reexport of Russian gas to third parties.[89] Gazprom acceded to the EU's main demands in exchange for unfettered access to the EU market. Gazprom announced the sale of its Latvian network assets in 2016.

The third energy package sought not to replace Russia as Europe's largest energy supplier, but rather to create common rules for companies operating in European markets. The EU wanted to balance objectives of energy security and maintaining access to an abundant supply of inexpensive Russian gas. Therefore, the EU allowed Gazprom to negotiate privileged access to some pipelines. The EU also exempted new infrastructure projects such as Nord Stream from some anti-monopoly rules, to encourage new investment.

Poland and other transit states had long disputed the wisdom of increasing EU reliance on Russian gas by constructing new pipeline capacity, arguing that it placed existing transit countries at risk of energy blackmail.[90] However, until 2022, the EU continued its policy of increasing access to cheap Russian gas, while diversifying supplies. This reflected a fine balance between the EU states that were worried about overreliance on Russian gas and those that wanted to ensure cheap supplies to boost the EU economy. The third energy package encouraged Russia to continue to sell to the EU market, while making it more difficult for Russia to exert leverage over European countries through gas geopolitics.[91]

Russia's 2022 invasion of Ukraine upended this arrangement. It showed that any reliance on Russia constituted a threat to the Union itself, as CEE states had long argued, and effectively subsidized Russia's invasions of the lands in between. In May 2022, the European Union swiftly published a new strategy, REPowerEU, which aimed to end EU dependence on Russian fossil fuels and simultaneously tackle the climate crisis by reducing energy usage, diversifying supplies, and accelerating the rollout of renewable energy.[92] Whereas the third energy package sought to provide Europe with relatively clean and inexpensive Russian gas, REPowerEU aimed toward a self-reliant green future through increasing investment in domestic renewables.[93] REPowerEU set a goal of 45 percent renewable energy in Europe by 2030. It encouraged member states to reduce energy consumption by 15 percent through conservation measures, cut red tape to approve green energy projects faster, and seek alternative supplies. In the interim, Europe rushed to build LNG terminals to enable gas imports from the United States, Qatar, and other suppliers. Polish prime minister Mateusz Morawiecki saluted the completion of the Baltic Pipe transporting Norwegian gas to Poland via Denmark in 2022, stating, "The era of Russian domination in the field of gas is coming to an end, the era that was marked by blackmail, threats, and extortion."[94] REPowerEU also promised to help Ukraine and other Eastern Partnership countries resist Russian energy blackmail. While gas prices initially spiked after Russia's invasion of Ukraine in February 2022, prices fell sharply after the summer as European countries enacted price caps on Russian oil and gas and LNG import capacity exceeded demand. European countries also compensated or protected consumers from high gas prices.[95]

Countering Russian Propaganda, Disinformation, and Hacking

In contrast to the gas wars in Europe, which the EU appears to have won, Western countries have faced greater difficulties in countering Russian propaganda and disinformation. Democracies find it difficult to ban media sources, even if they distribute Russian government propaganda. Within the European Union and the United States, almost all speech is protected by laws on press freedom and freedom of expression, though the EU did ban Russian government propaganda networks Russia Today and Sputnik in 2022. Ukraine banned all Russian television and social media and even some journalists from its territory for national security reasons, but it is not a member of the EU, where such actions would face scrutiny from the European Court of Justice.

The EU sought to counter Russian propaganda by shoring up cyber defenses, identifying propaganda through public education campaigns, and trying to debunk it. For instance, when Germany was hit with Russian hacking in advance of its parliamentary election in 2017, Chancellor Angela Merkel warned that the election would be undermined by Russia. Hans-Georg Maassen, head of Germany's domestic intelligence agency, announced in 2017, "There's increasing evidence of attempts to influence the election" by Russia. "We expect another jump in cyber-attacks ahead of the vote," he said after Russian hackers tried to gain access to computers belonging to political-party-connected think tanks. Hackers connected to Russian intelligence previously accessed the computer system of the German parliament. Russia's objective was clear: to harm the electoral chances of Angela Merkel, Russia's main opponent in Europe, to bolster Alternative for Germany and other anti-EU parties, and to decrease confidence in elections. According to press reports, Germany responded forcefully:

> Merkel's Christian Democratic Union (CDU) is calling for a law that would allow the country to "hack back" and wipe out attacking servers. The BSI [Federal Office for Information Security] this year is hiring 180 people—from lawyers to coders—and will embed experts with the election watchdog to protect the vote. The agency has set up cybersecurity response teams to clean up after attacks and help infiltrated government agencies keep computer systems from collapsing. In May the BSI held talks with counterparts such as France's online security agency to gather information on thwarting attacks like one that targeted the presidential campaign of Emmanuel Macron.[96]

After Russia's hacking during the US presidential elections in 2016, EU governments began to take Russian covert intervention in elections far more seriously. France's presidential election produced a decisive win for candidate Emmanuel Macron, despite WikiLeaks dumping his emails days before the election.

To call out Russian propaganda and dispel myths, the EU created a strategic communications strategy in 2016. The European Parliament resolution "notes with regret that Russia uses contacts and meetings with EU counterparts for propaganda purposes and to publicly weaken the EU's joint position, rather than for establishing a real dialogue." It further alleges that "the Russian Government is employing a wide range of tools and instruments, such as think tanks and special foundations (e.g. Russkiy Mir), special authorities (Rossotrudnichestvo), multilingual TV stations (e.g. RT), pseudo news agencies and multimedia services (e.g. Sputnik), cross-border social and religious groups, as the regime wants to present itself as the only defender of traditional Christian values, social media and internet trolls to challenge democratic values, divide Europe, gather domestic support and create the perception of failed states in the EU's eastern neighbourhood."[97]

To counteract this, the EU proposed a wide variety of measures, including the creation of an EU Strategic Communication Task Force and the dissemination of its publication *Disinformation Digest*, which challenges the veracity of Russian propaganda. The EU seeks to raise public awareness of propaganda and to develop citizens' ability to discern propaganda from regular news, to encourage quality journalism and journalism training, and to monitor social media and other media sources to encourage good journalism practices. While the EU is still groping toward a comprehensive strategy to counter Russian and other propaganda, it has begun to take concerted action.

The United States has also taken some initial steps in the public domain. The US foreign news agency, Radio Free Europe

/ Radio Liberty, regularly debunks Russian disinformation. In 2020, the US State Department's Global Engagement Center published a useful report on how Russian disinformation works through a "collection of official, proxy, and unattributed communication channels and platforms"—for instance, by finding "obscure Western fringe thinkers and conspiracy theorists" and giving their anti-Western views a broad international platform. It shows that the entire Russian ecosystem, from official government communications to proxy sources to Twitter bots, works together to echo and amplify disinformation.[98] In 2022, however, the US Department of Homeland Security's creation of a Disinformation Governance Board to coordinate its efforts to respond to false information had to be put on hold due to attacks on its inaugural director, Nina Jankowicz, and right-wing accusations that it was a "ministry of truth" that would infringe free speech.[99]

Public companies such as Facebook have come under pressure to regulate political advertisements and prevent the spread of fake news, particularly sponsored by foreign sources. In 2018, Facebook began requiring political advertisers "to state who is paying for the message," and said that "it will verify the identity of the advertiser," making it harder for anonymous trolls to disseminate political messages on the widely used social media site.[100] These efforts remain in their infancy, but much more could be done to strengthen the information space in Western countries and make it less vulnerable to outside attack during election campaigns, while upholding principles of free speech.[101]

Military Responses

Since Russia poses a military threat to Europe, Western countries have increased military spending, preparedness, and coordination to respond to Russia's increasing aggressiveness. Russia has not pursued its war on the West mainly by traditional military means. Rather, Russia hopes to achieve its objectives by influencing or destabilizing the politics of its opponents with minimal use of direct military force.[102] However, direct military action has always been part of the equation, as in Georgia and Ukraine. Generally, Russia has used military force where its overmatched opponents had little chance of resistance and casualties remained low.[103] Though Russia appears to either have changed its approach or miscalculated in its 2022 invasion of Ukraine. Russia frequently threatens nuclear warfare and reminds the West of its nuclear capabilities but shows little sign of wanting a massive conflagration. Instead, Russia uses military threats to intimidate and deter opponents and force them to the negotiating table. Russia likewise sought to blackmail Ukraine with the destruction of Ukraine's Zaporizhzhia nuclear plant in 2022.[104]

Russia also began to take limited military actions against EU and NATO states themselves. Russia has repeatedly penetrated the airspace of the Baltic states, sent submarines into European and North American waters, flown its long-range bombers into UK and US airspace, and buzzed NATO warplanes and warships in the Baltic and Mediterranean Seas. In 2014, shortly after the United States and Canada welcomed Ukrainian president Petro Poroshenko and the United States promised $46 million in non-lethal aid to the Ukrainian military, US and Canadian fighter jets were forced to intercept Russian nuclear-capable long-range bombers flying toward North American airspace.[105] In 2015, Russia threatened to target Danish warships with nuclear missiles if Denmark joined a NATO missile defense program.[106] Since 2014, Russian nuclear-capable bombers have repeatedly flown by or into UK airspace, forcing the Royal Air Force and other European air forces to scramble jet fighters. Russia also sailed an aircraft carrier through the English Channel in 2017.[107]

All of this made NATO states feel less secure, particularly after Russia's invasions of Ukraine in 2014 and 2022. After the 2014 invasion, NATO responded with a range of measures designed to increase confidence in the West's ability to confront a renewed Russian threat. NATO created a Readiness Action Plan that aims "to convey a strong message: that NATO will stand by its members if and when these are threatened—or actually attacked." In 2014 and 2015, NATO devoted sixteen fighter jets to air policing in the Baltic states, began air surveillance flights over eastern NATO territory, sent more patrol ships to the Black, Mediterranean, and Baltic Seas, deployed ground troops to eastern NATO states on a rotational basis, conducted hundreds of NATO / national exercises, created a Very High Readiness Joint Task Force of several thousand troops to respond to an invasion of a NATO state within a few days, and built permanent national command and control stations in the most vulnerable eastern NATO states.[108] Together, these measures were not intended to return to the days of the Cold War, when hundreds of thousands of US troops were stationed in Europe to counter a massive Russian invasion. Nor were they intended to enable NATO to invade Russia. Instead, they sent a clear message that NATO would respond if one of its member states was invaded and that Russia would be fighting NATO militaries, rather than a single national army, as in Georgia or Ukraine. Though some criticized these responses as doing the bare minimum to deter an invasion, they appear to have deterred Russia from invading a NATO country.

NATO's response, however, was hampered by a general decline in military spending in Europe after the end of the Cold War. After the collapse of the Soviet Union, most European countries believed that they faced no serious military threat. While the United States reduced its military spending from 6 percent of GDP in 1989 to 3.6 percent in 2017, spending by European NATO allies dropped from an average of 3 percent in

1989 to 1.5 percent in 2017, below the 2 percent threshold set by NATO.[109] Since 2000, the United States has criticized European states' failure to meet the 2 percent threshold.

US president Donald Trump stepped up that criticism to new levels, threatening that the United States would not support the alliance unless European countries pay up.[110] At the same time, Russia's hybrid war began to change European threat perceptions, so average NATO defense expenditures crept up after 2014, particularly in front-line countries like Poland, the Baltic states, and Romania, which felt most exposed to Russian aggression.[111] Other countries came face-to-face with their lack of preparedness. For instance, after a presumed Russian submarine invaded Swedish waters in 2014, Sweden realized that it could not adequately respond to such a threat because it had scrapped its anti-submarine helicopter program and reduced its naval fleet after the end of the Cold War.[112] After Russia's annexation of Crimea, Sweden and Finland began to consider abandoning their long tradition of neutrality and joining NATO.

Russia's 2022 invasion of Ukraine changed the situation dramatically. Germany announced a major turning point (*Zeitenwende*) in its relations with Russia together with a €100 billion increase in defense expenditures.[113] The European Union immediately provided €2.5 billion in defense assistance to Ukraine through the new European Peace Facility.[114] NATO countries began arming Ukraine in earnest and adopted a new strategic concept, while Sweden and Finland applied for membership. According to NATO, Russia's invasion broke Europe's security architecture, forcing Western countries to bolster their defense preparedness after decades of limited threat perceptions.[115]

In addition to increasing preparedness for a Russian invasion, NATO continued to offer membership to CEE states, despite Russian opposition. Albania and Croatia joined in 2009. Russia fought to prevent Montenegro, a small nation of only

622,000 inhabitants with a strategic location on the Adriatic Sea, from joining NATO. Russian politicians and oligarchs own an estimated 40 percent of the real estate in Montenegro. In 2015, Russia sought an agreement to use Montenegrin ports to refuel and maintain its navy. When Montenegro refused, and elections in October 2016 threatened to bring a new government to power that would join NATO, Russian intelligence operatives planned an election-day coup. The coup failed, however, and Montenegro joined NATO in 2017.[116] NATO also insisted on leaving the door open for any European countries that wanted to join. In the run-up to Russia's 2022 invasion of Ukraine, NATO rejected Russia's demand for a legally binding agreement that Ukraine would never join the alliance. NATO remained dedicated to a European security architecture in which individual countries can choose their own alliances, without coercion from larger states—its so-called open-door policy.[117]

However, Western resolve did not deter Russia. Instead, it further aggravated Russia and caused it to intensify its hybrid war on the West, with a host of negative consequences for frontline states, particularly Ukraine. As described in chapter 2, Russia and Europe appear to be locked in a classical security dilemma. The more one side seeks to address its perceived security needs, the more the other side feels threatened.

A Europe Whole and Free

Throughout this period of increasing tensions, the EU continued to try to deepen relations with former Soviet republics such as Ukraine, Moldova, Belarus, Georgia, Azerbaijan, and Armenia.[118] The EU launched its Eastern Partnership in 2009 after two waves of enlargement in 2004 and 2007 brought in ten new member states in Central and Eastern Europe. Suddenly, the EU had a host of new neighbors in the former Soviet states. The EU did not wish to offer membership to these relatively underdeveloped states, but rather wanted to support their economic integration with the EU over the long term. The EU offered DCFTAs to all the Eastern Partnership states.

Russia sharply opposed the Eastern Partnership program from the beginning, seeing it as an unwanted intrusion into its own zone of influence. Yet the EU refused to be deterred by Russia, either before or after its 2014 intervention in Ukraine. Emboldened, perhaps, by the Euromaidan movement, the EU signed a DCFTA with Ukraine in 2015 that came into force on September 1, 2017, after a year's delay sought by Russia. The EU reached similar DCFTAs with Georgia and Moldova that came into force in 2016.[119] Belarus, Armenia, and Azerbaijan chose not to conclude DCFTAs with the EU, considering determined opposition from Russia. By contrast, Armenia concluded a "comprehensive and enhanced partnership agreement" with the EU in 2017, after it joined the Russia-sponsored Eurasian Economic Union.[120] In all Eastern Partnership countries, the EU monitors and encourages progress on democratization and human rights. EU support for the partnership countries only increased after Russia's 2022 full-scale invasion of Ukraine. After some debate, the EU made Ukraine, Moldova, and Georgia candidates for EU membership and opened negotiations with Ukraine and Moldova in 2023.

The EU's persistent projection of its economic and democratization projects in the Eastern Partnership countries continues to aggravate Russia. Yet the EU persists because it views Russia's objectives as imperialist and illegitimate. The EU maintains a vision of peace through economic interconnectedness; it wishes to strengthen political and economic relations with countries on its periphery. The EU has stood up to Russian aggression. Thus Europe today is defined by two competing integration projects: EU Europe and the Russian world. In the following chapter, we will explore how the lands in between Russia and the European Union—countries like Ukraine and

Moldova that are neither colonies of Russia nor member states of the European Union—have coped with the pressures and opportunities presented by both sides.

CONCLUSIONS

Though Western leaders failed to understand the full nature of Russia's hybrid threat from 2008 to 2012, Western institutions began to respond starting in 2012, particularly after Russia's invasions of Crimea and Ukraine in 2014 and 2022. Western institutions now display considerable unity, presenting a strong but measured response. NATO has so far deterred Russia from invading any NATO member state. And while Russia has treated the EU as an organization without teeth, a Venus compared to the martial nations of the United States and Russia, the EU has exhibited surprising strength in opposing Russia's imperialist aggression, primarily in the economic realm. The EU has hit Russia where it is vulnerable, in its weak, resource-dependent economy. Whereas Putin sought to use Russia's oil and gas resources as a geopolitical asset in the 2000s, the European Union fought back successfully, forcing Russia to obey EU regulations and thwarting the divide-and-rule tactics of its powerful eastern neighbor. Western economic sanctions seriously damaged the Russian economy. However, the West still struggles to counter Russian propaganda, and efforts have only begun to protect the integrity of Western electoral systems. Western leaders have taken steps to bolster its cybersecurity and military infrastructure to withstand a Russian assault. The EU has also continued its policy of economic integration of former Soviet states in between Russia and the European Union, in the face of determined Russian opposition, extending the prospect of membership to Ukraine, Moldova, and Georgia. In short, the West has reacted more strongly than often recognized.

Yet Russia has not backed down. Still reeling from the impact of sanctions, Russia nonetheless redoubled its efforts to undermine Western institutions and Western elections, hoping for a breakthrough in its struggle to disable Western opponents from within. Russia accelerated its military conquest of Ukrainian territory in 2022. In Western countries, Russia moved from quiet support of extremist parties to blatant undermining of EU and Western elections. These attacks take place not because the EU and NATO are weak, as commonly suspected, but rather because Russia perceives them to be too strong. Unable to rely on small, malleable Trojan horse governments in Cyprus, Greece, or Hungary, Russia now aims to recruit politicians and dismantle support for the EU in the largest member states. Brexit handed a major victory to Russia by taking one of its largest opponents out of the EU. Russia, meanwhile, sought to elect a pro-Russian government in France, Germany, or the United States. Russia has not succeeded in dismantling Western institutions yet; quite to the contrary, its aggression fostered greater Western unity. But Russia has managed to transform every Western election into a high-stakes referendum on the future of democracy and the international system.

With the stakes raised, Russia and the West are entering a dangerous time in their relations. They are engaged in a pitched battle to determine the political future of Europe. Either the West's vision of a rule-bound, liberal order or Russia's vision of a great-power Europe dominated by authoritarian rulers will prevail. Nowhere is this conflict felt more than in the lands in between Russia and the EU, which sit balanced on a knife's edge between two competing geopolitical zones, creating a tense politics of polarization.

POLARIZING THE LANDS

IN BETWEEN

IN MARCH 2016, BELARUS'S DICTATOR, President Aleksander Lukashenko, addressed the geopolitical forces dividing his country. "If the partners which we're in dialogue with try to insist that we have to choose between Russia, Poland or the EU, we don't want to be put in this position," he said. At that moment, Belarus, closely aligned with Moscow, was in talks with the Washington, DC–based IMF for a $3 billion loan to bolster its currency reserves in exchange for implementing a raft of liberal economic reforms.[1]

Aleksander Lukashenko exemplifies how some leading politicians have sought to navigate the divisive politics of hybrid war in the lands in between. Lukashenko, frequently demonized in the West and in Russia, is a virtuoso at managing his country's reliance on Moscow while tacking toward the West when needed. Belarus long has deferred to Russia when necessary. Lukashenko chose not to sign a DCFTA with the EU in 2013 when it became clear that this would incur sanctions from Russia. At the same time, until 2021, on those occasions when Russia has tried to force Lukashenko to take actions that would compromise Belarusian sovereignty or independence, such as selling a strategic enterprise to a Russian oligarch or hosting a permanent Russian military base, Lukashenko leaned toward Brussels and Washington. "Rejection, resistance, oscillation and 'non-commitment' have defined Lukashenko's regime," according to one analyst.[2] In 2014, Lukashenko positioned himself as an honest broker between Russia and the West by hosting the Minsk talks that sought to end the conflict in Ukraine. Yet, with the disastrous results of Belarus's presidential election in 2020 and Russia's full-scale invasion of Ukraine in 2022, non-commitment became more difficult to maintain. In 2021, Lukashenko gave in to Russian pressure to use Belarus to launch its invasion of Ukraine. Yet, determined to hang on to a thin shred of sovereignty, Lukashenko persistently evaded Russia's demands to deploy Belarusian troops in Ukraine, even after Russia became desperate for reinforcements.[3]

Lukashenko embodies the political paradoxes that haunt the lands in between. Caught between powerful neighbors pulling in different directions, politics in these countries has become sharply, intensely polarized. Some talk of a "civilizational choice" between East and West, a battle between a world of Orthodox and post-Soviet fellowship and a European future of liberal democracy. People and political parties are sharply divided into pro-European and pro-Russian camps. Each watches its own television stations, lives in its own media and information bubble, and feels threatened by the other. Some people work and study abroad in Europe, others in Russia. It often seems that two different civilizations exist in the same place. No wonder some scholars have called Eastern Europe the "shatterzone of empires."[4]

Yet the paradox is this. While political parties and public media fight a pitched battle for the hearts and minds of the population, things look different at the pinnacle of power. Many key power brokers in these societies share one important characteristic: an ability to profit from both sides—and from the conflict that divides them.

In some cases, these power brokers are presidents, who may align primarily with Russia or the West but always hedge their bets and maintain room for maneuver to protect their own sovereignty. In other cases, these power brokers are not presidents but oligarchs, leading businesspeople with substantial political influence. For instance, most Ukrainian oligarchs have proven enormously flexible, enriching themselves under the pro-Russian Yanukovich presidency before switching their support to the pro-Western Poroshenko or Zelensky. Oligarch Victor Pinchuk is famous for having opposed NATO membership for Ukraine before supporting it when a new regime came to power in Kyiv. He does not seem to be a man of principle. Pinchuk was a close associate of the Clintons who later switched allegiances and donated to Donald Trump's election campaign. He knows how to stay close to power.[5] Moldova's leading oligarch, Vlad Plahotniuc, maneuvered himself into the leadership of his country's governing pro-EU alliance while profiting from rebroadcasting the main Russian TV stations and their political propaganda. Georgia's Bidzina Ivanishvili entered politics on a platform of closer ties with Russia, while also maintaining Georgia's pro-EU direction. The paradoxes are endless and hard to comprehend.

Yet there is a simple explanation. In countries where mass politics is extremely polarized—fought out between media and political forces that are fiercely pro-EU or pro-Russia—the greatest power and wealth often flow not to ideological partisans, but to the power brokers who position themselves to profit from the passions and insecurities of both sides. In a war such as this, there is always a catch-22—and a Milo Minderbinder armed with greed, self-preservation instincts, and flexibility who deftly seeks to transcend it.

War makes the position of these power brokers both more profitable and precarious. As the stakes rise, both sides in a conflict scrutinize their allies' behavior more carefully, making it more difficult to bridge the divide. Yet, paradoxically, the potential spoils also rise, since both sides are willing to pay more for political loyalty, especially to those who might defect.

This paradoxical politics of polarization and power brokers is most visible in the lands in between, vulnerable states caught up in a geopolitical struggle between two "civilizations"—West and East. However, it is becoming increasingly visible in the West as well. As Western countries get caught up in Russia's hybrid war, the lessons of the lands in between become more relevant. Often seen as poor, backward states, these countries' greater vulnerability to Russian influence puts them ahead in this instance. They have much to teach us about the disorienting politics of hybrid war that we in the West are experiencing today.

VULNERABILITY TO RUSSIA

Compared to other European or Western states, the lands in between are highly vulnerable to Russian influence: military, economic, and cultural. This greater vulnerability sets them apart from CEE states that joined the European Union and NATO in the 2000s and from developed Western countries of Europe and North America, addressed in following chapters.

On the military side, many lands in between have suffered Russian military intervention in recent years. Georgia, Moldova, and Ukraine all have parts of their territory occupied by the Russian military or breakaway republics under the protection of Russia. While other European countries may be concerned about Russian military threats, the lands in between live with the reality of being relatively small states in Russia's backyard and, in some cases, ongoing occupation. This threat has persisted since the end of the Soviet Union in 1991.

Moldova's experience of occupation dates from 1991, when its attempts to exercise military control over its entire territory were repulsed by the Soviet Fourteenth Army, stationed in Transnistria, a sliver of land across the Dniester River from the rest of Moldova. The Soviet Fourteenth Army fought to keep Transnistria—with its larger Russian-speaking population—independent from a newly sovereign and mostly Romanian-speaking Moldova. This short war ended with a frozen conflict between Russia and Moldova and the creation of the Transnistrian Moldovan Republic, propped up by a small 1,500-troop Russian occupation force that has persisted to the present day.

Russia invaded Georgia in 2008 and forced it to cede control of two territories to the Russian army: Abkhazia and South Ossetia.[6] Russia invaded Ukraine in 2014, annexing the Crimean peninsula and occupying the Donbas region, establishing breakaway republics in Donetsk and Luhansk. Russia invaded Ukraine again in 2022 and declared the annexation of four regions, Donetsk, Kherson, Luhansk, and Zaporizhzhia, but none of these regions is fully under the control of Russian forces at the time of this writing.

While other lands in between have not experienced occupation directly, the possibility of Russian military intervention remains an ever-present reality. Armenia has long hosted a Russian military base at Gyumri and has a close security relationship with Russia. After pro-democracy protests in Armenia overturned a dictatorial, pro-Russian government in 2018, new prime minister Nikol Pashinyan immediately felt compelled to reaffirm the "strategic alliance" between Russia and Armenia.[7] No surprise there. Armenian leaders long believed that a close relationship with Russia would deter neighboring Azerbaijan from invading and retaking the territory of Nagorno-Karabakh. Armenia had seized Nagorno-Karabakh, formerly an Armenian enclave within Azerbaijan, in a war in the 1990s. Yet as Azerbaijan grew wealthy with oil revenues, it overtook Armenia in economic development and sought to retake

Nagorno-Karabakh in 2020.[8] A second offensive in September 2023, while Russia was distracted with its invasion of Ukraine, returned Nagorno-Karabakh to Azerbaijan. Azerbaijan has no Russian military base and tries to maintain good relations with both Russia and the West.

Economically, these countries have historically been heavily dependent on Russia, as relatively small countries bordering the much larger Russian economy. In most cases, Russia is one of their largest trading partners. Moreover, this trade dependence is "asymmetric": they depend on Russia far more than Russia does on them.[9] This gives Russia the ability to use trade sanctions to severely punish or reward the lands in between.

For instance, Russia halted the import of Moldovan wine in 2006–7 and 2013–17, along with other food products, to punish it for increasing ties with the EU.[10] When Belarus violated Russian countersanctions against the EU in 2014–15, Russia intercepted and destroyed suspected (often rebranded) EU products moving through Belarus to the Russian market.[11] These enforcement actions occurred despite Belarus's membership in the Eurasian customs union with Russia. Russia imposed a series of trade sanctions on Ukraine in 2013–14, declaring all imports from Ukraine "high-risk" to justify extensive scrutiny that effectively shut down trade for several weeks, along with targeted sanctions on particular industries and companies.[12] After the Rose Revolution that brought Mikheil Saakashvili to power, Russia blocked imports of Georgian agricultural products from 2006 to 2013.[13] Despite its supposed commitment to free trade within the Eurasian Economic Union and the World Trade Organization, Russia frequently uses trade embargoes and sanctions to force the lands in between to reckon with their economic vulnerability to Russia.

Culturally, the lands in between remain exceptionally vulnerable to Russian influence. As former Soviet republics, all have substantial Russian-speaking populations, a legacy of

Soviet imperialism that provides an entry point for Russian state media and political propaganda.[14] Russian state media creates an alternative worldview for its spectators. Conspiracy theories abound. Enemies are identified and berated. Facts are covered up. Heroes—especially Russian president Vladimir Putin—are built up. The Kremlin controls the content of news stories and metanarratives daily.[15] Its intent is to create a population that believes Russian narratives—including seeing America and the EU as enemies and Russia as an innocent victim—and to use them to influence the politics of target countries.

As a result of this information warfare, Ukraine, one of the biggest targets of Russian propaganda, banned the broadcast of Russian TV channels and prevented certain Russian journalists from entering Ukraine. Similarly, Ukraine banned Russian social media websites, claiming that they were being used to transmit Kremlin propaganda messages to Ukraine's large Russian-speaking population.[16]

While Russia's media campaigns have gained enormous attention in the West, its use of the Orthodox Church as a mechanism of foreign cultural influence has not. Yet not only do most of the lands in between share the Orthodox faith, but many churches have been under the direct control of the Moscow patriarchate of the Orthodox Church, which deploys its priests to deliver political messages, particularly at election time. In Ukraine, Moldova, and Belarus, Russia has enjoyed direct control over one of the most trusted institutions in the country.[17] Russia uses the church to emphasize conservative family values, spread anti-EU and anti-US messages, and encourage parishioners to vote for pro-Russian political parties that espouse these views, while emphasizing a common Orthodox culture in the lands in between.[18]

To counter this influence, Ukraine founded a Kyiv patriarchate of the Orthodox Church, separate from Moscow. The Kyiv patriarchate rapidly gained ground, establishing thousands of churches and parishes throughout the country attended by approximately 15 million Ukrainian parishioners, compared to 10 million for the Moscow patriarchate in 2017. Many Ukrainians regarded both as legitimate Orthodox churches. Yet there was one important difference: the Kyiv patriarchate declared itself firmly in favor of Ukrainian national independence and sovereignty.[19] In 2018, Orthodoxy's world center, the Patriarchate of Constantinople, finally recognized the Kyiv patriarchate as sovereign in Ukraine, despite protests and threats of retaliation from Moscow. Moscow retains an important influence through the churches of the Moscow patriarchate.[20]

In summary, Russia has a number of tools of geopolitical influence in the lands in between that it does not have elsewhere in Europe or in North America. The EU constitutes a strong countervailing cultural and economic influence among its members. The lands in between, however, did not seize the opportunity to join the EU and NATO immediately after the collapse of the Soviet Union in 1991. Politically, these countries have remained divided between those who want a European future for their countries and those who wish to affiliate with the more familiar Russian sphere of influence. Because of Russia's greater military, economic, and cultural influence in the lands in between, these countries' experience seems irrelevant to the West. But now that Russian malign influences affect all Western countries, particularly at election time, the experience of lands in between requires careful consideration.

EUROPEAN UNION INFLUENCE

After the collapse of the Soviet empire in 1991, the lands in between opened to the West and found that their prosperity depends on integration with Western economies. As a result, these countries embraced neoliberal economic reforms in the 1990s and 2000s, to varying degrees.[21] As their CEE neighbors joined the EU in the 2000s, the lands in between required closer ties with the EU common market just to maintain preexisting trade and investment relationships with neighboring countries. For instance, Moldova and Romania, which share a common language and history, suddenly found themselves on opposite sides of the EU customs frontier. To maintain historic ties, the lands in between needed closer relations with the EU.

The EU responded by launching the Eastern Partnership program in 2009. According to an official EU website, "The Eastern Partnership aims at building a common area of shared democracy, prosperity, stability and increased cooperation." While the EU does not offer a prospect of membership to Eastern Partnership countries, it does offer a closer economic and political relationship for countries willing to adopt EU practices and institutions, which could lead toward membership. On the political side, the heads of state or government from the six Eastern Partnership countries convene at summit meetings with their EU counterparts twice per year. The EU also sponsors civil society, local and regional government, parliamentary, and business partnership meetings. Since the Eastern Partnership is part of a wider European Neighborhood Policy, the partner countries and the EU produce "action plans" and "progress reports" on integration on a yearly basis. These provide an opportunity for countries to set integration objectives and for the EU to critique progress toward integration.

On the economic side, the EU sought to conclude DCFTAs with all Eastern Partnership countries in 2014, agreements that offered substantial access to EU markets in exchange for regulatory harmonization with EU rules. Because of Russian opposition, Armenia, Azerbaijan, and Belarus declined to sign such agreements—as did Ukraine under President Yanukovich. However, Georgia, Moldova, and ultimately Ukraine, after the Maidan revolution, concluded DCFTAs with the EU in

2016 and 2017.[22] Armenia joined Russia's Eurasian Economic Union, but it also signed a more limited partnership agreement with the EU in 2017. At the 2015 Riga Summit, the Eastern Partnership countries decided on four "priority areas of cooperation": stronger governance, stronger economy, better connectivity, and stronger society. These mirror the requirements of EU membership. In addition, the EU provides significant financial support to Eastern Partnership countries, amounting to €2.8 billion between 2014 and 2017,[23] and the prospect of visa-free travel to the EU, a major incentive for citizens who seek to study or work abroad.

The EU also exerts significant influence over the lands in between as a major trading partner and model of economic prosperity and good governance. Many citizens of Eastern Partnership countries see that EU membership dramatically boosted the economic prospects of neighbors such as Poland and Romania, whose wages continue to converge with EU averages.[24] They want the same. Still, while Russian influence in the lands in between works primarily through cultural and military means, EU influence works primarily through the attraction of its enormous and highly developed economy. This helps to explain why EU integration seems to appeal to different population groups, primarily those best positioned to take advantage of the economic opportunities it offers. Some argue that EU influence would be higher still if the EU had explicitly offered the prospect of membership to all Eastern Partnership countries.[25]

Countervailing influences of Russia and the West have left people in the lands in between divided. Some prefer a pro-Russian direction for their countries, while others advocate rapid integration with the EU. Overall, Georgia, Ukraine, and Moldova have taken the most pro-EU perspective, while Armenia, Belarus, and Azerbaijan have shown less enthusiasm. Yet in each country, these choices have spawned sharp divisions that have become sharper still as geopolitical conflict between Russia and the EU grows.

THE POLITICS OF "CIVILIZATIONAL CHOICE"

Between Russia's extensive influence operations and the EU's push to integrate countries through DCFTAs, it should be no surprise that politics in these countries has become increasingly polarized. In Moldova and Ukraine, many politicians feel that their countries are at a crossroads and speak of a "civilizational choice" between the EU and Russia, language increasingly common in Russia itself.[26] For instance, in 2017, the prime ministers of Ukraine and Moldova held a press conference to reaffirm a European direction for their countries. Ukrainian prime minister Volodymyr Groysman stated, "A stable political situation in Moldova and preserving the course of Chisinau towards European integration poses great interest for Ukraine. Successful realization of our joint civilizational choice shall facilitate the stability and security in the region, the effectiveness of our cooperation and the prosperity and development of our peoples."[27] Similarly, on the brink of Moldova's 2014 parliamentary election, Moldova's prime minister, Iurie Leancă, told the *Financial Times*, "This election is critical and crucial for the future of the country. Do we want to move the country forward? It is a civilizational choice."[28]

When each election becomes a referendum on a "civilizational choice" between Russia and the EU, it is hard to find an in-between position. On the one hand, the lands in between can choose closer relations with the EU, a huge and successful market characterized by rule of law, freedom of speech, anti-corruption campaigns, visa-free travel, educational opportunities, and a path toward Western prosperity, at the risk of high inequality and increasing internationalism. On the other, they can choose to be part of the new Russian empire, where they share a common culture and history and benefit from long-standing trade and employment ties, but also suffer from a top-down system of corruption, a weaker economy, and a state propaganda machine that feeds a debilitating belief in conspiracy theories.

Given the stark nature of this choice, it is not surprising that geopolitics has become the number-one political issue in these countries. Not left versus right, which has been the dominant political cleavage in Western countries for hundreds of years. Nor liberal versus conservative. Not even the divide between former communist and anti-communist, though these divisions sometimes overlap. The main issue in national politics is whether to rejoin Soviet Union 2.0 or to achieve national independence in an EU framework. Because this is the most fundamental issue for voters—one that will determine their economic futures, their life chances, and the manner in which their country and economy are governed—political parties tend to provide a clear choice. At election time, politicians remind voters what is at stake and beg them to forgive minor transgressions, such as endemic corruption, in service of a greater good.

"Civilizational choice" has thus become a defining issue for political parties. As one analyst puts it, "Most of the elections in Ukraine's recent political history have not only been hotly contested but have also manifested the clash between two visions for the country's future, one anchored on the European political model of liberal democracy and the other associated with Russia and its illiberal political tradition of state paternalism and centralized leadership."[29] Voters in these countries look first at the overall direction of a party, then secondarily at its positions on domestic policy issues. Geopolitics dominates politics in the lands in between. For countries caught in the middle of an intensifying geopolitical competition, it is hard to find middle ground, even though, for many politicians, "this is not the position we want to be in."[30] Many politicians would rather debate the substance of domestic political issues or economic development than an abstract civilizational choice.

While the whole idea of "civilizational choice" may seem abstract to some, both the EU and Russia consciously promote their own opposing visions of European civilization. While the EU presents a world of "European values," prosperity, and human rights, Russia emphasizes traditional values that it believes are shared by the lands in between due to a common connection to the Orthodox Christian Church. In Ukraine, "Patriarch Kirill I of the Russian Orthodox Church, a true spokesperson of Kremlin political worldviews, has . . . persistently emphasized the cultural and spiritual unity of Russians and Ukrainians."[31] Russia wants Ukraine, Moldova, Belarus, and other Orthodox countries to remain part of a common Orthodox civilization centered in Moscow.

Russia's appeal to the existence of a common Orthodox civilization and the language of "civilizational choice" and the "Russian world" has become a key aspect of Russia's attempts to influence the lands in between. On the eve of the Ukraine conflict in 2013, Vladimir Putin attended an Orthodox Church conference on the "civilizational choice" facing Ukraine and underlined Ukraine's and Russia's common heritage in the medieval state of Kyivan Rus. Putin said, "We know today's reality of course, know that there are the Ukrainian people and the Belarusian people, and other peoples too, and we respect all the parts of this heritage, but at the same time, at the foundations of this heritage are the common spiritual values that make us a single people. The Ukrainian Orthodox Church leaders spoke about this today. It would be hard to deny this. We can only agree with it. . . . We must remember this brotherhood and preserve our ancestors' traditions. Together, they built a unique system of Orthodox values and strengthened themselves in their faith."[32] Putin reiterated these themes on the eve of his 2022 invasion of Ukraine in an essay titled "On the Historical Unity of Russians and Ukrainians."[33]

In this perspective, for Ukraine or Belarus to join the EU undermines Orthodox tradition by adopting corrupt Western values of individual freedom and self-expression. Russian politicians often deploy gay marriage as a symbol of Western wrongheadedness and decadence, referring to Europe as "Gayropa." Increasingly, Russian leaders no longer see themselves as European, instead considering themselves Eurasian. As Kremlin aide and thinker Vladislav Surkov put it, Russia's culture is a "mixed breed" that incorporates elements of both the East and the West, like "someone born of a mixed marriage . . . He is everyone's relative, but nobody's family. Treated by foreigners like one of their own, an outcast among his own people. He understands everyone and is understood by no one."[34] In short, Russians are not European, but from a different civilization.

Armed conflict, or the threat thereof, only makes these political divides more intense. Choosing between civilizations increasingly means deciding on which side to fight.

THE FRONT LINES

Ukraine

The hottest war in the lands in between is of course the one in Ukraine. Russia's brutal full-scale invasion in 2022 claimed tens of thousands of victims. Russia's war crimes and physical and cultural genocide sharpened political polarization, forcing most

Ukrainians to choose the West over Russia. This had not always been the case.

Prior to 2014, the median voter in Ukraine wanted closer relations with the EU and Russia simultaneously and did not worry if these goals were mutually exclusive. Ukrainians simply wanted good relations with both sides. Top leaders reflected these priorities. Pro-Russian president Viktor Yanukovich, for instance, negotiated a DCFTA with the EU throughout 2012 and 2013 while also pursuing a "multivector" foreign policy that would allow Ukraine to balance between Russia and the EU.

Russia's 2014 invasion convinced the median voter in Ukraine that Russia was an aggressor, not a friend, and that Ukraine's future lies with the West. The old political middle ground was suddenly gone. It was replaced by a pro-Western majority that believes an independent Ukraine must ally with the West. In public opinion polls conducted in September 2014, a few months into the conflict, a vast majority of Ukrainians supported joining the EU for the first time, with 59 percent in favor compared to 17 percent for joining Russia's Eurasian Economic Union.[35] After Russia's 2022 invasion of Ukraine, support for EU and NATO membership reached 92 and 86 percent respectively, and only 9 percent wanted Ukraine to be part of the Eurasian Economic Union.[36] Russia's repeated invasions forced millions of Ukrainians to make a civilizational choice. A vast majority chose the West. As a result, Ukrainian national identity now means independence from Russia.

Celebrating the launch of visa-free travel for Ukrainians to the EU in June 2017, Ukrainian president Petro Poroshenko hailed it as a "final break" with the Russian empire and quoted Russian poet Mikhail Lermontov saying, "Farewell, unwashed Russia."[37] The middle ground that many Ukrainians once occupied, of being friendly to both the EU and Russia, no longer existed.

Belarus

Belarus, the former Soviet republic to the north of Ukraine, chose a different path. Belarus has remained clearly aligned with Russia since the 1990s, even joining together with Russia in a "union state" with a common customs border. EU influence in Belarus has been minimal. However, politics in Belarus remains polarized between those who support alliance with Russia and those who want Belarus to move closer to EU Europe and democratic rule.

President Aleksander Lukashenko's regime in Belarus rests on two pillars: a repressive security apparatus closely aligned with Russia and a liberal intelligentsia that provides a modicum of good governance and holds out the hope of closer relations with the West. Belarus has a small but active opposition movement made up of Belarusian nationalists who oppose subservience to Moscow and liberals who wish to see Belarus integrate into the European Union. The opposition led mass demonstrations in 2020 and 2021 after a presidential election in which the opposition candidate, Sviatlana Tsikhanouskaya, claimed to have won 60–70 percent of the votes, but Lukashenko was declared the victor. Belarusian security forces blackmailed Tsikhanouskaya into leaving the country and tortured, imprisoned, and beat thousands of protesters to suppress months of nationwide protests.[38] As in Ukraine, Belarusian independence increasingly means opposing Russia and supporting the EU.

Meanwhile, the Lukashenko regime adopts Russia's anti-EU propaganda, railing against "Gayropa" and in favor of conservative cultural values. Belarusian state ideology emphasizes that Belarus is vulnerable to invasion from the west, using its disastrous experience as a battlefield between the Nazi and Red armies during World War II as a justification for why Belarus needs authoritarian rule—to protect Belarus, promote stability, and prevent war.[39] Lukashenko sees himself as a bulwark of stability and sovereignty between East and West.

Moldova

Similarly in Moldova, politics has become increasingly polarized, breaking down into clearly identified pro-Russia and pro-EU camps. On one side are former presidents Igor Dodon and Vladimir Voronin in the Bloc of Communists and Socialists, supportive of Russia. During the 2016 election, Dodon promised to rule "like Putin" and declared that Crimea is Russian territory.[40] On the other is current president Maia Sandu, a former World Bank employee and minister of education, and the Party of Action and Solidarity, dedicated to working toward EU integration by 2030. Approximately 10 percent of Moldovans would like to see Moldova merge with Romania, a fast track to EU membership. The Moldovan language is Romanian, and many Moldovans qualify for Romanian passports, which provide access to the EU for work or travel. However, non-Romanian minority groups distrust Romania and feel safer with Russia. Most Moldovans wish to preserve their country and support integration into the EU as an independent state. The EU granted Moldova (and Ukraine) candidate status in June 2023.[41]

The battle between pro-EU and pro-Russia forces in Moldova has intensified since 2014, with both Russia and the EU pushing hard for domestic allies, providing monetary and media support. According to one analyst, "Playing on the East-West geopolitical divisions within society represents the favorite and most effective way to manipulate atomized public opinion in Moldova."[42] Russia clearly wants to integrate Moldova into a new Russian empire. Pro-EU governments of Moldova, by contrast, want fast-track accession to the EU, with visa-free travel and greater possibilities for work and study, but also greater competition and opportunities from the massive EU economy.

In 2017, approximately equal shares of the population supported both options.[43] By 2023, about two-thirds of Moldovans supported EU membership, while one-third opposed it.[44]

Unfortunately for the West, opposition to joining the EU was fed by corruption among ostensibly pro-EU politicians in Moldova. While the Alliance for European Integration, which governed Moldova from 2009 to 2018, promised progress toward EU trade, travel, and eventual membership, it proved to be exceptionally corrupt. In one notorious case, $1 billion went missing from the Moldovan banking system. While pro-Russia businessman Ilan Shor ultimately was convicted of this crime, former Moldovan prime minister Vlad Filat, head of a pro-EU government, was sentenced to nine years in jail for taking bribes from Shor in connection with this case.[45] This dampened voters' enthusiasm for the EU integration coalition. Maia Sandu won the 2019 parliamentary and 2020 presidential elections promising a clean pro-EU choice. She defeated the pro-Russia presidential candidate Igor Dodon with 57 percent of the vote in 2020. New elections will take place in 2024.

As support for the EU has risen in Moldova, parties that campaigned on a "multivector" approach to Russia and the West have been sidelined. For instance, Renato Usati's Our Party, which identifies itself as pro-Moldovan and seeks to avoid being identified too closely with either Russia or the EU, saw its support wither in recent years. In a political spectrum sharply divided between pro-EU and pro-Russian forces, voters want to know which side parties are on. And Usati has increasingly been identified with Russia, since he moved to Russia after being threatened with arrest in Moldova and is rumored to have links to Russian secret services. Ethnic parties face the same problem of being forced to identify as either pro-EU or pro-Russia. As Daniel Cadier and Samuel Charap write, "The Ukraine crisis seems to have reinforced the tendency to approach the region through a binary geopolitical lens, which is detrimental to political and economic reform. . . . Worse, this binarization of regional politics exacerbates internal divides in the countries of the common neighbourhood and allows elites to instrumentalise competition among external actors to their benefit."[46]

Summary

In sum, the intensifying geopolitical conflict between Russia and the West has forced political parties and voters in the front-line states to choose. Either their country can seek prosperity and freedom in the European Union, with all the good and bad that entails, or they can join the Eurasian Economic Union, which offers closer political and economic integration with Russia. Geopolitics overwhelms politics. In most countries, politics revolves around domestic issues such as jobs, economic growth, healthcare, and public services. In the lands in between, the big question is: what civilization do we belong to?

POLARIZATION AND POWER BROKERS

This sharp polarization, however, creates a paradox. In a context of geopolitical competition, sharp polarization, and "civilizational choice," the big winners often are the ones who play both sides. This is a dangerous game. Some win and some lose. All play it differently. But the ability to profit from both sides is a surprisingly common feature of the power brokers who dominate these divided societies. As one author remarked, "Politicians exhibit cold pragmatism, healthy manipulative skills, and a praiseworthy inclination to exploit the animosity between great powers to the fullest."[47]

Here is how it works. In polarized societies, competing sides offer opposing ideological visions. In the case of the pro-Europe camp, it is the vision of a state ruled by law, individual freedoms, and self-expression. In the case of the pro-Russian side, it is a vision of traditional Christian culture, family values, and Orthodox spirituality. External actors—the European Union or the Russian state—encourage and reward those who support these value systems. Obviously, individual interests come into play. Those who speak European languages and have a higher degree of education may support pro-EU parties. Those who have lived and worked in Russia may support a pro-Russian orientation. However, both sides in this struggle combine an appeal based on values with an economic message: Believe in Europe and enjoy prosperity. Believe in a unity of Slavic or Orthodox people and enjoy the patronage of Russia.

Yet in polarized societies, neither side thoroughly dominates.[48] A significant minority is always aggrieved. This introduces volatility into political life. To maintain control, the most successful politicians—or businesspeople—find a way to diversify their appeal and cater to all sides. Think of it this way: If one were running a company that wanted to dominate the media market in the lands in between, it would be helpful to own newspapers and TV stations on opposite sides of the civilizational divide. To take a pure ideological position would be to cede market share to someone else. The same is true in politics. The most successful politician is the one who wins votes—or campaign contributions or economic support—from both sides. This requires sacrificing ideological consistency.

While political parties often traffic in ideas—selling the idea of a Ukrainian, Georgian, or Belarusian nation or the ideals of rule of law or good government—power brokers prioritize material concerns. They are concentrated on achieving real gains in the here and now. As David Cadier and Samuel Charap point out, both Russia and the EU share a "willingness to subsidize political loyalty."[49] Russians pay good money for compliance with their wishes and desires. The EU devotes substantial sums to international development programs designed to bring countries closer to Europe. Many politicians and party leaders gravitate to one side or the other out of deeply held beliefs. Other leading politicians and businesspeople seek to win resources from both sides by pursuing a dangerously ambiguous or flexible approach.

The lands in between provide plenty of fascinating examples. Each has distinctive characteristics, strategies, and circumstances. While the Western media tend to focus on pro-Western heroes like Mikheil Saakashvili, who imposed liberal reforms on the Republic of Georgia before later losing power and even his Georgian passport, it says less about his successor as major domo of Georgian politics, Bidzina Ivanishvili. Yet Ivanishvili has dominated Georgian politics for many years and he is no hero.

Ivanishvili is the most powerful Georgian oligarch. He lives in a 108,000-square-foot modernist compound situated on a hill above the capital city, Tbilisi. He made his money in Russia, starting in the 1990s as an importer of computer and phone equipment. He founded a bank and participated in voucher privatization, acquiring ore and metals companies and rising in the *Forbes* ranks of global billionaires. He is a Russian oligarch who, during his election campaign in 2011–12, made a point of arguing that Georgia needed to normalize relations with Russia after the 2008 Russo-Georgian war, which he blamed on Saakashvili. He told the British daily *Telegraph*, "The government encourages hysteria about Russian aggression. They want to frighten people, and use it [the Russian issue] as part of a political game. But we will be obliged to forge relations with Russia, whether we like it or not. We should not forget that Russia is our biggest neighbour and we should use that."[50]

However, Ivanishvili and his Georgian Dream Party did not mean to abandon Georgia's Western orientation, which a majority see as central to Georgia's future economic success. Instead, he emphasized that he would continue to seek closer relations with the EU and NATO, while at the same time improving relations with Russia. He told the *Guardian*, "Our policy is European and Euro-Atlantic integration. There is no substitute for NATO." While this may seem contradictory, Ivanishvili was able to put an end to the Russian embargo on Georgian agricultural products in 2013 and normalize business ties with Russia, despite continued Russian land grabs and occupation of parts of the country. Personally, Ivanishvili claims to have sold most of his Russian holdings after entering politics but retained a sizable share of Gazprom stock. He showed up in the Panama Papers as the holder of an offshore company. Yet Georgia has not relinquished its Western aspirations under his rule. Georgia signed a DCFTA with the EU in June 2014, won visa-free travel to the EU for its citizens in 2017, and was officially recognized as a candidate for EU membership in 2023, although the EU elected not to open membership negotiations with Georgia.[51] This seemingly contradictory set of policies is underpinned by public opinion. "Georgians overwhelmingly desire a good political relationship with Russia" (54 percent) and supported close relations with the United States (71 percent) and the EU (65 percent) in a poll conducted in 2009, soon after the Russo-Georgian war.[52] On both sides of the divide, Georgians can find something to love and to hate about their leading oligarch, who, after winning election as prime minister in 2012, resigned in 2013 to stand behind the scenes. In 2018, he was forced to return to lead his Georgian Dream Party after a power struggle broke out between its prime minister and mayor of Tbilisi. Ivanishvili's chosen candidate, Salome Zourabichvili, won the presidency in 2018 with 60 percent of the vote.

Russia's 2022 invasion of Ukraine complicated Georgia's multivector foreign policy. Like other lands in between, Georgia came under serious pressure to choose sides. In April 2023, Francis Fukuyama and Nino Evgenidze in *Foreign Affairs* criticized the Georgian government as it "ramped up anti-Western propaganda efforts, earned praise from Moscow for not joining

Western sanctions and trade restrictions on Russia, and emulated a Russian-style crackdown on Georgia's vibrant civil
society."[53] As a consequence, the EU initially decided not to ele-
vate Georgia to candidate status in 2022 along with Ukraine and
Moldova, but later reversed its decision.[54] Opening of membership talks, however, will be contingent on Georgia exhibiting a
clearer pro-Western direction. Yet Georgia continues to push
a multivector approach. The financial returns of smuggling
sanctioned Western goods into Russia may be too tempting to
resist. Ukrainian intelligence issued a statement in April 2022
claiming that "representatives of Georgian special services were
instructed by the political leadership not to interfere with the
activities of smugglers."[55] Georgia also has a close and growing
business relationship with China.

Ivanishvili is one of the most dramatic examples of a power
broker in the lands in between, in part because he lives in a
James Bond–style futurist mansion and owns a $1 billion art
collection, but he is not alone. Many leading politicians in the
lands in between manage a similar balancing act, earning fortunes in business with Russia while running a pro-EU government, or vice versa.

These power brokers try to achieve the unachievable: at-
taining closer ties with the West while maintaining friendly relations with the regional superpower, Russia. For smaller states,
analysts believe that agility and responsiveness are natural advantages as they seek to navigate the minefield of great-power
politics.[56] Flexibility is not only a necessity, but an opportunity
that may be richly rewarded. The EU provides billions of euros
in assistance that can be controlled by political leaders. Russia
offers business deals and payoffs to its political allies. As geopolitics becomes more polarized and violent, the amount that
the EU and Russia are willing to pay for loyalty increases, while
balancing between them becomes more difficult to sustain.
How do oligarchs, presidents, and other power brokers walk
that line?

Flexibility is the ultimate resource for power brokers in the lands in between. In a recent academic take on this subject, Stanislav Markus and Volha Charnysh investigated the political activities of oligarchs in Ukraine.[57] They found that oligarchs—super-wealthy and often politically connected business leaders—benefit from flexibility. While some become governors (or presidents) and adopt political roles themselves, these positions do not enhance an oligarch's personal wealth. Oligarchs do best when they remain in the background, providing donations to one or more parties. This allows them to hedge their bets between different parts of the political spectrum and change positions as circumstances change. Markus and Charnysh find that many of the same oligarchs who fared extremely well economically under the pro-Russian Yanukovich government also fared extremely well under the pro-EU Poroshenko government. Indeed, there was very little change in the ranks of Ukrainian oligarchs between 2012 and 2016. After Russia's invasion of Crimea, most Ukrainian oligarchs adopted pro-EU messaging, promoted pro-Ukrainian parties, and even sponsored pro-Ukrainian militias. However, their allegiance is, first and foremost, to their own power. Flexibility is a great asset in a highly polarized and volatile political climate.

But oligarchs' efforts to play both sides sometimes fail spectacularly. Take the case of Vladimir Plahotniuc. Plahotniuc was the richest man and most powerful oligarch in Moldova, a small country perched between Ukraine and Romania and a model of flexibility. As leader of one of Moldova's pro-EU parties, the Democratic Party, he advocated for Moldovan accession to the European Union in Brussels. At the same time, his business interests were heavily aligned with Moscow. Plahotniuc owned the most prominent Russian-language TV channels in Moldova, which pump out Russian propaganda,[58] and was rumored to support the pro-Russian Socialist Party, led by Igor Dodon. For a time, Plahotniuc was on top of the world. He dominated Moldovan politics, passing EU legislation in parliament and benefiting from EU contracts, while also entertaining and helping to indoctrinate the pro-Russian population. With cynical ideological inconsistency and a willingness to play both sides, Plahotniuc walked a fine line. Until the ground gave out under his feet. In June 2019, both his EU and Russian patrons withdrew their support. Plahotniuc lost the elections to a more genuine pro-EU party. He left the country and fled to the United States. However, the United States declared him persona non grata in 2020, and his present whereabouts are unknown. The United States and United Kingdom sanctioned Plahotniuc in 2022 and sought to freeze his assets, in part because of concerns he might be plotting to overturn the Moldovan government.[59] Tightrope walking puts power brokers at risk of falling.

Former president of Moldova Igor Dodon took a different route through the minefield of Moldovan politics. One of Putin's greatest allies in the region, Dodon made his career as a pro-EU reformer in the leadership of Moldova's Ministry of Economy and Trade from 2006 to 2009. In 2007, he advocated that Moldova sign an association agreement with the European Union that he later promised to scrap. As a member of parliament in 2012, Dodon was one of three members to cross party lines to support the Alliance for European Integration candidate for prime minister, Nicolae Timofti, ending a long deadlock.[60] Dodon abandoned the pro-EU parties, however, when the political winds began to turn and founded a party funded by Moscow, espousing a pro-Kremlin line. Dodon was the only foreign leader to observe Russia's Victory Day celebrations in Moscow in 2017. Putin called him a court jester. Dodon subsequently accepted US money to refurbish a military base close to Transnistria, the Russian-occupied breakaway region of Moldova.[61] Dodon may lack strong or consistent values, but he has a keen sense of how to tack from side to side, taking advantage of prevailing winds.

Azerbaijan too has carefully managed relations with both Russia and Europe. An oil dictatorship run by the Aliev family, father and son, Azerbaijan signed contracts with Western firms to exploit its oil resources in 1994. The country refused to join Russia's Eurasian Economic Union or the Collective Security Treaty Organization, which includes both Moscow and Beijing. Azerbaijan forced the last Russian troops off its territory when it refused to extend a lease on a radar station in Gabala. However, it also joined the Russian trans-Adriatic pipeline project and decided not to conclude a DCFTA with the European Union. Amanda Paul calls this strategy "choosing not to choose" between the EU and Russia, a policy enabled by Azerbaijan's oil wealth, which gives it the resources to pursue an independent policy.[62]

Armenia likewise has sought to follow a path between Russia and the EU that is remarkable for its flexibility. While Armenia made great progress toward signing a DCFTA with the EU, it suddenly pulled out of negotiations in 2013 at Russia's insistence and joined the Eurasian Economic Union in 2015. It further granted Gazprom monopoly control over its pipeline network. Yet, soon after, Armenia began negotiating an amended trade agreement with the EU.[63] President Nikol Pashinyan, elected after the Armenian revolution of 2018 that asserted European values of democracy and civil rights, has continued the multivector foreign policy of past governments and remained in the Eurasian Economic Union.[64]

LANDS IN BETWEEN?

What relevance does this experience of polarization and power brokers have for the West? Perhaps it afflicts the lands in between—small, vulnerable states on the front lines of great-power conflict in a "shatterzone of empires."[65] But what does it have to do with politics in the developed West?

More than you might expect. As Western countries have become targets of Russia's hybrid war, similar phenomena have arisen in the West as well. Of course, the lands in between remain more vulnerable, for all the reasons previously listed—their economic, cultural, and military closeness to Russia. Yet as Russia's hybrid war deploys disinformation, political chaos, and encouragement of extreme parties, patterns of politics in the small, weak states in between Russia and Europe are increasingly visible in the developed West.

I build this argument in the next chapter, which demonstrates that the politics of polarization and power brokers afflicts not only the lands in between, but also member states of the European Union in Central and Eastern Europe. These countries were once seen as major success stories of transition, having escaped the Soviet bloc and founded successful democracies. Yet as they have been caught up in this new conflict, they exhibit a growing polarization and the rise of cynical power brokers. Now EU member states such as Hungary have created a problem of "civilizational choice" in the EU itself. A subsequent chapter shows the same patterns to be present in the core of Europe and in the United States. Exploring the paradoxical politics of the lands in between can help us to better understand how hybrid warfare affects politics throughout Europe and the developed West.

CONTESTING CENTRAL AND

EASTERN EUROPE

WOULD ANYONE HAVE IMAGINED IN 2008 that Czechia in 2018 would have a pro-Russian president? Or that this pro-Russian president would be the same leader who opposed the Russian invasion of Czechoslovakia in 1968, ushered his country into NATO in 2001 as prime minister, and negotiated the country's European Union membership? Yet the case of Miloš Zeman shows that even EU and NATO member states in Central Europe, whose geopolitical orientation appeared settled until recently, often experience the same politics of flexibility as the lands in between.

Elected for five-year terms as president in 2013 and 2018, Miloš Zeman has a long history in Czech politics. Zeman first rose to prominence as a "1968er," a Czech communist who favored the Prague Spring economic reforms and opposed the Russian invasion of Czechoslovakia. Like other reform communists who were ejected from the party, his career suffered, and Zeman remains critical of the 1968 invasion and current Russian disinformation on the topic.[1] After helping to overturn communism in 1989, Zeman rose to become the leader of the Czech Social Democratic Party and, as prime minister from 1998 to 2002, helped to negotiate Czechia's accession to the European Union and NATO. On the eve of Czech accession to NATO in 1999, he stated, "We have finally embarked on the path leading us to the Europe which is undivided and free. This year will be remembered as a turning point in our history. . . . [T]he direction we have chosen is the right one. We consider it as a vote of confidence in our future, in the future of Central Europe and in the future of Europe."

Yet after Zeman was deposed as leader of the Social Democratic Party and defeated in his run for the presidency in 2003, he began a period of soul-searching, and a new Miloš Zeman emerged. Zeman joined a wave of populist politicians in Central and Eastern Europe, adopting anti-Muslim, anti-immigration, and pro-Russian political views. He was recruited to attend a pro-Russian Dialogue of Civilizations by Vladimir Yakunin, head of Russian Railways. Zeman also acquired a close aide, Martin Nejedlý, a Czech businessman with extensive Russian connections who had previously run a subsidiary of the Russian oil company Lukoil and financed Zeman's return to politics.[2] In 2015, when Nejedlý was fined $1.4 million by a Czech court in a business dispute, Lukoil came forward to pay the fine.[3]

With this new financing and populist line, Zeman won the Czech presidency in 2013. After being elected president, Zeman aligned himself with the European far right. He lauded Russia's annexation of Crimea and stated that there were no Russian troops in eastern Ukraine after 2014. From 2014 to 2022, he spoke out against Western sanctions on Russia. Zeman endorsed Russian actions in Syria and called for a "Czechxit" referendum on leaving the EU in 2016. In 2018, Zeman won his campaign for reelection against Jiří Drahoš, a pro-EU academic who was subjected to a massive trolling and disinformation campaign, reminiscent of Russian electoral manipulation. Zeman worked to legitimize Russia's foreign policy messages and business interests in Europe.[4] While it is impossible to know Zeman's true motivations, some suspect that he modeled himself on Hungary's Viktor Orbán, seeking to extend his power with Russian help, while milking resources and investment from the European Union. Haunted by the ghosts of 1968, Zeman condemned Russia's 2022 invasion of Ukraine as an "unprovoked act of aggression." He was succeeded as president in 2023 by Petr Pavel, a retired general who is strongly pro-EU and pro-NATO.[5]

With the success of Zeman and similar leaders, Central and Eastern Europe once again became contested terrain in Russia's hybrid war with the West. Countries that had joined the European Union and seemingly made a civilizational choice to join the West began to turn east. Political leaders in these countries do not necessarily seek to break from their EU membership and Western orientation, but they see an opportunity to profit from the resources and opportunities Moscow offers and to accommodate Russian foreign policy demands. For the West, it feels as if the ground has shifted under its feet.

As with the lands in between, Russia has many tools of influence in Central and Eastern Europe, including energy exports, media, support for anti-EU parties, and military operations. While Central and East European states enjoy membership in the EU and NATO, they remain more vulnerable to Russian influence. First, Central and East European countries have oil and gas infrastructures that make them heavily dependent on Russia for energy supplies. Second, they have population segments that are sympathetic to Russian messages. Third, Russia has a long history of intervention in these countries and deep knowledge of domestic politics and economics that it can exploit in influence operations. Together, these factors have enabled Russia to undermine the EU from within using a variety of strategies, including energy blackmail, funding for anti-EU extremist parties, and recruitment of "Trojan horse" government leaders to advance Russia's agenda inside the EU.[6] Not surprisingly, Russia's campaign has exacerbated political polarization and played into the hands of power brokers in Central and Eastern Europe who seek to reinforce their political positions with the resources that they gain from both sides, as in the lands in between.[7]

ENERGY POLITICS

Energy has played an outsized role in the contest for Central and Eastern Europe. Lacking energy supplies outside of abundant coal, considered a dirty fuel by the European Union, Central and East European states are crisscrossed by pipelines bringing Russian oil and gas to the West. These transit states were historically almost entirely reliant on Russia for gas, as well as pipeline transit fees. Russia's gas cutoffs to Ukraine in 2006 and 2009 demonstrated that most Central and East European member states were vulnerable to gas blackmail. Scandinavian scholars found fifty-five instances of Russian attempts to use energy blackmail for political ends before 2007.[8] Putin's Russia uses this reliance and the promise of new gas pipelines and nuclear facilities to pressure Central and East European states to befriend Russia and tie themselves to Russian business interests.[9]

Of course, EU membership exerts a powerful countervailing influence on CEE member states, enabling them to diversify energy supplies well before Russia's full-scale invasion of Ukraine in 2022, as described in chapter 2. Most countries took advantage of the diversification opportunities. In 2011 Lithuania, hit hard by Russian pipeline shutoffs, became the first EU state to require Gazprom to "unbundle" production and distribution, forcing the sale of Gazprom's pipeline network in Lithuania. Russian president Vladimir Putin protested, calling it "uncivilized robbery."[10] Yet the EU gave Lithuania the legal basis and political backing to succeed. Similarly, Poland and Lithuania built LNG terminals on the Baltic Sea coast to facilitate import of Qatari and US natural gas.[11] Lithuania named its LNG terminal "Independence." With EU encouragement, CEE countries created interconnectors among themselves that allow them to receive gas from multiple sources, reducing reliance on Russia. A few countries, such as Bulgaria, proved slower to build interconnectors and diversify supplies, though even Bulgaria mostly completed a two-way connection with Romania in 2016 under the Danube River.[12] It finished a long-planned interconnector with Greece in 2022.

Russia tried to respond to EU attempts to diversify fossil fuel sources with its own pipeline projects in Central and Eastern Europe designed to reinforce reliance on Russia. A key element of this strategy was the South Stream (later TurkStream) pipeline. Like Nord Stream, which connected Russia directly with Germany, cutting out Poland, Belarus, and Ukraine, South Stream sought to replace Ukraine as a transit country for both business and political reasons. To build South Stream, Gazprom reached agreements on pipeline routes with EU states, perhaps the most important being Bulgaria, where the pipeline was planned to make landfall after traveling from Russia (and Crimea) under the Black Sea. However, Russia wanted to construct the pipeline without obeying EU rules on procurement, pipeline access, financing, and usage. This was a business decision with a political dimension, intended to demonstrate that the EU is a paper tiger. As prominent Russian opposition figure and energy analyst Vladimir Milov put it, "The Kremlin, as always, is trying to achieve its goals and overcome European regulations through political means."[13] Russia bribed Bulgarian parliamentarians and government officials to take its side in these matters, causing the cost of the project to quadruple between 2008 and 2015.[14] However, after the 2014 annexation of Crimea, the EU put its foot down and pressured Bulgaria into canceling the South Stream pipeline unless Russia complied with EU regulations, thus saving Bulgaria from becoming "Gazprom's new preferred transit banana republic," in the words of Milov. Russia then moved its pipeline route to make landfall in Turkey.

Though Bulgaria is an EU member state, the EU had to fight hard to keep Bulgaria on its side.[15] Russian companies and individuals bought a substantial share of the Bulgarian economy in recent years. Russian Duma deputy Piotr Tolstoy raised eyebrows in 2016 when he stated on Russian TV, "We will just buy out the entire [country]. Half of its coastline we have already bought." Bulgarians were offended at his "arrogance." Yet he is apparently right that Russian (followed by Armenian) investors are far and away the most important in Bulgaria. Russians own an estimated half a million mostly seaside homes in Bulgaria. Tolstoy, a great-grandson of novelist Leo Tolstoy, added that the EU needed deep reform and should abandon its policy of enlargement to countries in "Russia's zone of national interest."[16]

Russia also has developed Hungary, another EU member state, as an energy ally, finding a willing partner in Prime Minister Viktor Orbán. Russia promised to make Hungary a hub for South Stream gas in 2015, providing transit fees and most likely bribes or slush funds to Hungarian officials in the process.[17] Orbán has proven open to Russian proposals and an enthusiastic partner, seeing an opportunity to increase gas supplies for the EU and to play an important economic role in Europe. Hungary also agreed to allow Russia to finance and build two new nuclear reactors at an estimated cost of some €12 billion at the site of an existing plant at Paks, 120 kilometers from the capital, Budapest. While this project proved controversial when Hungary awarded Rosatom, a Russian state company, a no-bid contract, normally a no-no in the EU, it managed to convince EU regulators to approve construction in 2017.[18] Orbán seeks to broker the demands of Russia and the EU, profiting from the desire of Russia to bolster its energy market in Europe, while accommodating EU regulatory demands and remaining on the inside of the European Union. Russia sealed the deal with generous financing for the Paks project. In 2015, Orbán stated, "Whoever thinks that Europe can be competitive, that the European economy can be competitive without economic cooperation with Russia, whoever thinks that energy security can exist in Europe without the energy that comes from Russia, is chasing ghosts."[19] Hungary continued to support Russian energy imports after Russia's 2022 invasion of Ukraine (see Introduction) and won an exception to EU sanctions that allows it to continue to import Russian oil via the Druzhba pipeline.

That Russia uses its diplomats and intelligence services to identify partners and win contracts indicates the priority that the Russian state accords its energy diplomacy in Central and Eastern Europe. In 2014, the Czech Security Information Service (BIS) wrote in its annual report that "Gazprom, the major exporter of Russian natural gas, made efforts to exert maximum control over natural gas transit, storage and trade in Central Europe," while advancing business interests and exerting political influence over the country. "Russia started perceiving Czech nuclear power engineering in a broader Central European context aiming to make good use of investments and efforts devoted to creating, managing, stabilizing and future exploitation of networks expanding Russian influence in Central Europe." Specifically, Russian intelligence attempted to influence "all entities even indirectly involved in fulfilling the goals of Czech energy policies" with a view to gaining or influencing control over Czech power plants, engineering companies, and supplies of nuclear fuel. Under President Putin, Russia has made no secret that it sees energy politics as a key to geopolitical influence, and it deploys its intelligence services to further its goals.[20]

Energy politics very often filters into normal politics because of its propensity to generate payoffs for top leaders. While rumors about extensive bribery of top officials and creation of slush funds for political parties abound throughout the EU, a *New York Times* investigation in Bulgaria showed how the system works. The *Times* reported that a Russian state-owned bank (VTB) "showered the country with politically strategic investments as Mr. Putin pushed the government to move forward on South Stream." Russia courted Bulgaria's far-right party, and a Russian Duma deputy (who also brokered a Kremlin loan to France's far-right National Front) came to Bulgaria and promised to make the deputy energy minister "very comfortable" if he would cooperate in the project. When Bulgaria awarded contracts for the construction of its portion of South Stream, these contracts went to Kremlin-connected Russian companies in partnership with Bulgarian insiders.[21]

In sum, while EU energy policy has enabled CEE member states to diversify fossil fuel supplies and reduce reliance on Russia, Russia has countered by offering profitable deals to governments willing to buck EU regulations. Russia has threatened cutoffs and dangled lucrative new energy deals, while developing cozy relations with CEE politicians and seeking to undermine EU policies from within. While the EU demonstrated its power to shut down Russian projects at will, as with the cancellation of South Stream construction in Bulgaria, Russia continued to rely heavily on energy blackmail to undermine EU support for Ukraine in 2022.

Prior to Russia's full-scale invasion of Ukraine, access to cheap Russian gas remained a key part of EU energy strategy, despite its countervailing emphasis on supply diversification. EU energy companies and regulators, for instance, took a benign view of the Nord Stream 1 and 2 pipeline projects, which connected Russia directly with Germany under the Baltic Sea, bypassing existing transit countries including Ukraine. Germany approved the project despite objections from EU partners such as Poland, who feared that it would increase EU reliance on

Russian gas, cut out Central European transit states, and make Germany more vulnerable to Russian influence.[22] The events of 2022 (see chapter 2) showed that Poland's warnings were right. Prior to that, the United States slowed the construction of Nord Stream 2 by passing legislation (under the Trump administration) to allow sanctions on companies doing business with Russia. President Biden reversed course in response to German pleas to enable construction to move forward. However, once Russia invaded Ukraine, Germany refused to certify the pipeline, and it remained unused until Nord Stream 1 and 2 were hit by mysterious explosions that disabled three of their four pipes. Russia lost much of its European energy trade in 2022 when the EU imposed sanctions to punish Russia for its invasion of Ukraine, but some Central European states continue to import Russian oil and Russia continues to play European states off against one another.

POLITICAL INFLUENCE

In addition to the energy weapon, Russia holds many other cards in the new EU member states of Central and Eastern Europe.

In some countries, particularly the Baltic republics of Estonia and Latvia, Russia has used large Russian-speaking minorities to exert influence on domestic politics. These Russian-speaking populations, made up of Belarusians, Russians, Ukrainians, and other, smaller ethnic groups, rely on Russian-language media and are influenced by Kremlin media messages. While most Russian-speakers in the Baltics appreciate living in the EU rather than in Russia, they are vulnerable to Russian propaganda: "In Estonia in 2007, following false reports in the Russian media about the destruction of a monument to Soviet soldiers in World War II, young Russian-speakers rioted and

protested holding signs with slogans like 'USSR Forever.'"
Whether or not Russian-speaking minorities believe Russian
propaganda or act upon it, "most Baltic Russian-speakers would
qualify for protection as outlined in Russia's laws and compatriot policies," giving Russia an excuse for intervention when-
ever it judges the interests of Russians abroad to be violated.
As a result, Baltic governments are on tenterhooks. Russia has
sought to intensify its links to Russian-speaking populations
in the Baltic republics by issuing them Russian passports and
many other measures. Agnia Grigas suggests that these are first
steps in a process that has led to armed intervention in other
parts of the former Russian empire.[23]

In addition, Russia has sought allies among fringe political
parties throughout Central and Eastern Europe to destabilize
domestic politics and governance. Strangely for a country that
frequently portrays itself as an opponent of fascism, and justi-
fies its invasion of Ukraine as a fight against fascism, many of
Russia's allies in Central and Eastern Europe hail from the far
right of the political spectrum. The main criterion for Russian
support of extremist parties is that they articulate anti-EU, anti-
NATO messages and vocally support controversial Russian
foreign policy goals, such as the annexation of Crimea. While
Russia certainly did not create far-right nationalism in Europe,
Russia is the greatest sponsor of neofascist and far-right parties
across Europe. Russia has supported the far-right Jobbik Party
in Hungary, Ataka in Bulgaria, the Freedom Party in Austria,
Golden Dawn in Greece, and many others. Russia provides financing, political advice, training, and technology to these
parties in exchange for adoption of a pro-Russia foreign policy
platform and statements in support of Russian positions on
foreign policy matters. Far-right parties legitimate Russia's discourse within the EU and destabilize mainstream parties. Some
analysts, like historian Tim Snyder, conclude that Russia's support for fascist parties is based on ideological affinity.[24] Others

suggest it is a marriage of convenience: Russia will support any party with an anti-EU ideology.[25] Whether Russia's leaders are fascistic or simply cynical, Russia uses far-right European nationalists to disable Western institutions from within.

Some CEE states take a hard line on Russia within the EU, particularly Poland and the Baltic states. For instance, Poland has supported Ukraine in its struggles with Russia and opposed Russian annexation of Crimea and the construction of the Nord Stream pipelines. Lithuania forced Gazprom to unbundle its energy assets in Lithuania and built a new LNG terminal to achieve energy independence. Both countries have been strong supporters of the Energy Union within the EU. Poland was a main author of the Eastern Partnership policy, together with Sweden, offering EU support to the lands in between. Poland and the Baltic states have long supported a stronger NATO presence in their countries, and the vast majority of Poles regarding Polish-Russian relations as negative.[26]

This has not stopped Russia, however, from trying to recruit fringe politicians in these front-line states to toe the Russian line. Until his imprisonment in Poland on charges of spying for Russia, Russia was funding Mateusz Piskorski and his far-right Change movement. Like most far-right movements funded by Russia, Piskorski criticized Ukrainians as "fascists" and supported Russia's annexation of Crimea. Piskorski helped to organize international observers for elections in territories seized by Russia, such as Transnistria and South Ossetia.[27]

In addition to extremist parties like Change, Russia finances and helps to train far-right paramilitary organizations in many EU member states. Its intelligence services sponsor fight clubs that teach the Russian style of hand-to-hand combat. These organizations provide a recruiting tool for Russian military intelligence and a means of creating connections with far-right groups. In Slovakia, the leader of a Facebook page promoting the "Russian fighting style" is also head of external relations of a Slovak far-right organization, the Slovak Revival Movement.[28] The Slovak Revival Movement articulates a pan-Slavic ideology and spreads Russian propaganda via its web presence. A similar group, the Slovak Conscripts, is "a paramilitary group providing military training combined with pan-Slavic and pro-Russian ideological indoctrination." It is based on the model of Russian military-patriotic clubs and often invites visiting instructors from Russia to assist with training.[29] While small, these pro-Russian paramilitary organizations operate throughout Central and East Europe.

Far-right parties supported by Russia have enjoyed significant success in CEE politics and Russia has stepped up support since its invasion of Ukraine. In Slovakia, the pro-Russian, neo-Nazi People's Party–Our Slovakia won 8 percent of the vote in parliamentary elections and 14 out of 150 seats in the Slovak parliament in 2016. Its leader, Marian Kotleba, was elected governor of the Banská Bystrica region. People's Party–Our Slovakia "labelled the Maidan revolution an act of 'terrorists' and . . . launched its petition to secede from the EU and NATO."[30] Hungary's far-right Jobbik Party became the second-largest party in Hungary in the 2010s after Viktor Orbán's Fidesz, gaining 17 percent of the vote in parliamentary elections in 2010 and 20 percent in 2014. The party founded and supported violent neofascist paramilitary organizations, including the Hungarian Guard, Sixty-Four Counties Youth Movement, Army of Outlaws, Hungarian Self-Defense Movement, and Wolves.

In 2014, Jobbik leader Zoltán Lázár wrote in support of a colleague accused of spying on the EU for Russia, "We stand for anti-globalization, we are Eurosceptic, anti-liberal and we believe in Eastern Opening. In that context, Russia doesn't appear to be all that threatening. In other words, if someone 'spies for them' on the EU, all we say is: hip-hip hurray." Russia's support for far-right parties in Central and Eastern Europe increases political polarization and erodes support for mainstream parties. Studies show that the share of the radical-right vote in Europe has increased in recent years, in part due to spiking illegal immigration into Europe in 2015–16. No doubt the far right existed in Europe long before Russia got into the game, but recent successes have been fed, in part, by Russian propaganda, financial support, and actions to exacerbate any current crises.[31] In September 2022, pro-Russian parties in Czechia organized protests in the center of Prague against rising energy prices, calling for an end to EU sanctions on Russia.

TROJAN HORSES IN EU GOVERNANCE

While Russia's support for far-right parties and paramilitaries is attention-grabbing, Russia also cultivates ties with mainstream political parties in Central and Eastern Europe to develop sympathetic leaders and governments that it can use to fracture the EU from the inside. The most important case in this regard is Hungary (see Introduction), where President Putin developed a close relationship with Prime Minister Viktor Orbán, a power broker cut from the same cloth as those in the lands in between.

Orbán, who began his career as a democratic, anti-communist political activist, has made no secret of his Russophilia, which began suddenly in 2009 after a personal meeting with Vladimir Putin.[32] Upon being elected prime minister in 2010,[33] Orbán promised an "Eastern winds" economic strategy that emphasized seizing opportunities in the East as well as the West. While seeking to remain a player within the European Union, Orbán has pushed the boundaries of what the EU will accept through authoritarian constitutional changes and frequent statements against the EU sanctions regime on Russia. As discussed earlier, the largest element of Orbán's relationship with Russia is in the energy sector. Hungary seeks to become a key pipeline terminus and transit country, which would ensure a constant flow of transit revenues and politically controlled rents to grease the wheels of what Bálint Magyar calls the "post-communist mafia state" in Hungary.[34] But Russia also coordinates policy with Hungary in Ukraine, where Hungary has a large minority population. Following Russia's invasions of Ukraine, Orbán advanced Hungary's own irredentist claims to a portion of western Ukraine and supported Hungarian separatist organizations.[35] These actions seem significant since Russia has frequently suggested that Ukraine's neighbors should join it in carving up Ukraine.[36]

While Hungary often delays or criticizes EU sanctions on Russia, it has little ability to defy the EU. A relatively small EU member state, Hungary needs to remain in good standing to ensure the inflow of EU loans and structural funds and to operate without discrimination within EU institutions. In 2022, the EU blocked COVID recovery and cohesion funds from Hungary over its rule-of-law violations and increasing authoritarianism.[37] So while Prime Minister Orbán frequently speaks out against sanctions on Russia, his government ultimately supports most sanctions packages, to avoid further deterioration of Hungary's standing within the EU. Likewise, Orbán dropped his opposition to a €50 billion aid package to Ukraine in 2024. Russia tolerates the fact that weaker EU states like Hungary cannot veto Russia sanctions.

Russia also cooperates with Hungary in more covert ways. In 2017, a former Hungarian counterintelligence agent, Ferenc Katrein, gave a press interview in which he alleged that the Orbán government in Hungary was facilitating Russian intelligence operations against the EU. He claimed that the Orbán government sought to obstruct Hungary's own counterintelligence operations against Russia by reassigning experienced agents and turning a blind eye to individuals suspected of espionage activities in Russian "state-owned or state-backed companies, airlines, travel agencies, cultural centers, educational institutions, and state-owned media." Katrein further accused the Hungarian government of not sharing information about Russian intelligence threats and support for far-right organizations with its NATO allies. He alleged that a "bond" program that allowed foreigners to buy Hungarian citizenship for a few hundred thousand dollars without proper background checks had enabled Russia and China to plant long-term illegal agents in the EU, with EU citizenship. Katrein stated unequivocally that Russia was fighting a secret intelligence war against the European Union that constituted a major threat—for instance, "aggravating the migration crisis" by blowing up anti-immigrant sentiment to undermine EU leaders.[38] He described a campaign consisting of gathering information, deploying agents of influence, and spreading disinformation designed to harm the EU and popularize Russian narratives.

Russian intelligence also targets other CEE countries. In its 2015 annual report, the Czech Security Information Service reported that "in 2015, Russian activities focused on the information war regarding the Ukrainian and Syrian conflicts and on political, scientific, technical and economic espionage." In its information war, Russia focused on "covert infiltration of Czech media and the Internet, massive production of Russian propaganda and disinformation controlled by the state," and "attempts to disrupt Czech-Polish relations, disinformation and alarming rumors defaming the US and NATO, [and] disinformation creating a virtual threat of a war with Russia." Russia also focused on "maintaining and strengthening Russian positions and outlooks in Czech power engineering" and other economic, scientific, and technological espionage.[39] Russia uses covert strategies to build political and economic ties with CEE countries and spread Russian narratives through various media.

MEDIA INFLUENCE

Except in the Baltic republics of Estonia and Latvia, where there is a sizable Russian-speaking population, Russia cannot rely on Russian-language media to distribute its political messages in Central and Eastern Europe. Instead, Russia spreads its propaganda on far-right websites and news organizations linked with sympathetic oligarchs.

Russia seeks to undo public confidence in the EU among those in Central and Eastern Europe by popularizing its own anti-EU, anti-NATO, and anti-US narratives. The objective is to turn CEE populations away from the EU and NATO and prepare the way for these countries eventually to leave NATO. Russian propaganda often suggests that the United States is the puppeteer behind NATO and controls European politics without the assent of Europeans. Russia publicizes Europeans who oppose sanctions against Russia, point out the economic costs of sanctions, and speak out against policies supposedly imposed on Europe by the United States. Russia argues that the sanctions are both unjustified and unlawful.

Russian propaganda in Central and Eastern Europe also espouses pan-Slavism as a connection between Slavic nations of Central and Eastern Europe and Russia. One Slovak outlet quoted the chairman of the Russian State Duma, Vyacheslav Volodin, as stating, "The West genetically despises Russia and basically all Slavic nations," evoking images of Nazi race rhetoric to defame the West. Russian propaganda has also tried to convince Central Europeans that the United States is conspiring to sell Europe expensive American gas, rather than cheap Russian gas. Another common theme has been to discredit Ukraine by portraying it as aggressive, full of Nazis (when in fact Russia is a primary sponsor of the far right in Europe), and chaotic, unable to govern itself. These messages are spread from multiple sources, including extremist news sites, but also by mainstream politicians allied with Russia.[40]

These narratives appeal to a section of Central and East Europeans who, like their counterparts in the lands in between, do not want an either-or choice of Russia versus the EU. Since the CEE countries have substantial historical ties with both East and West, many wish for good relations with both sides. For instance, in Hungary in 2017, a majority of voters polled supported NATO membership for Hungary, but Vladimir Putin was more popular than Western leaders such as Angela Merkel. Nearly half of Czech respondents to a survey in 2016 believed that, notwithstanding strong support for Western institutions, Czechia should be somewhere in between West and East.[41] Many Central Europeans clearly see their countries as a bridge between East and West and thus sympathize with Russian narratives to some extent, though as in Ukraine, Russophile sentiments diminished after 2022.

MILITARY INTERVENTIONS AND THREATS

While Russia designs its influence techniques to avoid detection and prevent a full-scale military response, Russia does threaten EU member states militarily. EU perceptions of the threat Russia poses to Europe increased dramatically after Russia's 2022 invasion of Ukraine.[42] But even before that, Russia launched military interventions in countries that border on the EU (such as Ukraine and Moldova) and directly threatened EU member states through military exercises, penetrations of member state airspace, cyberattacks, and other means, with a particular emphasis on the Baltic republics of Estonia, Latvia, and Lithuania.

The Baltic republics were formerly incorporated into the Soviet Union from 1940 to 1991, occupy a vulnerable position between Russia, Belarus, and the Baltic Sea, and fear a possible Russian intervention. Their large Russian-speaking populations give Russia a potential excuse to intervene, particularly in Estonia and Latvia, where the Russian-speaking population reaches 25 and 35 percent, respectively. Due to having been part of the Soviet Union, the Baltic states' infrastructure is more closely connected to Russia than that of other CEE member states of the EU. Russia's aggression toward the Baltic states includes a cyberattack on Estonia in 2007 that shut down a number of government services and a 2014 abduction of an Estonian border guard seized in Estonian territory and transported to Russia, where he was imprisoned. Russia has also confronted the Baltic republics over World War II memory, protesting the relocation of a statue commemorating the Soviet "liberation" of Estonia from the Nazi regime, which resulted in Estonia's incorporation into the USSR, an event that is not remembered fondly in Estonia. Russian military exercises regularly target the Baltic states by practicing a beach landing in the Baltic Sea. Russia has placed nuclear-capable missiles in Russia's Baltic enclave, Kaliningrad. Russia illegally penetrated Baltic airspace many times since the Ukraine crisis. Russian incursions into NATO airspace and dangerous overflights of NATO ships and airplanes occurred at a rate of forty to fifty per year after 2014.[43]

Some speculate whether Russia might someday seek to invade the Baltic states—for instance, the Russian-speaking enclave of Narva in Estonia. While the Baltic states are vulnerable, their status as NATO states means that an invasion would provoke a unified response, a major deterrent. Russia seeks more covert and deniable forms of influence, but the threat of military intervention is keenly felt in CEE states that border on Russia or Belarus. Russian military threats also concern Poland, the largest CEE member state of the EU. One Russian exercise in 2009 simulated a tactical nuclear strike on Warsaw and subsequent invasion.[44] Poland tripled its defense spending from

2000 to 2018 to counter the Russian threat, striving to have one of the most capable militaries in Europe.[45]

POLARIZATION AND POWER BROKERS

Russia's hybrid war on CEE member states of the European Union has a number of objectives. Russia seeks to sow conflict within the EU, end the sanctions regime, and produce a more pro-Russian EU while diminishing US influence in Europe. Subject to this campaign, CEE countries share some of the same political pathologies as the lands in between, including political polarization and infiltration of Russian narratives in political discourse.

While Russia's 2022 invasion of Ukraine forced many politicians to choose sides between Russia and the West, some CEE power brokers continue to position themselves between the EU and Russia. These power brokers are far from ideological. They may change positions over time, seeking maximum advantage. One year, they may bring their country into NATO. Another year, they may acclaim the annexation of Crimea or seal a massive energy deal with Russia. While many regard power brokers such as Zeman or Orbán as Russian agents, they are more likely guided by self-interest. They do not care to join the Russian empire, but rather seek to maximize their own political power and resources. They do not wish to break with the EU, but rather want to continue to profit from the EU and Russia at the same time. Not all countries in Central and Eastern Europe have such power brokers at the helm. Russia's 2022 invasion of Ukraine made these power brokers' position more precarious. But they are surprisingly common in countries once assumed to have made a decisive "civilizational choice" to join the Western world when they signed up for NATO and the EU.

CONCLUSIONS

Russia has launched a comprehensive campaign to influence CEE member state governments within the EU. Its intent is clear—to destroy the EU from within by destabilizing and controlling CEE governments. CEE governments are, from the Russian perspective, the soft underbelly of the EU, since democracy and rule of law are weaker and Russia's historical ties stronger in these countries compared to other EU states. Since CEE countries made a "civilizational choice" when joining the EU, Russia faces considerable headwinds when trying to bring them back under its influence. Support for EU and NATO membership remains strong throughout Central and Eastern Europe, and EU institutions have mobilized to fight back. Yet, despite this, Russia continues to try to tear these countries away from the EU, realizing this might be a long game. Russia seeks to bribe mainstream politicians and fund radical extremists to voice controversial Russian foreign policy positions or support Russian energy projects. Russia has targeted the information space by recruiting a wide range of outlets for its state propaganda and seizing on controversial issues such as migration. Where possible, Russia uses energy blackmail, cyberattacks, and the threat of military intervention to scare people into cooperation with Russia. Russian covert activities in CEE states that are new members of NATO have reached Cold War levels to develop levers of influence—over energy businesses, fringe political parties, governing parties, criminal networks, and intelligence services.[46] Russia's campaign against the EU has contributed to a polarization of the political scene as well as to the rise of power brokers, like Viktor Orbán in Hungary, who seek rents from Russia in addition to the benefits of EU membership.

However, these strategies have their limits. As Russia learned when encouraging its Trojan horses to dismantle EU sanctions policy, CEE member states simply do not have the power to undermine strategic decisions by the EU and NATO. For this reason, Russia has intensified its efforts to exert a strong influence on the politics of the largest member states of the European Union—and the United States.

DESTABILIZING THE

DEVELOPED WEST

WHEN I BEGAN WORKING ON THIS book in 2014, I thought that Russian influence campaigns only affected weak and vulnerable countries between the EU and Russia, where Russia had stronger links and greater leverage.[1] But the events of 2016 shocked me out of complacency. It never occurred to me that Russia might bring its hybrid war to Western countries and that Russia might use the lands in between as a training ground for more ambitious targets. The US presidential election of 2016 shattered America's sense of invulnerability to Russia's covert destabilization. It also proved that policymakers and analysts could learn a lot from what was going on in the lands in between.

Now that the United States, Britain, France, Germany, and other Western countries face regular electoral attacks from Russia, threat perceptions have changed, and countries openly debate how to respond. While the tenor of this debate is often anxious, it reflects a vigorous response to an unexpected challenge, a response that may eventually enable the West to fight back with strong public support. Democracies have a hard time countering hybrid war techniques, especially since people have underestimated the threat for so long and continue to do so. Waging a conflict against subversion entails sacrifices, and in a democracy, citizens need to have understanding of and input into decisions on priorities and trade-offs. Public support is crucial to success in countering disinformation and election disruption. Thus, public debate is essential.

When I recovered from my shock, I realized that Russia's hybrid attacks have a similar effect in the most powerful countries in the world and that politics in advanced countries increasingly mirrors politics in the lands in between. The lands in between can no longer be perceived as exotic or unique,[2] but rather should be seen as providing a vital—and so far largely unheeded—early warning of the challenges the developed West now faces.

In this chapter, I spell out the threat posed by Russian covert influence in Western democracies while exploring the resources and strategies by which the West is fighting back. Western countries were initially surprised and unprepared for a covert Russian onslaught.[3] However, leading Western countries have many more tools to deploy, including economic sanctions, energy diversification policies, and financial regulations against money laundering. The battle for the soul of the West is on, and while Russia has scored some impressive victories, it has also awakened determined opposition.

A COVERT CAMPAIGN

While Russian attempts to influence the developed West are similar to those in Central and Eastern Europe and the lands in between, Russia lacks some forms of leverage over the more distant and powerful Western countries. For instance, Western countries are far less susceptible to gas and energy blackmail; they are not contiguous with Russia or as reliant on Russian pipelines. Although Russia certainly tried in 2022, it has less ability to use gas deliveries as an instrument of geopolitics in Western countries. Russia must work harder to build intelligence assets in Western countries than in former Warsaw Pact nations or former Soviet republics and cannot rely on preexisting ties. Russia therefore has less ability to organize supportive paramilitary organizations in the West, though Russian fight clubs are present in Germany and the United States.[4] Russian businesses own a smaller proportion of the economy in developed Western countries and have less opportunity for economic leverage, though Russian ownership of substantial stakes in Facebook and Twitter (now X) has raised concerns.[5] As a result, the main avenue of Russian influence in Western Europe and the United States has been via hearts and minds—distributing Russian narratives through fringe and mass media, spreading disinformation, mobilizing agents of influence, and supporting extremist, anti-EU, and anti-NATO political parties, leaders, and movements, such as France's National Rally (formerly National Front), Germany's Alliance for Germany, the Brexit campaign, and, of course, Donald Trump. Russia's ultimate goal is to break up the Western alliance and its institutions.[6]

In spreading its media messages to the West, Russia has relied on foreign-language broadcast services, especially Russia Today and Sputnik. Both were de-platformed in the United States and banned in the European Union in March 2022.[7] Both are Kremlin-controlled operations that put out news and disinformation carefully tailored by Russian intelligence services. One study based on interviews with current and former RT staff found that RT was "used as an instrument of state defense policy to meddle in the politics of other states."[8] RT also provided a conduit for payments to Western analysts and politicians who took a pro-Russian line. Former UK Independence Party leader and Brexit campaigner Nigel Farage, for instance, was a paid commentator for Russia Today. He refused to disclose how much he was paid. In countries where it operates, RT amplifies the views of fringe politicians, normally on the far right, but also on the far left. Western politicians who appear regularly on RT develop and articulate anti-EU positions, whether or not they held them before, and support controversial Russian foreign policies such as the annexation of Crimea. France's Prorussie television, a branch of Russia's Voice of Russia,[9] was closely connected to Marine Le Pen's National Front (now National Rally) and frequently included National Front politicians in its news segments, making up for their infrequent appearances in mainstream news media.[10] In the United States, Russia Today gave airtime to the Libertarian and Green Parties, as well as other fringe politicians. During the 2016 US presidential election campaign, both Green Party candidate Jill Stein and Libertarian Party candidate Gary Johnson opposed US support for Ukraine and favored Brexit.[11] In sum, RT seeks to mainstream fringe and extremist views that are anti-EU and anti-NATO or that will toe the Russian line on controversial foreign policy issues and polarize Western politics.

Whereas RT looks and feels a lot like CNN in its production values, Russia's other foreign-language state media network, Sputnik, is more of a down-market conspiracy tabloid. It is through Sputnik radio that the Kremlin publishes sensational, whole-cloth fabrications, similar to what one finds in much of the Russian-language state-controlled media. Andrew Feinberg, a journalist who worked as Sputnik's White House correspondent before he quit, wrote that "Sputnik's mission wasn't really to report the news as much as it was to push a narrative that would either sow doubts about situations that weren't flattering to Russia or its allies, or hurt the reputation of the United States and its allies."[12] For instance, Sputnik lead stories included reports that the United States and United Kingdom sent chemical weapons to terrorists in Syria. The rest of the news consists of mostly unfavorable stories about disasters and problems that occur in the United States or Europe, with heavy coverage of riots and floods. RT comments pages also provide a venue for far-right extremists. Feinberg reports that he was fired from Sputnik after refusing to promote the Seth Rich conspiracy theory at a time when Fox News had already repudiated the story. Seth Rich was a US campaign worker killed in a robbery; Fox News alleged that he was killed by Hillary Clinton in a grand conspiracy that was revealed as a hoax.

There has been a vigorous debate over the visibility and impact of these foreign-language propaganda networks. Some accounts suggest that RT's reach is rather limited, with 8 million viewers per week in the United States, for instance, and 70 million worldwide. However, others suggest that their broadcasts are amplified by a strong social media presence with billions of views and their stories sometimes get picked up by local media outlets, especially those of the far-right and extremist media in countries worldwide.[13] In essence, these pseudo-news stations have become Kremlin tools for directing coverage worldwide. With them, the Kremlin can influence the news in target countries, at least to some extent, while building actively engaged audiences.[14] In addition, these networks create an opportunity for Russia to recruit and pay agents of influence, including Western politicians and media figures.

As part of the Russian media's broader purpose of spreading alternative narratives and propaganda messages, it also purveys politically targeted disinformation, most likely cooked up by Russian intelligence agencies to disrupt and polarize Western polities. One of the most prominent attacks was the "Lisa" case in Germany. At the height of the European refugee crisis in January 2016,[15] when the German government was facing public criticism for its lenient approach to admitting migrants, reports originating in Russia alleged that a group of migrants had kidnapped and gang-raped a German teenager of Russian origin. These reports targeted the Russian-speaking community in Germany, made up primarily of ethnic Germans who lived throughout the Soviet Union and left after 1991. Street protests, possibly organized by Russian intelligence operatives, then broke out in Germany; mainstream German media began to cover the story. However, a police investigation quickly discovered that "Lisa" had not been kidnapped or raped. Instead, she had run away from home for a few days to stay with a German boyfriend of Turkish origin. Yet even after German police announced the results of their investigation, Russian government officials, including Foreign Minister Sergei Lavrov, continued to insist that Germany strengthen its position on minorities and to allege that Russians were at risk in Germany. Since Russia had justified its 2014 intervention in Ukraine on similar grounds, this claim was potentially explosive. Russia's creation from whole cloth of the "Lisa" case heightened tensions in Germany at the peak of the refugee crisis, a difficult time for Chancellor Angela Merkel. It was easy to see why Russian intelligence focused on Merkel: she was the linchpin behind European Union sanctions against Russia. It was Merkel who decided that Putin was "on another planet" and moved Germany from supporting a "modernization partnership" with Russia to advocating a tough EU sanctions regime. The "Lisa" case amounted to a hybrid attack using disinformation, street protests, and official government statements to denigrate a Western politician supportive of Russia sanctions.

Germany has not been the only target. Similar cases of disinformation have popped up in multiple Western countries. In August 2017, a fake *Guardian* (UK) news article appeared on a website that had a URL and look similar to those of the official *Guardian* page but was clearly written by a non-native speaker of English. The fake article purported to quote former British MI6 head Sir John Scarlett admitting that British and American intelligence agencies had organized Georgia's Rose Revolution in 2003 as part of a broader, but failed, effort to cause Russia to disintegrate. This fake article served to bolster Russian propaganda messages at home, as articles citing it were distributed widely in Russia. It sought to frighten Russians into believing that the West was out to get Russia, convince people that domestic pro-democracy protests were paid for by the West, and disseminate rumors that the West plans to use a color revolution in Russia to undermine the Putin regime. By identifying pro-democracy movements as unpatriotic, it seeks to head off an existential threat to the Putin regime posed by Western support for democratization.

In one bizarre instance of Russian blatant disinformation, on September 11, 2014, Russian intelligence organized a social media campaign to spread fake rumors of an explosion at a US chemical plant. Russian Twitter bots distributed fake news stories of an explosion at the Columbian Chemicals plant in Centerville, Louisiana, accompanied by a fake YouTube video purporting to show a man watching a TV news report stating that ISIS had claimed responsibility. People in the area received texts stating, "Toxic fume hazard warning in this area until 1:30 PM." According to the *New York Times*, "Dozens of journalists, media outlets and politicians, from Louisiana to New York City, found their Twitter accounts inundated with messages about the disaster." An investigative report found that this cyberattack and others—including reports of an Ebola outbreak in Atlanta—had been ginned up by a "troll factory" in St. Petersburg, Russia, where hundreds of paid trolls regularly used social media to conduct information warfare against the United States. This may have been a precursor to Russian intervention in the 2016 presidential election, or an exercise that allowed Russian intelligence to hone their techniques in destabilizing polities, sowing confusion, and spreading fake information, particularly during a crisis.[16]

As a core part of their mission, RT and other Russian media foster anti-Western conspiracy theories, such as that the 9/11 attacks were an "inside job."[17] Russia seeks to undermine faith in democratic government in the West and turn as many of its viewers as possible against the EU, NATO, and the Western international system. It seeks to provide "a televisual home for disaffected viewers in the west." Russia encourages any possible source of disaffection. RT, for instance, initially built its reputation covering the Occupy Wall Street protests. Tearing down the West also serves to build up Russia. As one *New Statesman* journalist in the UK concluded, the Russian government "funds RT to persuade everyone else that their own countries are no better" than Russia.[18] Russia hopes that by doing so, people will regard Russia as a normal country, not a deeply defective authoritarian state. It is not clear that this campaign works so well, however, as public opinion polls show Russia to be deeply unpopular in other countries.[19] Disapproval of Russia's leadership increased from 38 to 57 percent worldwide after Russia's 2022 invasion of Ukraine, according to one Gallup poll.[20]

HACKING ELECTIONS

Awareness of Russia's tactics has grown exponentially since the US presidential elections of 2016, when the world learned of Russia's expertise in hacking and influencing elections by electronic means.[21] It was not the first time, however, that Russia used such tactics. Russia's cyberwar on democratic elections has been going on at least since 2004, when Russia hacked the Central Election Commission of Ukraine to produce a fake victory for candidate Viktor Yanukovich.[22] While Russia learned from the Orange Revolution that erupted in response to this blatant electoral fraud, and does not appear to have directly falsified election results in the United States in 2016, it did infiltrate voter systems in a majority of US states, giving it the capability to do so.[23] Instead, Russia concentrated on equipping Facebook and Twitter accounts and bots with the ability to quickly disseminate fake news reports originating from Russian or conservative media and using its intelligence services to hack and disseminate opponents' emails at maximally embarrassing times. Robert Mueller profiled these tactics in his famous report on Russian interference in the 2016 US presidential election. Russia deployed them in other Western countries as well.

During the 2017 French presidential election, Russia openly supported far-right candidate Marine Le Pen. Le Pen won the largest share of votes in the first round of the election, only to fall to challenger Emmanuel Macron by a wide margin in the second round. Nonetheless, Russia had high hopes for Le Pen. Russian banks lent her party €9 million for the presidential campaign,[24] and Le Pen made a high-profile visit to the Kremlin during the height of the election campaign. She repeatedly emphasized her support for key Russian foreign policy goals, such as the annexation of Crimea. Le Pen had previously visited Russia in 2014 and 2015, even taking a side trip to sanctioned Crimea. She has long supported replacing the EU with a nationalist great-power alliance including France and Russia.[25] Le Pen also supported US president Donald Trump. Her overtures were rewarded when many of the same Twitter bots that supported Trump in the United States came to life again to support Le Pen in the 2017 French election.[26] During the 2017 presidential election campaign in France, Russian hackers stole Le Pen opponent Emmanuel Macron's emails and dumped them on WikiLeaks just before the election. WikiLeaks has cooperated closely with Russian intelligence agencies, and founder Julian Assange has been a paid TV host on Russia Today, making him a paid employee of the Russian state.[27] During the election campaign and after, victorious candidate Emmanuel Macron denounced Russia Today and Sputnik as Russian propaganda channels whose "agents of influence" spread "falsehoods" about him. He made headlines when he refused to accredit RT and Sputnik "journalists" to his presidential campaign and denounced their activity at a press conference with Vladimir Putin.[28] Even

though Macron's emails were dumped on WikiLeaks a day before the final round of the election, they had little impact since
they revealed no serious scandals. Macron, it seems, was clean.

Another potentially damaging Russian hacking attack took
place in Germany in May 2015 in the German Bundestag, as
its parliament is called. The Russian hacker group Fancy Bear,
associated with Russian military intelligence, successfully
phished, and broke into the email accounts of, several German
parliamentarians using fake look-alike websites, eventually
taking over five of six administrator accounts of the Bundestag.
Russian hackers then copied whole computers and roamed
at will throughout the German parliament's systems until the
hack was discovered some two weeks later. While the executive branch had protections in place to prevent such an attack,
Germany's parliament did not. It remains unclear what files
the hackers stole, but the German intelligence service believed
that the most damaging information would be leaked during
the 2017 parliamentary election campaign, when the ruling
Christian Democrats and Chancellor Angela Merkel, who
took a tough line on Russia sanctions, were up for reelection.
However, while Russia supported the far-right Alliance for
Germany party, which nearly tripled its share of the vote from
4.7 to 12.6 percent to become Germany's third-largest party,
Russia abstained from dumping stolen information against the
Christian Democrats, perhaps because of the negative pub-
licity from previous attacks or threats of a proactive defense by
German intelligence.[29]

The November 2016 presidential election in the United
States and subsequent investigations shone a light on Russian
electoral hacking. Candidate Hillary Clinton called Donald
Trump Putin's "puppet" during a televised debate on October
19, 2016.[30] On July 27, Donald Trump had invited the Russian
government to release Hillary Clinton's emails in a talk broadcast on national TV. He said, "Russia, if you're listening, I hope

you're able to find the 30,000 emails that are missing. . . . I think you will probably be rewarded mightily by our press."[31] Robert Mueller found that the Russian military intelligence service (GRU) had hacked Democratic servers in April 2016 and released them through the online personas Guccifer 2.0 and DCLeaks before dumping them on WikiLeaks.[32] The hacked emails received extensive media coverage. In addition, Russian trolls had a strong presence on US social media, attacking commentators they disliked and promoting fake news, often created by Russian media and broadcast to the world via US fringe websites and conservative and far-right media. Revelations that the Trump campaign may have coordinated some aspects of this campaign with Russian intelligence services led to FBI and congressional investigations.[33] President Trump then fired FBI director James Comey and the Justice Department appointed Special Counsel Robert Mueller to investigate further. Mueller concluded that Trump campaign chairman Paul Manafort shared internal polling data with Oleg Deripaska, a Russian oligarch with whom he had previously invested, and discussed a potential deal to end the war in Ukraine on terms favorable to Russia. As a result, the world became fully aware of Russian attempts to influence the US presidential elections.[34]

Russia has also sought to influence elections through more standard means, such as campaign contributions. For instance,[35] a British parliamentary investigation suggested that Russia supported the Brexit campaign,[36] which did significant damage to the EU, removing a key military and economic power and plunging it into political and economic crisis. Trolls from Russia's infamous Internet Research Agency tweeted on behalf of Brexit, creating a large portion of the Brexit discussion on Twitter. "Britons who considered their choices had no idea at the time that they were reading material disseminated by bots, nor that the bots were part of a Russian foreign policy to weaken their country."[37] Nigel Farage, the UKIP leader who was the most visible Brexit campaigner, received valuable airtime from Russia Today (RT), at a time when few British outlets carried his interviews[38] Farage began mouthing Kremlin talking points on foreign policy, notably supporting the Crimea annexation and also making positive statements about the strong leadership of President Putin. Arron Banks, the largest funder of the Brexit campaign, met repeatedly with Russia's ambassador to the UK in the run-up to the Brexit campaign.[39] UK political finance laws ban foreign entities from donating to political campaigns but allow UK companies to do so. Therefore, Russian entities seeking to donate to the Brexit campaign may have used proxy companies, including those related to Arron Banks.[40] Another top aide of Nigel Farage, George Cottrell, was arrested in an FBI sting operation in Chicago in 2017 and convicted by a US court of money laundering.[41] Arron Banks accompanied Farage when he became the first foreign official to meet with Donald Trump after his 2016 election.

SUPPORT FOR THE EXTREMES

To further polarize politics in the developed West and render democratic political systems dysfunctional, Russia provides support to extremist parties and paramilitary organizations on the far right and far left. Russia has supported separatist groups in Western countries, extremist paramilitaries, and fight clubs, in addition to using its intelligence agencies to develop pro-Russian political and business networks, mirroring their operations in Central and Eastern Europe and the lands in between.

Key to this effort is Russia's material support for far-right parties and movements in Europe and the United States. In addition to the case of the French National Front (now National Rally), mentioned earlier, Russia has supported Jobbik in Hungary, which started out as a neofascist movement. One of

Jobbik's European parliamentarians was convicted of spying for Russia.[42] Russia also has funded the neofascist party Golden Dawn in Greece, as well as Ataka in Bulgaria. Ataka, a small anti-EU party, joined a pro-EU coalition government in Bulgaria from 2017 to 2019.[43] During the 2017 elections in Germany, Russian social media supported Alliance for Germany, the first far-right party elected to the German parliament in the postwar era. In 2023, the *Washington Post* obtained Russian documents that showed it sought to build an anti-war coalition between the far-right Alliance for Germany and far-left politician Sahra Wagenknecht.[44] Austria's far-right Freedom Party openly concluded a partnership agreement with Putin's United Russia Party in 2016.[45] Russia's support for the far right in Europe is designed to draw voters away from mainstream parties, undermine political support for the EU, provide a voice for Russian foreign policy views in European parliaments, distribute Russian propaganda, sow dissent, and cause or exacerbate various crises.[46] To the extent that extremist parties win seats in parliament, mainstream parties face greater difficulties forming governments, undermining political stability.

Russia also establishes pro-Russia paramilitary organizations in Western states. A Germany-based researcher found that the Russian military intelligence service GRU had organized sixty-three "systema" fight clubs across the EU and North America, teaching Russian hand-to-hand combat methods. The founders of these clubs were all GRU or FSB (the Russian federal security service) agents. He alleged that these clubs were being used to recruit agents in sleeper cells that could be used to stage violent provocations.[47] An Estonian intelligence agent pointed out that Russia has gone beyond media influence operations to organize protests, noting that the International Convention of German-Russians organized a protest of some seven hundred people in front of German chancellor Angela Merkel's office, coordinated with the "Lisa" case disinformation.[48] Mark Galeotti, an American expert on Russian intelligence operations, issued a report alleging that the "highly criminalized" Russian state was using Russian crime organizations to carry out intelligence work throughout Western nations. He advised Western states to crack down on Russian criminal networks and view them as instruments of the Russian state, noting that prominent Russian underworld financier Semion Mogilevich continues to live and work openly in Russia.[49] Timothy Snyder writes that "Russia's support of the NRA [National Rifle Association] resembled its support of right-wing paramilitaries in Hungary, Slovakia, and the Czech Republic," noting that the NRA complained that the United States took too soft a line on Russia through 2015, when it accepted Russian financial support.[50]

Russia has also frequently supported secessionist movements in Western states to create political crises and weaken democratic polities through internal dissent. In the United States, the California secession movement California Yes, launched during the Trump election campaign to sow discord in America by detaching a pro-Hillary state, has well-documented ties to Russia. The founder of California Yes, Louis Marinelli, was a right-wing activist (though the movement is avowedly leftist) based in Yekaterinburg, Russia. He has a Russian wife and opened a Russian "embassy" for his organization with Russian financing. He has spent more time living in Russia than California.[51] Shortly after the election, Marinelli closed down California Yes and returned to Russia.[52] He admitted to receiving office space and travel expenses from a far-right Russian group.[53] Russian support for "Calexit" appears to be only one element of a worldwide campaign to undermine democratic states through secession. In 2018, the head of the German Federal Office for the Protection of the Constitution (BfV) stated that it was "very plausible" that Russia had carried out a disinformation campaign in Spain in 2017 to encourage voters to support Catalan independence.[54]

LEVERAGING BUSINESS TIES

In addition, Russia financed and built networks of ties with mainstream political parties in Europe, such as the French Republicans, the British Conservative Party, and, in Germany, the Social Democrats and the Left (Die Linke). In several European countries, Russia used associations designed to support bilateral cooperation as platforms for developing relations with Russia-friendly corporate leaders and politicians. These included the German-Russian Forum and the Petersburg Dialog, funded mainly by the German Foreign Ministry. During the 2000s and 2010s, Russia used these organizations to develop supporters at the top level of German industry, people with strong business ties with Russia who could influence German and EU policy against sanctions and in favor of continued engagement.[55] In 2021, however, Russia began to blacklist German NGOs under its foreign agent law if they spoke out against Russia's 2014 annexation of Crimea or mentioned the 1939 Molotov-Ribbentrop Pact.[56] The powerful Petersburg Dialog, established by Putin and German chancellor Gerhard Schroeder, closed its doors in 2023 "given the criminal and aggressive war" Russia waged on Ukraine and Russia's "front-line position against Western democracies."[57]

But for a long time, these cooperation mechanisms worked. In a 2017 Atlantic Council report, Stefan Meister showed that the Eastern Committee of Germany's powerful business lobby "continues to try to influence decision makers to alter their position on Russia," organizing a trip to Moscow in 2016 "to give representatives of leading German companies the opportunity to meet with Putin and hear arguments for the improvement of relations through a common economic space and the lifting of sanctions." In France, where far-left, far-right, and center-right Republicans all supported closer relations with Russia until 2022, the business community led the way. Analyst Marlene

Laruelle wrote that "many chief executive officers (CEOs) of these big industrial groups have close connections to the Kremlin's inner circle and have been acting as intermediaries of Russian interests and worldviews for the Republicans." French businesses developed close ties in "the defense industry (Thales, Dassault, Alstom), the energy sector (Total, Areva, Gaz de France), the food and luxury industry (Danone, Leroy-Merlin, Auchan, Yves Rocher, Bonduelle), the transport industry (Vinci, Renault), and the banking system (Société Générale)."[58] Laruelle argues that, at least for the center-right, France's alignment with Moscow sought to balance between the United States and Russia, in the Gaullist tradition. German Social Democrats long supported an "Ostpolitik" of rapprochement with Russia. In the United States, Russian intelligence also tried to develop support among the think tank community in Washington, DC, recruiting individuals and institutions to support a Russian foreign policy line and cultivating support among business leaders.

As a result, European countries—and the United States—often seem to be one election away from electing a pro-Russian government that would significantly alter their positions toward Russia, starting with the sanctions regime. French president Emmanuel Macron accused Russia of undermining his 2016 presidential campaign and criticized the pro-Russia stances taken by the far-right National Front, far-left candidate Jean-Luc Mélenchon, and mainstream Republicans. In the 2017 German elections, Chancellor Angela Merkel's Christian Democratic Union faced growing opposition from Alternative for Germany, a far-right party that has strong sympathies with the authoritarian Russian president and strong support among Germany's Russian-speaking minority.[59] Through 2022, it seemed that Russia's campaign of influence and alignment might help to elect a government in a major European country that would reverse the sanctions regime. Yet the scale and brutality of Russia's aggression against Ukraine in 2022 convinced most Europeans that Russia constituted a threat that could not be ignored. Whereas Italian populist Five-Star Movement leader Beppe Grillo became a vocal supporter of Putin's policies, populist prime minister Giorgia Meloni took a firm anti-Putin line and encouraged the EU to integrate Moldova, Ukraine, and the western Balkan countries.[60] Yet Russia continued to try to foster European opposition to the war in Ukraine and the high gas prices and inflation it brought on in 2022. In 2023, Alternative for Germany's public support reached new heights, while the populist Freedom Party in Austria led public opinion polls. Russia's efforts to ignite an anti-war coalition in Germany suggest that it still hopes this strategy may succeed. In 2024, Germans took to the streets in mass demonstrations against Alternative for Germany.

MILITARY THREATS

Few wish to recognize that Russia's interventions in Western politics include not only support for political parties and movements and the dissemination of Kremlin propaganda and disinformation, but also the threat of military force against Western countries. Starting in 2010, Russia declared the Western countries to be the primary source of "military dangers" in its official military security doctrine, in a move that puzzled EU countries that had been trying to develop a partnership with Russia. Russia increased unauthorized overflights of NATO airspace, particularly in the Baltic states. Reports counted some thirty-nine unauthorized overflights in 2014 and fifty in 2015.[61] Overflights accelerated with Russia's 2022 invasion of Ukraine.[62] Russia has also attempted overflights of US, Canadian, and British airspace, timed to political events. Russia flew close to Canadian airspace during a visit by Ukrainian president Petro Poroshenko in 2014 and simulated an attack on Denmark in 2014.[63] Russian bombers, anti-submarine aircraft, and intelligence-collection planes penetrated US airspace in Alaska more than sixty times in 2021.[64] In 2014, a Russian submarine was sighted in Swedish waters.[65] Russian officials have also reminded their Western counterparts of the possibility of nuclear war, threatening to aim nuclear weapons at Danish ships should the country join NATO's missile defense shield and to retaliate with nuclear force over an attack on Crimea or Kaliningrad, Russia's Baltic territory.[66] Russia has coupled its influence campaign in the developed West with provocative military measures and rhetoric designed to ensure that Western countries fear Russia.

Western perceptions of Russian military threats increased exponentially in February 2022. Russian tanks rolling into Ukraine represented the greatest military invasion in Europe since World War II and forced not only front-line states like Poland, Finland, and the Baltics, but also the rest of Europe, to contemplate the possibility of a major land war. German chancellor Olaf Scholz announced a turning point (*Zeitenwende*) in European security together with a €100 billion defense spending package. French president Emmanuel Macron announced a 30 percent increase in military spending from 2023 to 2030.[67] The Stockholm International Peace Research Institute found that the outbreak of war in Ukraine triggered the steepest increase in military expenditure in Europe in three decades.[68]

Russia's frequent nuclear threats gave developed Western nations the impression that Russia's leadership under Vladimir Putin had become unhinged. In March 2023, former Russian president Dmitry Medvedev warned that a "nuclear apocalypse" is drawing closer, one of only a wide range of threats "that are loud, frequent, and extreme," according to a report by the Carnegie Endowment for International Peace. The report concludes that "not only does the regime see its current position as deeply precarious but also that the regime is willing to take severe risks to improve its security."[69] Russia uses these threats to force developed Western nations to think twice before arming Ukraine. They remind the West that Russia's hybrid war has always included a military dimension.

IMPACT

While the nature and extent of Russian hybrid war on the developed Western countries has become clear in recent years, its effect on politics has been hotly debated. Some argue it that has had unintended consequences. In its efforts to disable Ukraine, Russia's attacks galvanized a pro-Western consensus in the country. In attempting to use energy blackmail against Europe, Russia caused the EU to invest more heavily in a green transition that will hurt Russia's interests over the long term.[70] Thomas Risse and Nelli Babayan argue that in some cases, "efforts by illiberal regimes [to oppose democracy] have the counterintuitive effect of fostering democracy by strengthening democratic elites and civil society."[71] Yet the main effects of Russia's hybrid war on the developed Western countries have been similar to its effects on the lands in between: to create a new politics of polarization and power brokers.

As in the lands in between, Russia has become a key issue in democratic elections in the West. A sort of "civilizational choice" discourse has grown in the West. In 2018, President Macron spoke of a "European civil war" between forces of liberal democracy and authoritarian nationalism. "We are seeing authoritarianism all around us. . . . In these times European democracy is our best chance."[72] Echoing these sentiments, outgoing US National Security Council director H. R. McMaster in 2018 warned that the West is "engaged in a fundamental contest between our free and open societies and closed and repressive systems," and that "revisionist and repressive powers are attempting to undermine our values, our institutions, and our way of life." He claimed that the United States had failed to be tough enough in addressing these challenges.[73] Hot on the heels of Russia's 2022 invasion of Ukraine, President Joseph Biden characterized the struggle against Russia as a "battle between democracy versus autocracy" (see Introduction). What are these statements if not an articulation of a civilizational choice facing Western democracies—as the lands in between faced years before?

Indeed, since Russia launched its hybrid war on the West in 2007, Western politics at each election seems to pose a choice between authoritarianism and democracy, free markets and crony capitalism, the quest for truth and reliance on propaganda. Political parties in most Western countries divide sharply along these lines, with distinct views of whether the West should continue to support the liberal international system or a new system based on great-power politics, prominent power brokers, and xenophobic nationalism.

Russian support for extremist parties in the West has contributed directly to this polarization of the political system, as in the lands in between. Germany is one example. Mainstream parties are losing support, while Russia-supported far-left and far-right parties rise. This weakens the pro-EU center of the political spectrum and enhances the power of the anti-EU parties—parties that seek to do away with the key institutions of the liberal international order, such as democratic checks and balances, NATO, and the European Union. Italy provides another example. The success of the Five Star Movement and Lega in the 2018 parliamentary elections made it difficult to form a coalition government because mainstream parties were sidelined, and extremist parties had trouble agreeing with one another's extreme positions on issues such as how to behave within the EU. Polarization makes coalition politics and government formation more difficult and threatens the stability and democratic character of Western countries.

This hybrid war has also elevated oligarchs and power brokers who seek to profit both from Russia and the West, taking rents from both sides.

President Donald Trump provides a key case in point. Trump rose to power with support from the Russian government, although the Mueller investigation did not find evidence of direct collusion. The Trump organization relied heavily on Russian money, often from sales to shell companies.[74] A *New Republic* article called Trump at least "a convenient patsy for Russian oligarchs and mobsters," implying that he may have known that condos in his buildings were being used to launder money from Russian mafia figures.[75] Trump's presidential campaign benefited from substantial Russian support, including the purchase of Facebook ads and the hacking of Democratic Party servers by Russian intelligence services. To some extent, Trump appeared to reward Russia for its support by speaking out against sanctions, lobbying to reinstate Russia to the G7, criticizing NATO, and accepting Russian annexation of Crimea. Yet at the same time, Trump claimed, "There's never been a president as tough on Russia as I have been."[76] Trump sent lethal weapons to Ukraine, funded the European Deterrence Initiative, and imposed sanctions on the Nord Stream 2 pipeline in 2019. Analysts have struggled to understand the contradictions of Trump's Russia policy.

Seen through the lens of the lands in between, Trump's actions from 2016 to 2020 make more sense. Like other power brokers profiled in this book, Trump did not take an ideological view of US-Russia relations. Instead, he saw them in terms of his own power, which could be maximized by kowtowing to Putin at some times, while at others aggressively pushing US interests to the detriment of Russia. These opposing stances may have reinforced each other. Trump willingly gave Putin things that he may have perceived as relatively costless, such as treating Russia like a great power, refusing to criticize Putin, and speaking approvingly of Russia's annexation of Crimea. But Trump did not shy away from conflict at other times, such as when Trump sought to promote US liquified natural gas exports to Europe by killing Nord Stream 2 or deterring Russian use of force by upgrading the US nuclear arsenal. Similarly to flexible oligarchs in the lands in between, Trump saw the advantage of sometimes supporting and sometimes opposing Russian interests, while retaining room to maneuver. Overall, Trump pushed the United States away from a firm commitment to NATO allies and toward a more transactional approach to foreign policy. But it would be hard to say that he was firmly in the pocket of Russia. Instead, he sought to manipulate both sides to achieve his own objectives.

Politics in core Europe and the United States now reflects the pathologies of politics as in the lands in between. Developed Western countries now perceive themselves as occupying a zone of insecurity. All face a "civilizational choice" between a liberal international order fraying at the edges and a brave new world of xenophobic nationalism and great-power order, between free markets and crony capitalism, between rule of law and oligarchy. Elections have become referenda on this civilizational choice. Political parties are polarizing along these lines. And yet power brokers are emerging to take advantage of opportunities presented by this new politics of polarization. Though the intensity of this conflict remains higher in Ukraine and other lands in between, with shooting wars, occupations, and provocations by Russia, we can see there the future of Western politics, a dystopia of division.

FIGHTING BACK

Yet Western countries, after being blindsided by Russia's assault on their institutions, have begun to fight back. As discussed in chapter 2, the United States, the European Union, and other

Western countries voted to impose damaging economic sanctions on Russia after its 2014 and 2022 invasions of Ukraine, sanctions Russia is desperate to remove. Intelligence services and law enforcement agencies now investigate and monitor Russian subversion of elections and the information space. The EU launched a counter-propaganda agency to debunk Russian propaganda and fake news. US special counsel Robert Mueller indicted thirty-four individuals and three Russian businesses on charges related to Russian influence on the 2016 presidential election. These included former Trump campaign chairman Paul Manafort, Trump campaign official Rick Gates, former national security advisor Michael Flynn, political operative Roger Stone, Trump's personal attorney Michael Cohen, thirteen Russian nationals (including Yevgeniy Prigozhin), and the infamous Russian troll farm, the Internet Research Agency. Russia's 2022 invasion of Ukraine turned Western public opinion decisively against Russia. Brexit dramatically increased support for the EU. So, despite everything, the developed West has shown resilience. But will this be enough? Russia's strategy of division depends on inaction in the West. Only with growing awareness can the West confront these challenges effectively.

▼

THE NEW POLITICS OF
HYBRID WAR

AT ITS HEART, THE STRUGGLE between Russia and the West is a struggle for Europe. On the one hand, the Western powers wish to pursue the project of an EU Europe: a vision of democratically governed nation-states coming together in a union that renders conflict unthinkable and promotes prosperity through free trade and common regulation. On the other hand, a revisionist Russia wants to create a great-power Europe: a Europe in which Russia and other large European powers have rightful spheres of influence and meet periodically to resolve European issues through summit negotiations. Such a great-power Europe would provide Russia with renewed influence in its "near abroad," and give Russia a seat at the table that it feels it has been lacking in European affairs. These visions are fundamentally incompatible: a "difference between a Europe of empire and a Europe of integration."[1] As a result, European affairs now are defined by a new confrontation between Russia and the West that some have compared to the Cold War.[2] But this is not like the Cold War.

In the Cold War, an agreement was reached at Yalta in 1945 on spheres of influence: one system on one side of the Iron Curtain and another system on the other. Each side threatened the other with nuclear weapons, but mutual assured destruction kept both sides in check and peace was maintained in Europe, though proxy wars were fought elsewhere. The current conflict does not respect defined borders. Governance of the West as a whole and the lands in between is at stake. The West is not content to allow Russia to dominate its former Soviet neighbors, since the West wishes to export its vision of European peace. The West believes that the former Soviet countries' choice of alliance is a fundamental sovereign right and they can benefit from economic integration with the EU. Meanwhile, Russia wants to dismantle the EU, which it regards as a geopolitical competitor, and undermine liberal democratic institutions. Initially fought largely through covert and indirect methods, this conflict now threatens everyone on either side of an emerging divide in Europe. Only after Russia's full-scale invasion of Ukraine in 2022 did this realization hit home for many Europeans.

There are many theories of why this conflict has occurred. Some blame the West for expanding NATO and enlarging the EU, which frightened Russia into a hostile reaction.[3] Some say the United States and Europe humiliated Russia by treating it like a defeated power and expanding Western institutions after 1989 rather than developing new institutions including Russia in a new European security structure.[4] Others point to Russia's failure to accept its own post-imperial situation after the collapse of the Soviet Union,[5] or to the incompatible geopolitical cultures of Russia and the West.[6] After Gorbachev declared an end to the Soviet empire, Russia and other successor states were plunged into a deep political, economic, and identity crisis. The Baltic states managed to integrate successfully into EU Europe, but the rest did not, suffering massive damage to their economies and their pride. Russia's revisionist hostility represents a reaction to this internal crisis, a time of troubles, expressed in a time-honored tradition of imperial aggression.

While many plausible theories of this conflict continue to be debated, the proximate cause is easy to identify. It began with the ascension of Vladimir Putin to the presidency of Russia in

1999–2000. Handpicked by President Boris Yeltsin in 1999, Putin rejected Yeltsin's pro-Western foreign policies in favor of a restoration of Soviet pride and tsarist nationalism. His first act was to crush Chechnya's drive for independence.

In 2000, the first year of the new millennium, I happened to be working at Moscow State University's Faculty of Public Administration, administering a technical assistance program for the US Department of State and teaching a course called Public Administration and Democracy. Moscow State University, Russia's greatest university, like other universities, had fallen to great depths during the 1990s. Professors had to work three or four jobs to make ends meet and had little time for research. Buildings were falling apart, and corruption had taken hold. To counter this, President Putin plowed money back into universities and scientific research institutes that had been the pride of the Soviet era. One of the first projects undertaken at Moscow State University was to sandblast the outside of the landmark university building in Sparrow Hills and burnish the Stalinist symbols of Soviet pride, restoring the massive crests of the CCCP on the four sides of the great tower and polishing the red star at its apex.[7] Clearly, Putin sought to restore Russian pride in the Soviet legacy, even adopting the Soviet anthem as the new Russian anthem, but with new words.

Putin called the collapse of the Soviet Union the greatest geopolitical catastrophe of the twentieth century.[8] In one of the defining moments of his career, he defended the KGB headquarters in East Germany from the ransacking that befell the East German Stasi building after the Berlin Wall came down. Upon coming to power in Russia as the successor to Yeltsin, Putin developed a popular but self-serving narrative about Russia and the West. He argued that the 1990s were a disastrous decade for Russia—and that the West was largely to blame. Trying to impose Western capitalism and democratic governance led Russia to terrible results: a social and economic catastrophe of unimaginable proportions. Russia's economy declined to less than half its 1989 level of production.[9] Death rates skyrocketed by 50 percent, with male life expectancy falling by nearly ten years from sixty-six to fifty-seven, a collapse unprecedented in peacetime in any country of the world.[10] The 1990s were a bizarre time in Russia, with promises of prosperity and Western governance linked with a flagrant growth of mafia activity, human trafficking, prostitution, and collapse of social institutions. Any country would be embarrassed and angry after what Russia endured in the 1990s. But was the West to blame?

While Western economists optimistically believed that neoliberal economic reforms would create a capitalist utopia in Russia, the West did not create the communist system. Western politicians did not create the mass corruption, failed leadership, and lack of public sentiment that fueled terrible abuses of public trust. The West was not responsible for cutting Russians off from the rest of the world. Russia did this itself. Russian economists played a key role in designing and implementing programs such as voucher privatization. Russian businesspeople and the Russian government developed the infamous "loans for shares" scheme that enabled President Yeltsin to win another term in office in exchange for transferring leading enterprises into the hands of oligarchs. Other transition countries, with similar Western-oriented economic programs, fared far better. Russia was, to a large extent, the author of its own fate.

Nonetheless, it was Putin's genius to turn Russia's anger and frustration over the transitions of the 1990s against the West. Putin offered Russians an opportunity to blame all their troubles on the West. It was wildly popular. Blaming the West for Russia's failure to thrive in democratic governance or market economics has become a core part of Kremlin propaganda and the worldview of most of the Russian population. As a corollary to this, Putin pined for a soft re-creation of the Soviet Union or the tsarist empire. From the beginning of his rule, he sought to revive the Soviet system, using many old techniques, values, approaches, and even personnel, with some updates derived from Russia's nationalist and tsarist legacies.

GREAT-POWER VERSUS EU EUROPE

Russia's hybrid war on the West arose from its aspirations to be a great power, and many have remarked on the fact that Putin's geopolitical vision is reminiscent of nineteenth-century imperialism.[11] Yet few have spelled out what this means.[12] Specifically, Putin's view of Russia's relations with the West is modeled on the world of post-Napoleonic Europe, in which the emissaries of the Russian tsar sat together with those of the German and Austrian emperors and the French and British kings to arrange European affairs in a series of "congresses," or meetings, to solve the international crises of the day. Putin aspires to be a modern day Metternich, the Austrian count and foreign minister who created the Congress of Vienna and what later evolved into the "Concert of Europe," or the "Congress system," which kept the peace in Europe from 1815 to 1848. Why? The reason is simple. Whereas Russia will never be a core member of Western institutions such as the European Union—Russia is not democratic and cannot tolerate either the legal culture or the pooled sovereignty required by the EU—it can be a key player, if not first among equals, of a new great-power Europe that fits its nationalist vision.

Russia's ideal is for the EU not to exist, or to be downgraded, and for the great powers of the European continent to manage affairs among themselves: Russia, Germany, France, and the UK, as independent nations. This is why Putin prefers the "Normandy format" as a mechanism to resolve the

Ukraine conflict. He prefers to sit with the German chancellor and the French president rather than with representatives of the European Union, who often represent smaller nations. This is why Russian president Dmitry Medvedev in 2008 proposed a new security architecture for Europe, based on "indivisible security" for all countries in Europe, regardless of their bloc affiliations. The proposal was not to set up a new institution, but rather to declare respect for the rights and interests of all European states—indeed, all states involved in European security—and agree to convene meetings when necessary to prevent conflict. Western leaders dismissed Medvedev's proposals as "vague, with uncertainty over whether the Russian president wanted to create a new institution or simply strengthen Moscow's means to oppose European security developments that it did not like."[13] In retrospect, we can see that these proposals were modeled on Congress Europe, an arrangement in which the Christian great powers of the day—Russia, Prussia, Austria, France, and Britain—met periodically to address security challenges as they arose. They divided responsibilities and spheres of influence among themselves and prevented a major war for thirty years. In essence, Medvedev preferred this loose form of coordination over the institutional structure and legal requirements of EU membership or the permanent alliance of NATO. In theory, every European country would have a voice. In reality, great powers would decide. Sergei Karaganov, a senior Russian government strategist, spoke of the "idea of forming a club of great powers, which would be able, on a par with the UN, to make the world at least a little more manageable."[14]

The problem, though, with Russia's vision of a great-power Europe is that most Europeans see it as a throwback to a nineteenth-century vision of international relations that catastrophically failed. While Congress Europe kept the peace for thirty years, the structure collapsed after the democratic revolutions of 1848 and then, decisively, in World War I. The complex balance of alliances between large and small powers in Europe finally imploded in a "war to end all wars." It failed to encompass smaller nations' desires for national independence. For most Europeans, great-power politics is and should be a thing of the past. By contrast, NATO and the European Union have kept the peace in Europe for seventy years and continue to protect member states large and small. Whereas Congress Europe was a club of autocracies, EU Europe is a club of democracies. Western institutions gained new relevance when a dozen or more countries of Eastern Europe, former satellites of the Soviet Union, clamored to enter the European Union and NATO after the end of the Cold War. Eleven new member states were admitted to the EU in the 2000s, having been previously admitted to NATO. An enlarged Europe confidently believed in institutional structures designed to forge peace through economic integration, democratic governance, respect for internationally recognized borders, and minority rights, all values that the conservative great powers of Europe's past fiercely opposed.

When Russia proposed what it thought was a legitimate security arrangement and was met by a blank stare from the West, it then sought to undermine EU Europe's efforts to expand its zone of influence. Russia opposed EU and NATO efforts to extend its integration project to the lands in between. Russia started its own campaign to shape the developed West in its own image. Realizing that confronting the West directly through military tactics would fail, Russia launched a hybrid war. It combined a political war on Western institutions with traditional wars and frozen conflicts in its near abroad. In this way, Russia sought to establish a sphere of influence in Europe and stem the advance of EU Europe, while preventing its enemies from reacting.

NEW POLITICS OF POLARIZATION AND POWER BROKERS

Russia's hybrid war on the West created serious problems for Western democracies. Russia's support for far-right and far-left parties exacerbated political polarization. Of course, Russia did not create political extremism in the West, but by funding and supporting it with media messaging, Russia enhanced its challenges to mainstream politics. Growing extremism has made it more difficult for mainstream parties to form governments in many countries. Russia planted divisive messages at the core of Western politics, aggravated the immigration crisis through its disinformation, as in the "Lisa" case in Germany, and fed a wide range of divisions between races, ethnicities, and regions. In the small, vulnerable countries in between Russia and the EU, people talk of "civilizational choice" between two worlds—one Eastern and autocratic, the other Western and democratic. They have lived with this for some time.

While some mock the notion of civilizational choice, seeing it as a reflection of Samuel Huntington's controversial work on the "clash of civilizations,"[15] similar language has become increasingly evident in the developed West itself. President Macron of France has pointed to an emerging "European civil war" between the forces of liberal democracy and authoritarian nationalism. Each Western election in this hybrid war era has become a referendum on the future of democracy, as authoritarian nationalists compete for power on xenophobic nationalist and pro-Russia platforms. The fundamental institutions that structure European politics and security—the European Union and NATO—are under constant attack. Timothy Snyder argues that we cannot take for granted Western democratic institutions and, instead, must fight to preserve them again and again.[16] The experience of Hungary reminds us that Western democratic institutions remain fragile. They can break down and a new civilization could be born at any time.

The perception that countries face a civilizational choice heightens the political stakes and contributes to polarization. Political parties divide sharply into those that support the liberal international order and those that do not. They pose a stark choice. A party like the National Rally (formerly National Front) wants to degrade or withdraw from the European Union, while Macron wants France to be a leader of EU Europe. This helps to explain why, even when the National Rally (National Front) candidate wins enough votes to enter the second round of the French presidential election, as Marine Le Pen did in 2017, voters on the right and the left combine to defeat the National Front. The same occurred in snap parliamentary elections in France in 2024. The most important aspect of politics is not right or left, but whether France stays in the European Union and remains a democracy and an open society. US president Joe Biden has used similar language to discuss his reelection campaign in 2024 versus Donald Trump, as did Vice President Kamala Harris.

Paradoxically, though, many of the big winners in this polarized political context are power brokers who find a way to profit from both sides. Such a strategy is high risk. Some might judge the task to be impossible. Yet politicians who care about the here and now rather than ideologies have found ways to benefit from the politics of civilizational choice by mobilizing resources from both sides.

Russia offers big rewards to politicians who cooperate, including preferential oil and real estate deals, media support, and funding for political campaigns. In the 2016 US presidential election, Russia sought a direct line into the Trump and Stein campaigns to defeat Hillary Clinton. Some candidates happily accepted the material support Russia provided. Russian social media manipulation and the hack-and-release attacks involving sensitive information played important roles in the campaign.

At the same time, politicians seemingly "bought" by Russia also seek material benefits from relations with or continued membership in the West. Hungarian Prime Minister Viktor Orbán does not wish to depart from the European Union and join the Eurasian Economic Union. He wishes to enrich himself, his party, and his country with structural funds from the European Union while also turning Hungary into a hub for Russian gas exports to Europe and winning Russian financing for a nuclear power station. Bidzina Ivanishvili does not seek to pull Georgia out of its Deep and Comprehensive Free Trade Agreement with the EU while strengthening relations with Russia and undermining EU sanctions. In fact, the EU granted Georgia candidacy for membership just as Georgia turned toward Moscow in 2023. The point of this game is to gain resources from both sides. And, strangely, a highly polarized political environment creates exceptional opportunities for profit. Each side is so afraid of the inroads made by the other side that they value the allegiance of an ally or potential ally even more, particularly when they seem disloyal. Small states understand these dynamics very well. In Czechia, the Good Soldier Schweik is a national literary hero. In Jaroslav Hašek's famous book, the seemingly dim-witted Schweik kowtows to the great powers of the day, joins the Austro-Hungarian army grudgingly during World War I, hilariously mocks all commands he is given, and, when the opportunity arises, defects to the Russian side to save his skin.[17] The moral: give the great powers the appearance of getting what they want, but serve yourself.

Politicians beyond ideology, concerned primarily with their own material interests, see only benefits in cooperating with geopolitical rivals. Small, vulnerable nations have played this game since time immemorial. Accommodating great powers has been a necessity for states unable to risk angering powerful neighbors. It is more surprising to see this politics of polarization and power brokers take shape in large, powerful states that are members of the European Union and the developed West. Yet politics in the West today increasingly mirrors the contradictions of politics in the lands in between. Why? Because today, we are all vulnerable.

WHAT IS TO BE DONE?

The West is not defenseless. NATO's military assistance to Ukraine in 2022 showed that the West has enormous capabilities, should it choose to use them. NATO coordinated the supply of weapons to Ukraine to resist Russia's invasion, helping to stop Russia's invading force in its tracks. The EU forcefully responded to Russia's aggression with punishing economic sanctions, boycotts and price caps on Russian fossil fuels, and humanitarian assistance to Ukrainians fleeing the war.[18] These measures seriously harmed the Russian economy and made it harder for Russia to supply its army. The RePowerEU energy strategy accelerated the EU's green transition and rapidly reduced its reliance on Russia. The West has the capacity to act. But will it use that capacity? Russia uses energy blackmail and political warfare to wear down the West's will to resist—with some effect, as the US Congress blocked additional aid to Ukraine in 2024. To succeed in this conflict, the West must help Ukraine to win, while confronting other aspects of Russia's hybrid war.

First, the West must commit to including Ukraine and Moldova in the EU and NATO. As a former adviser to President Macron of France was quoted as saying, enlargement has become a "geopolitical necessity . . . there is no longer a stable grey zone possible between the Union and Russia."[19] Indeed, the EU acted on this sentiment, opening membership negotiations with Ukraine and Moldova in 2024. NATO also needs to put Ukraine on the track to full membership. Whether or not

Russia succeeds in occupying part of Ukraine's territory over the long term, Russia has lost the hearts and minds of Ukrainians, convincing an overwhelming majority of the population that its statehood can only be protected within the Western community of nations. The West must clarify its boundaries with Russia.

At the same time, Russia's conflict with the West goes far beyond the borders of Ukraine. Since 2022, Russia has intensified efforts to target elections and political systems throughout the Western world, in order to discredit, polarize, and disable opposing polities and gain advantage in Ukraine. Russia's history of electoral intervention in the United States "points to a tumultuous 2024 election cycle."[20] It requires Western countries to combat money laundering, respond to disinformation, and react more aggressively to cyberattacks. Western leaders have ignored Russia's hybrid threat for so long and in many cases remain unwilling to address it. The United States has been disabled from within. Many Americans willfully spread Kremlin propaganda, such as Tucker Carlson accusing Ukraine of blowing up the Nova Kakhovka Dam, which drowned hundreds of Ukrainians, or doing softball interviews with Vladimir Putin and praising supermarkets in Russia.[21] Despite this, the outlines of an effective response have become clearer and remain within reach.

One of the most effective responses to Russia's hybrid war would be to limit Russia's ability to use Western countries for money laundering and influence operations. While Western countries imposed tough sanctions on Russia after its 2022 invasion of Ukraine, Russian oligarchs and government figures still use London and other Western capitals as a safe place to park their money, transferring ill-gotten gains to bank accounts and funds based in the West and buying expensive real estate and political influence. Many send their children to study or live in the West. After 2022, many Russians sought refuge in the Persian Gulf states, Turkey, Central Asia, and the Caucasus.[22]

However, the West can still respond by "ending anonymity in shell companies and trusts; demanding basic anti-money-laundering checks for lawyers, art gallerists, and auction-house managers; and closing loopholes that allow anonymity in the real-estate, private-equity, and hedge-fund industries."[23]

After the Brexit debacle, Britain began to scrutinize the sources of the money that Russian oligarchs used to win UK "investor" visas.[24] In 2018, the UK refused to allow Roman Abramovich, the owner of the Chelsea football club, back into the country until it investigated his financial dealings. However, Britain and other Western countries overall have struggled with requiring greater transparency in financial transactions. "UK governments have shied away from hitting the moneyed Kremlin-linked interests that, by an extraordinary coincidence, enrich a well-connected stratum of UK-based bankers, accountants, solicitors, and estate agents."[25] In 2018, a British parliamentary report titled "Moscow's Gold" concluded that "measures to combat money laundering should therefore form a central aspect of Government strategy towards hostile regimes, including that of President Putin."[26] Yet, in 2022, the treasurer of the governing Conservative Party, Ehud Sheleg, was accused of fueling a surge of Russian donations from 2019 to 2021, including from his Russian father-in-law, a senior politician in the pro-Kremlin government of Crimea.[27] Until the West requires transparency in financial transactions, Russian and other foreign money will continue to influence Western politicians.

The West also can do more to confront Russian disinformation, propaganda, and information warfare. This is difficult in democratic societies, where free flow of information is a core principle. Western countries were reluctant to ban Russian news sources like Russia Today or Sputnik until Russia's 2022 attack on Ukraine, which clarified the stakes for national security. Then the EU banned the Russian propaganda networks and encouraged social media companies to do the same. EU

Commission president Ursula von der Leyen stated, "Russia Today and Sputnik, as well as their subsidiaries, will no longer be able to spread their lies to justify Putin's war and to sow division in our union. So we are developing tools to ban their toxic and harmful disinformation in Europe." Google banned RT and Sputnik worldwide, though Russia continues to subvert the ban by posting its propaganda videos on YouTube, playing a game of cat and mouse with content moderators.[28] Baltic countries that have borne the brunt of information warfare for years have taken a different approach, bolstering public information campaigns in response. They have sought to inform the entire population that they are subject to Russian disinformation campaigns and to "emphasize media literacy and critical-thinking skills" in elementary schools to "inoculate future citizens against misinformation," including Russian-speakers.[29] In an effort to address the problem of Russian-funded disinformation spread in the 2016 US presidential election, Facebook instituted a rule that political and policy ads in the United States must identify their source. In 2018, Facebook began requiring that political advertisers verify their identity by producing government ID and disclosing their addresses.[30] However, changes enacted after Elon Musk bought Twitter in October 2022 led to a surge in Russian and Chinese propaganda on that platform.[31]

Western institutions could respond more forcefully, making it more difficult to hack into and disable public infrastructure, enabling critical infrastructure systems to get back online as quickly as possible after an attack, and allowing cyber defenders to wipe out attacking computer systems. Australia recently passed an important law aimed at safeguarding democratic elections from foreign interference.[32] The real problem is not that the West lacks defenses, but rather that Russia's hybrid war has delayed and disabled responses by sowing confusion in the West about the nature of Russia's challenge and cultivating pro-Russia allies. If Western countries act, much could be done to blunt the impact of Russia's hybrid war.

Russia's hybrid war on the West may be a feature of our politics for a long time to come. Relations between Russia and the West will not substantially improve without a change in government in Moscow. As a House of Lords report on EU-Russia relations noted, "The EU and Member States face a strategic question of whether Europe can be secure and prosperous if Russia continues to be governed as it is today."[33] Russia continues to prioritize interference in Western elections to promote pro-Russia politicians and sow division. This campaign continues despite a massive backlash against Russian electoral meddling in the West. The current regime in Moscow supports policies that are unacceptable to Western governments. Meanwhile, the EU and NATO insist that independent states bordering Russia have the right to join whatever economic and security organizations they choose, and that Russia does not have a legitimate right to veto those choices. Russia cannot change the European Union's current strategy of integration. Its war on Ukraine caused NATO to expand to include Finland and Sweden and reignited EU enlargement. The most important question in EU-Russian relations today, then, is which will outlast the other: President Putin or the EU and NATO?

In this context, the EU and NATO have little choice but to confront Russia on issues where they strenuously disagree. As David Kramer put it, "Nobody wants war with Putin's regime, but calling for a strong stand against his egregious behavior is not tantamount to launching World War III. . . . [It] is not only necessary but also the right, moral thing to do."[34] Core Western institutions must develop techniques of opposing Russia's attempts to co-opt Western elites, as well as its disinformation, cyberwarfare, and other forms of hybrid war, in the hopes of surviving Russia's assault. The West must help Ukraine to fight back. And wait for a change of government in Moscow.

AFTER PUTIN?

Some question whether Russian foreign policy will change after Putin and suggest that Russia's foreign policy could remain anti-Western or become more nationalistic still.[35] History counsels that we should anticipate change. Over the last century, every Russian leader has taken a different foreign policy approach, reflecting individual preferences. Gorbachev, Yeltsin, and Putin pursued incomparable foreign policies, with the first two strongly pro-Western and the latter anti-Western and aggressive. Soviet leaders also took very different foreign policy approaches. Think of the transition from Stalin to Khrushchev. As a result, it is very likely that any future president of Russia will take a different approach toward the West, changing from the hyperaggressive stance of President Putin. This change is likely to lead toward moderation. It is hard to imagine a Russian president embracing a more aggressive and warlike stance than what we have today.

Russia's political system suffers from a fundamental weakness: the lack of any succession strategy. Russia today is a personalistic dictatorship. That means that when political change comes, it could lead to catastrophic instability. The Soviet regime had a system of leadership transition that, while not perfect, worked reasonably well. In the event of the death of a leader, the Politburo would choose a new leader from among its ranks. There were controversies and disagreements, but there was a clear and widely accepted process that determined who got to choose the new leader and how, similar to China today.

In Putin's dictatorship, there is just Putin. No strategy or policy on succession. Putin came to power when the previous president, Boris Yeltsin, resigned early and appointed him to the presidency prior to an election, on the theory that people would vote for the incumbent. Will Putin follow the same strategy? Will he avoid leaving office at all costs, ultimately dying in office as his Soviet forebears did, or be ousted in a palace coup? President Putin is paranoid about the United States sponsoring a color revolution in Russia: he worries that he could be turned out in a wave of popular protest. Russia's political system is fundamentally unstable. While its centralization is a strength, it creates the ever-present possibility of a descent into chaos, as Russia experienced in the 1990s.[36]

Which will go first, Putin or the EU and NATO? It is possible that Russia's attempts to undermine Western institutions will succeed. With a wave of populist politics rising, coinciding with growing nationalism and concerns about immigration and globalization, pro-Russia populists have scored significant victories in the West. Britain opted to leave the EU in a campaign likely financed in part by Russia. Pro-Russia populists continue to rise in the polls in various countries throughout Europe, lately in Austria and Germany. It remains conceivable that the EU will break apart or radically change its policy on Russia. Russia may win on the battlefield in Ukraine. On the other hand, recent setbacks for the EU, such as Brexit and the clash with Russia, have created more unity in the EU. Public opinion polls show that EU voters expressed more allegiance to the EU after Brexit. In many countries, support for remaining in the EU increased by 10–20 percent.[37] Similarly, EU member states united to oppose Russia's invasion of Ukraine in 2022, notwithstanding frequent criticisms of sanctions from Russia's Trojan horses.[38] Putin has his back up against the wall. Russia's failure to achieve its objectives by invading Ukraine, so closely associated with Putin personally, decimated the Russian military with hundreds of thousands of casualties and raised questions about Putin's political future.

The West cannot live with Putin, but it cannot actively pursue regime change in Russia either. No regime that comes to power with Western assistance will be seen as legitimate in Russia. In the past it has been a mistake for the United States to support particular candidates in Russian elections, as it did in 1996, backing an extremely unpopular and incompetent Boris Yeltsin in a campaign against the communist candidate Gennady Zyuganov.[39] Zyuganov would have been preferable to the situation we face today. Russians need to make their own choices and mistakes, and learn from them. The West should do far more to make its messages heard in Russia in defense of liberal values, in opposition to Russian aggression, and in defiance of Putin's campaign against the EU, but it should not seek to influence democratic elections or the course of any palace coup. Russia will choose another leader, at another time.

The West could do more to defeat Putin on the battlefield, however. After Russia's 2022 invasion of Ukraine, Western governments chose to confront Russia using a variety of tactics, from economic sanctions and energy policy to provision of military equipment and training for Ukrainian soldiers. Yet some analysts criticized this approach for being too limited, arguing that "the United States has suffered from a deliberate fuzziness in formulating its objectives in the Russian war in Ukraine." In this critique, the Biden administration did enough to prevent Russia from succeeding in Ukraine, but not to defeat it.[40] Like Russia, many in the West welcome the ambiguity of hybrid warfare because the risks of a direct military confrontation between NATO and Russia are so great. The Biden administration has opted to prevent World War III, survive to play another day, and deal with a different Russian government in two, ten, twenty, or thirty years. That too could change.

LOOKING IN THE MIRROR

Ultimately, the struggle for Europe may be won not in Russia, but in the West itself. The West needs to work on bettering its own socioeconomic model and addressing the underlying reasons for the discontent that Russia and other powers exploit. The rise of populism in the West is fueled by two sources. The first is a xenophobic anger at those who, either through trade or through migration, are claimed to be "stealing our jobs" and changing our way of life. The second is rising inequality, fueled by forty years of neoliberal economic policy, which has reduced safety nets and rendered workers more vulnerable to economic risks. Europe and the United States need to develop new policies to address these problems through values discourse and economic policy.

While populist parties focus on nationalism as the answer, liberals must redefine nationalism and revamp economic policy. When workers feel more secure, they are less likely to buy into xenophobia. According to economist Dani Rodrik, "Senior US policymakers now believe that the post-1990 model of globalization, which prioritized free trade and free markets over national security, climate change, and the economic security of the middle class, has undermined the socioeconomic foundations of healthy democracies." The West needs to broaden economic opportunities through investment in critical industries, a return of full employment as a key policy target, job training, affordable childcare, and continuing education. Government needs to make sure the economy works for everyone; this is a key part of the populist challenge. Populist governments in Europe have clawed back control from foreign banks and initiated social welfare programs that guarantee a minimum income to families with young children and pensioners, while building domestic industries and a domestic capital class. In short, populists stole a good part of the traditional social democratic agenda while the EU embraced austerity. The results have been poisonous for European politics.[41]

Western societies also must rearticulate the values of political liberalism, equality before the law, protection of minorities, and the benefits of democracy, values that are under attack. It may be a long struggle, but the West needs to vigorously defend them. This war can be fought in the marketplace of ideas as well as in economic policy. Ultimately, the West is challenged to demonstrate the superiority of its international system, its economic model, and its values.

Until a leadership change in the Kremlin occurs, EU-Russia relations will remain marked by sanctions, military conflict, difficulty in the lands in between, and counterespionage. The West will defend the institutions that have worked to ensure peace in Europe for decades. Eventually—we know not when—a government will come to power in Moscow that seeks to close this divide between Russia and the West and work toward greater peace and cooperation on the continent.

CAUGHT IN BETWEEN?

Until that time, Europe faces serious tensions in its eastern borderlands. Prior to 2022, many people in the lands in between preferred an independent existence and chafed at being forced to choose between Russia and the EU. As one Opposition Bloc politician told me in Kyiv in 2017 when I asked to interview her for a book about the lands in between, "Your title made me sad." Ukraine, she said, wanted to be its own independent country, achieving a happy coexistence with both the European Union and Russia. This option is no longer on the table.

Instead, the lands in between face a stark choice: either trying to leave the Russian empire behind and fight for independence, or being reincorporated into Soviet Union 2.0. To guard their independence, they must adopt the laws of the European Union and engage in a thorough transformation of their economies and governance systems to make them compatible with the rest of the continent—a clear civilizational choice.

Some groups advocate a beautiful future within the EU, one that may not be fully attainable due to Russia's opposition. Others believe everything will be simpler with Russia, with fewer demands, fewer transformations, but a constrained future and a fundamental loss of sovereignty. Given this polarization, countries often have fallen prey to their own oligarchs and power brokers, who concentrate on material gains in the present. These leaders profit from the dreams and aspirations of both pro-EU and pro-Russia compatriots. If the EU wants legislation and is willing to pay for development programs, power brokers pocket part of the money while pretending to pass laws. If Russia wants to broadcast its propaganda and subvert EU trade through smuggling, power brokers pocket a share while resisting Russian buyouts. The result is a tense and fearful politics dominated by power brokers seeking to profit now and change sides in the future.

People in the West often pity the lands in between and regard these countries as backward, but what I have learned from researching this book, conducting interviews throughout the former Soviet space and Central and Eastern Europe over the course of more than a decade, is that their politics has prefigured our own. While we in the West blithely ignored Russian influence for years, pretending that President Dmitry Medvedev represented a liberal Russian future or that we could reset relations with Russia, the lands in between suffered the politics of polarization and power brokers. Now we too find ourselves vulnerable to false news stories spread by dubious social media accounts. We too find ourselves on the brink of civil war due to an extreme polarization of politics fostered by the rise of far-right parties. We too face a civilizational choice between living in a liberal democracy and subverting it in the name of nationalistic, great-power politics. We too find ourselves in the midst of a war between two conceptions of the international order—one Western and democratic, another Eastern and autocratic; one that adheres to rule of law and another based on crony capitalist links between top leaders. We too find ourselves governed by power brokers who enrich themselves while maneuvering between the two sides.

In this battle to the finish, the stakes are very high indeed—"too high for both sides to back down," in the words of one analyst.[42] The challenge of our age is to fight this hybrid conflict while bolstering a liberal democratic civilization that is increasingly under threat.

We too are lands in between.

NOTES

Chapter 1

1. The White House, "Remarks by President Biden on the United States Efforts of the Free World to Support the People of Ukraine," March 26, 2022, https://www.whitehouse.gov/briefing-room/speeches-remarks/2022/03/26/remarks-by-president-biden-on-the-united-efforts-of-the-free-world-to-support-the-people-of-ukraine/.
2. Caroline De Camaret and Dominique Baillard, " 'Democracy Is Standing Up Against Autocracy' in Ukraine, EU's von der Leyen Says," *Talking Europe*, France 24, March 18, 2022, https://www.france24.com/en/tv-shows/talking-europe/20220318-democracy-is-standing-up-against-autocracy-in-ukraine-eu-s-von-der-leyen-says.
3. Prime Minister's Office, "Prime Minister Boris Johnson's Address to the Ukrainian Parliament: 3 May 2022," May 3, 2022, https://www.gov.uk/government/speeches/prime-minister-boris-johnsons-address-to-the-ukrainian-parliament-3-may-2022.
4. Viktor Orbán, "Speech by Prime Minister Viktor Orbán at the Opening of CPAC Hungary," May 19, 2022, https://abouthungary.hu/speeches-and-remarks/speech-by-prime-minister-viktor-orban-at-the-opening-of-cpac-hungary.

5. Matina Stevis-Gridneff, "In a Speech to the E.U., Zelensky Singles Out Hungary over Sanctions," *New York Times*, March 25, 2022, https://www.nytimes.com/2022/03/25/world/europe/eu-zelen sky-hungary-sanctions-ukraine.html.
6. Justin Spike, "Hungary's Orban Criticized for 'Neutrality' in Ukraine War," Associated Press, March 26, 2022, https://apn ews.com/article/russia-ukraine-putin-business-budapest-viktor-orban-c289237f0c626ce9447bd1c78ebcd8ae.
7. Leszek Szymański, "Polish, Czech PMs Call on Hungary to Condemn Russian Crimes in Ukraine," The First News, April 29, 2022, https://www.thefirstnews.com/article/polish-czech-pms-call-on-hungary-to-condemn-russian-crimes-in-ukraine-30067.
8. Victor Jack, "Poland's Kaczyński Slams Orbán for Refusing to Condemn Bucha Killings," Politico, April 8, 2022, https://www.politico.eu/article/poland-kaczynski-slams-hungary-orban-for-refusing-to-condemn-bucha-killings/.
9. Kata Abnett, Jan Strupczewski, and Ingrid Melander, "EU Agrees Russia Oil Embargo, Give Hungary Exemptions; Zelenskiy Vows More Sanctions," Reuters, May 31, 2022, https://www.reuters.com/world/europe/best-we-could-get-eu-bows-hungarian-dema nds-agree-russian-oil-ban-2022-05-31/.
10. András Rácz, "Russia's Hybrid War in Ukraine: Breaking the Enemy's Ability to Resist," Finnish Institute of International Affairs, report no. 43, 2015, 27–43, https://www.files.ethz.ch/isn/191590/FIIAReport43.pdf.
11. Erik Reichborn-Kjennerud and Patrick Cullen, "What Is Hybrid Warfare," Norwegian Institute of International Affairs policy brief, 2016, 1–4, http://www.jstor.org/stable/resrep07978.
12. Frank G. Hoffman, "Hybrid Warfare and Challenges," *Joint Forces Quarterly* 52 (Winter 2009): 34–39, https://apps.dtic.mil/sti/pdfs/ADA516871.pdf.
13. "Warsaw Summit Comminqué," North Atlantic Treaty Organization, July 9, 2016, https://www.nato.int/cps/en/natohq/official_texts_133169.htm.
14. "Countering Hybrid Threats," North Atlantic Treaty Organization, June 21, 2022, https://www.nato.int/cps/en/natohq/topics_156338.
15. Reichborn-Kjennerud and Cullen, "What Is Hybrid Warfare," 2.

16. Mark Galeotti, "Russia's Hybrid Warfare as a Byproduct of a Hybrid State," War on the Rocks, December 6, 2016, https://warontherocks.com/2016/12/russias-hybrid-war-as-a-byproduct-of-a-hybrid-state/.

17. Reichborn-Kjennerud and Cullen, "What Is Hybrid Warfare."

18. "NATO's Response to Hybrid Threats," North Atlantic Treaty Organization, June 21, 2022, https://www.nato.int/cps/en/natohq/topics_156338.htm.

19. Elena Tislova, "Lavrov Says Hybrid War Waged Against Russia Aimed at Demonizing Country," Anatolia Agency, March 14, 2023, https://www.aa.com.tr/en/russia-ukraine-war/lavrov-says-hybrid-war-waged-against-russia-aimed-at-demonizing-country/2845468.

20. Stephen F. Cohen, "Patriotic Heresy vs. the New Cold War," *The Nation*, August 27, 2014, https://www.thenation.com/article/archive/patriotic-heresy-vs-new-cold-war/; Samuel Charap and Jeremy Shapiro, "Consequences of a New Cold War," *Survival* 57, no. 2 (2015): 37–46; Richard Sakwa, "New Cold War or Twenty Years' Crisis? Russia and International Politics," *International Affairs* 84, no. 2 (2008): 241–267; Robert Legvold, "Managing the New Cold War: What Moscow and Washington Can Learn from the Last One," *Foreign Affairs* 93, no. 4 (2014): 74–84; Robert Legvold, *Return to Cold War* (Cambridge, UK: Polity Press, 2016); Sergey Karaganov, "The New Cold War and the Emerging Greater Eurasia," *Journal of Eurasian Studies* 9, no. 2 (2018): 85–93.

21. Ravi Agrawal, "Fiona Hill: Putin's Running Out of Time," *Foreign Policy*, July 14, 2022, https://foreignpolicy.com/2022/07/14/putin-russia-war-fiona-hill-future-west-nato/.

22. Sean Monaghan, "Bad Idea: Winning the Gray Zone," Defense360, December 17, 2021, https://defense360.csis.org/bad-idea-winning-the-gray-zone/.

Chapter 2

1. "An Open Letter to the Obama Administration from Central and Eastern Europe," Radio Free Europe / Radio Liberty, July

16, 2009, https://www.rferl.org/a/An_Open_Letter_To_The_Obama_Administration_From_Central_And_Eastern_Europe/1778449.html.

2. David J. Kramer, *Back to Containment: Dealing with Putin's Regime* (Washington, DC: McCain Institute, 2017); Angela Stent, *The Limits of Partnership: U.S.-Russian Relations in the Twentieth Century* (Princeton, NJ: Princeton University Press, 2015). Stent shows on p. 163 that President George W. Bush and his secretary of state, Condoleezza Rice, also believed that Medvedev could turn Russia in a liberal direction.

3. Katie Sanders, "Romney: Obama Stopped Missile Defense Shield as a 'Gift to Russia,'" PolitiFact, March 23, 2014, http://www.politifact.com/punditfact/statements/2014/mar/23/mitt-romney/romney-obama-stopped-missile-defense-shield-gift-r/.

4. Martin Dangerfield, "Visegrad Group Cooperation and Russia," *Journal of Common Market Studies* 50, no. 6 (2012): 958–74.

5. Geir Hågen Karlsen, "Divide and Rule: Ten Lessons About Russian Political Influence Activities in Europe," *Palgrave Communications* 5, no. 19 (Winter 2019): 1–14, https://doi.org/10.1057/s41599-019-0227-8.

6. Samuel Charap, in "The Ghost of Hybrid War," *Survival* 57, no. 6 (2015): 52, states, "Western analysis gives the impression that Russia is already conducting hybrid war against the West. This is a dangerous misuse of the word 'war.'"

7. Steve Lee Myers, *The New Tsar: The Rise and Reign of Vladimir Putin* (New York: Vintage, 2015), 51.

8. Timothy Snyder, *The Road to Unfreedom: Russia, Europe, America* (New York: Tim Duggan Books, 2018).

9. Bobo Lo, *Russia and the New World Disorder* (London: Royal Institute of International Affairs, 2015), 101.

10. David Satter, *The Less You Know, The Better You Sleep: Russia's Road to Terror and Dictatorship Under Yeltsin and Putin* (New Haven, CT: Yale University Press, 2016), 163. See also Karen Dawisha, *Putin's Kleptocracy: Who Owns Russia?* (New York: Simon and Schuster, 2014); Garry Kasparov, *Winter Is Coming* (New York: Public Affairs, 2015); Janusz Bugajski, *Dismantling the West: Russia's Atlantic Agenda* (Washington, DC: Potomac Books, 2009); Marcel H. Van Herpen, *Putin's Wars: The Rise of*

Russia's New Imperialism, 2nd ed. (Lanham, MD: Rowman and Littlefield, 2015).

11. Putin's responsibility for souring relations with the West is attested to by a number of excellent studies, including Kramer, *Back to Containment*; Lilia Shevtsova, *Putin's Russia*, rev. ed. (Washington, DC: Carnegie Endowment for International Peace, 2010); Walter Laqueur, *Putinism: Russia and Its Future with the West* (New York: Macmillan, 2015); Katherine Stoner and Michael McFaul, "Who Lost Russia (This Time)? Vladimir Putin," *Washington Quarterly* 38, no. 2 (2015): 167–87.

12. John J. Mearsheimer, "Why the Ukraine Crisis Is the West's Fault: The Liberal Delusions That Provoked Putin," *Foreign Affairs*, September–October 2014, 1–12; Joshua R. Itzkowitz Shifrinson, "Deal or No Deal? The End of the Cold War and the U.S. Offer to Limit NATO Expansion," *International Security* 40, no. 4 (Spring 2016): 7–44; f; Michael E. O'Hanlon, *Beyond NATO: A New Security Architecture for Eastern Europe* (Washington, DC: Brookings Institution Press, 2017); James Dobbins and Andrei Zagorski, "Lessons Learned from Russia-West Interactions on European Security," in *Getting Out from "In Between": Perspectives on the Regional Order in Post-Soviet Europe and Eurasia*, ed. Samuel Charap, Alyssa Demus, and Jeremy Shapiro (Santa Monica, CA: RAND Corporation, 2018).

13. Stephen M. Walt, "Why Arming Kiev Is a Really, Really Bad Idea," *Foreign Policy*, February 9, 2015, http://foreig npolicy.com/2015/02/09/how-not-to-save-ukraine-arm ing-kiev-is-a-bad-idea.

14. Oleksander Chalyi writes, "All parties, including Ukraine, Russia, and the West, should acknowledge responsibility for the security crisis in and around Ukraine. The West and Russia should take responsibility for not reaching a consensus on a mutually acceptable security arrangement for Ukraine." "Approaches to Resolving the Conflict over the States In Between," in in *Getting Out from "In Between": Perspectives on the Regional Order in Post-Soviet Europe and Eurasia*, ed. Samuel Charap, Alyssa Demus, and Jeremy Shapiro (Santa Monica, CA: RAND Corporation, 2018), 36.

15. Andrei P. Tsygankov, *Russia and the West from Alexander to Putin: Honor in International Relations* (New York: Cambridge University Press, 2012).

16. Dmitri Trenin, *Should We Fear Russia?* (Cambridge: Polity Press, 2016); Dmitri Trenin, *Post-Imperium: A Eurasian Story* (Washington, DC: Carnegie Endowment for International Peace, 2011); Celeste Wallander, "Russian Transimperialism and Its Implications," *Washington Quarterly* 30, no. 2 (Spring 2007): 107–22; Van Herpen, *Putin's Wars*; Lo, *Russia and the New World Disorder*.

17. Charles A. Kupchan, "NATO's Final Frontier: Why Russia Should Join the Atlantic Alliance," *Foreign Affairs* 89, no. 3 (May–June 2010): 100–112; Bill Clinton, "I Tried to Put Russia on Another Path," *The Atlantic*, April 7, 2022, https://www.theatlantic.com/ideas/archive/2022/04/bill-clinton-nato-expansion-ukraine/629499/.

18. See also O'Hanlon, *Beyond NATO*, 20; he points to "a confluence of events in 2007 and 2008 that probably marked the decisive turning point in relations between Vladimir Putin and the West." Peter Reddaway, in *Russia's Domestic Security Wars: Putin's Use of Divide and Rule Against His Hardline Allies* (Cham, Switzerland: Palgrave MacMillan, 2018), 57, argues that Western outcry over the killings of Anna Politkovskaya and Alexander Litvinenko in 2006 "fed the anti-Western attitudes that had been intensifying since 2003 in the hardline sections of Russian elite opinion. These attitudes pushed Putin and his administration 'to the right' in foreign and domestic policy."

19. Transcript, "Putin's Prepared Remarks at the 43rd Munich Conference on Security Policy," *Washington Post*, February 12, 2007, http://www.washingtonpost.com/wp-dyn/content/article/2007/02/12/AR2007021200555.html.

20. Dobbins and Zagorski, "Lessons Learned," 9.

21. Stent, *The Limits of Partnership*, ch. 7.

22. Dmitry Medvedev, "Why I Had to Recognize Georgia's Breakaway Regions," *Financial Times*, August 26, 2008, https://www.ft.com/content/9c7ad792-7395-11dd-8a66-0000779fd18c.

23. Meghann Myers, "Back to Europe: The Army Is Sending More Troops, Tanks and Helicopters to Deter Russia," *Army Times*, March 19, 2017, https://www.armytimes.com/news/your-army/

2017/03/19/back-to-europe-the-army-is-sending-more-troops-tanks-and-helicopters-to-deter-russia/.

24. "Nobel Peace Prize Awarded to European Union," BBC, October 12, 2012, http://www.bbc.com/news/world-europe-19921072.

25. Dawisha, *Putin's Kleptocracy*; Vladimir Gel'man, *Authoritarian Russia: Analyzing Post-Soviet Regime Changes* (Pittsburgh: University of Pittsburgh Press, 2015).

26. Milada Anna Vachudova, "Democratization in Postcommunist Europe: Illiberal Regimes and the Leverage of International Actors," University of Pittsburgh Center for European Studies Working Paper no. 138, 2006, http://aei.pitt.edu/9023/1/Vachud ova.pdf.

27. Trenin, *Should We Fear Russia?*, 49. For a full analysis, see Gel'man, *Authoritarian Russia*; M. Stephen Fish, *Democracy Derailed in Russia: The Failure of Open Politics* (New York: Cambridge University Press, 2005).

28. Steven Levitsky and Lucan A. Way, "The Rise of Competitive Authoritarianism," *Journal of Democracy* 13, no. 2 (April 2002): 51–65.

29. Committee on Foreign Relations of the United States Senate, 115th Congress, "Putin's Asymmetric Assault on Democracy in Russia and Europe: Implications for U.S. National Security," January 10, 2018.

30. Marc Bennetts, "Russian TV Launches Series Following Putin's Weekly Activities," *Guardian*, September 3, 2018, https://www.theguardian.com/world/2018/sep/03/russian-tv-launches-series-devoted-vladimir-putins-weekly-activities.

31. Dawisha, *Putin's Kleptocracy*; Bálint Magyar, *Post-Communist Mafia State: The Case of Hungary* (Budapest: Central European University Press, 2016); Reddaway, *Russia's Domestic Security Wars*, 7.

32. Satter, *The Less You Know*.

33. Thomas Ambrosio, *Authoritarian Backlash: Russian Resistance to Democratization in the Former Soviet Union* (New York: Routledge, 2016), 6.

34. Graeme P. Herd, "Russian and the 'Orange Revolution': Response, Rhetoric, Reality?," *Connections* 4, no. 2 (Summer 2005): 15–28, https://www.jstor.org/stable/26323167.

35. Dobbins and Zagorski, "Lessons Learned," 9.
36. Ambrosio, *Authoritarian Backlash*.
37. Mark Leonard and Nicu Popescu, "A Power Audit of EU-Russia Relations," European Council on Foreign Relations, November 2007, 53.
38. Margot Light, "Russia and the EU: Strategic Partners or Strategic Rivals?," *Journal of Common Market Studies* 46 (2008): 7–27, https://doi.org/10.1111/j.1468-5965.2008.00808.x.
39. Light, "Russia and the EU."
40. Vladimir Putin, "Article by Vladimir Putin 'On the Historical Unity of Russians and Ukrainians," President of Russia, July 12, 2021, http://www.en.kremlin.ru/events/president/news/66181.
41. Katja Richters, *The Post-Soviet Russian Orthodox Church: Politics, Culture and Greater Russia* (London: Routledge, 2013).
42. Mitchell A. Orenstein, "Putin's Western Allies: Why Europe's Far Right Is on the Kremlin's Side," *Foreign Affairs*, March 25, 2014.
43. Mitchell A. Orenstein, Péter Krekó, and Attila Juhász, "The Hungarian Putin? Viktor Orbán and the Kremlin's Playbook," *Foreign Affairs*, February 8, 2015.
44. Andrei P. Tsygankov, "The Irony of Western Ideas in a Multicultural World: Russians' Intellectual Engagement with the 'End of History' and 'Clash of Civilizations,'" *International Studies Review* 5, no. 1 (March 2003): 53–76.
45. Bugajski, *Dismantling the West*.
46. teleSUR/capc, "Sergey Lavrov: Russia Is Under a Hybrid War from the West," teleSUR, May 15, 2022, https://www.telesurenglish.net/news/Sergey-Lavrov-Russia-Is-Under-a-Hybrid-War-From-the-West-20220515-0001.html.
47. Ofer Fridman, "On the 'Gerisamov Doctrine': Why the West Fails to Beat Russia's Punch," *Prism* 8, no. 2 (Fall 2019): 100–113, https://www.jstor.org/stable/10.2307/26803233; Roger N. McDermott, "Does Russia Have a Gerasimov Doctrine?," *Parameters* 46, no. 1 (Spring 2016): 97–105, doi:10.55540/0031-1723.2827.
48. Mark Galeotti, *Russian Political War: Moving Beyond the Hybrid* (London: Routledge, 2019).
49. A number of authors have pointed out that Russia has no official military strategy of "hybrid war," but what Western analysts

call hybrid war is sometimes referred to within Russia's defense ministry as "strategic deterrence," described as "a coordinated system of military and non-military (political, diplomatic, legal, economic, ideological, scientific-technical and others) measures taken consecutively or simultaneously . . . with the goal of deterring military action entailing damage of a strategic character." See Kristin Ven Bruusgaard, "Russian Strategic Deterrence," *Survival* 58, no. 4 (2016): 7–26. Maria Snegovaya, in *Putin's Information in Ukraine: Soviet Origins of Russia's Hybrid Warfare* (Washington, DC: Institute for the Study of War, 2015), uses the term "reflexive control" to denote Russia's hybrid warfare. A well-researched French report claims that Russia uses the term "new generation warfare": Jean-Baptiste Jeangène Vilmer et al., "Information Manipulation: A Challenge for Our Democracies," report by the Policy Planning Staff (CAPS, Ministry for Europe and Foreign Affairs) and the Institute for Strategic Research (IRSEM, Ministry for the Armed Forces), Republic of France, 2018, 55.

50. "What Does Putin Really Want?," Politico, February 25, 2022, https://www.politico.com/news/magazine/2022/02/25/putin-rus sia-ukraine-invasion-endgame-experts-00011652.

51. Bobo Lo, "Medvedev and the New European Security Architecture," Centre for European Reform, July 1, 2009, https://www.cer.eu/sites/default/files/publications/attachments/pdf/2011/pbrief_medvedev_july09-741.pdf.

52. Alexander Thomas, "Energy Transformation After the Second Russo-Ukrainian War," Foreign Policy Research Institute, July 21, 2022, https://www.fpri.org/article/2022/07/energy-transformat ion-after-the-second-russo-ukrainian-war/; Mitchell Orenstein, "Putin the Green? The Unintended Consequences of Russia's Energy War on Europe," Foreign Policy Research Institute, February 15, 2023, https://www.fpri.org/article/2023/02/putin-the-green-the-unintended-consequences-of-russias-energy-war-on-europe/.

53. Scott Boston, Michael Johnson, Nathan Beauchamp-Mustafaga, and Yvonne K. Crane, "Assessing the Conventional Force Imbalance in Europe: Implications for Countering Russian Local Superiority," RAND Corporation, Spring 2019, https://doi.org/10.7249/RR2402.

54. Eugene Rumer, "Russian and the Security of Europe," Carnegie Endowment for International Peace, June 30, 2016, https://carnegieendowment.org/files/CP_276_Rumer_Russia_Final.pdf.

55. For a more comprehensive description, see Committee on Foreign Relations, "Putin's Asymmetric Assault."

56. Bugajski, *Dismantling the West*, 17–18.

57. Satter, *The Less You Know*.

58. Alexey Kovalev, "Russia's Brutal Honesty Has Destroyed the West's Appeasers," *Foreign Policy*, August 12, 2022, https://foreignpolicy.com/2022/08/12/russia-ukraine-war-crimes-genocide-appeasement-mearsheimer-putin/.

59. Andrew Rettman, "Belgian Intelligence Chief Talks to EUobserver: Transcript," EUobserver, September 17, 2012, https://euobserver.com/secret-ue/117554.

60. Tom Van Rentergem, "From Russia with Love—Brussels at the Center of Foreign Intelligence Activities," Egmont: Royal Institute for International Relations, April 7, 2022, https://www.egmontinstitute.be/from-russia-with-love-brussels-at-the-center-of-foreign-intelligence-activities/. See also Euractiv with AFP and Reuters, "Spying for Russia: Europeans Recruited for Putin's Hybrid War," Euractiv, January 20, 2023, https://www.euractiv.com/section/global-europe/news/spying-for-russia-europeans-recruited-for-putins-hybrid-war/.

61. Bruce Auster, "A Possible Explanation for How U.S. Diplomatic Call Was Tapped," NPR, February 8, 2014, https://www.npr.org/2014/02/08/273181826/a-possible-explanation-for-how-u-s-diplomats-call-was-tapped.

62. Jakob Hanke Vela and Nicolas Camut, "There Are More Russian Spies in EU Parliament, Latvian Lawmakers Say," Politico, January 31, 2024, https://www.politico.eu/article/russia-spies-european-parliament-latvia-meps-eu/

63. Tim Mak, "FBI Warned of Russian Intelligence Links to Oligarch in Cohen Payment Allegation," NPR, May 11, 2018, https://www.npr.org/2018/05/11/610381368/fbi-warned-of-russian-intelligence-links-to-oligarch-in-cohen-payment-allegation.

64. Andrew Wilson, "Meeting Medvedev: The Politics of the Putin Succession," European Council on Foreign Relations, February

28, 2008, https://ecfr.eu/archive/page/-/ECFR-05_MEETING_ MEDVEDEV_-_THE_POLITICS_OF_THE_PUTIN_SUCCESS ION.pdf.

65. The concept of "false Dmitry" refers to several pretenders to the Russian throne during Russia's "time of troubles" from 1598 to 1613, all of whom claimed to be the youngest son of Ivan the Terrible.

66. Phillip Martin, "MIT Abandons Russian High-Tech Campus Partnership in Light of Ukraine Invasion," WGBH, February 25, 2022, https://www.wgbh.org/news/local-news/2022/02/25/mit- abandons-russian-high-tech-campus-partnership-in-light-of- ukraine-invasion.

67. Richard Field, "Jobbik MEP 'KGBéla' Kovács and Wife Outed as Russian Spies," *Budapest Beacon*, September 24, 2014, https:// budapestbeacon.com/jobbik-mep-kgbela-kovacs-and-wife-out ted-as-russian-spies/; Mitchell A. Orenstein and Péter Krekó, "A Russian Spy in Brussels? The Case of 'KGBéla'—and What It Means for Europe," *Foreign Affairs*, May 29, 2014, https://www. foreignaffairs.com/articles/hungary/2014-05-29/russian-spy- brussels; Euractiv with AFP, "Parliament Lifts Hungarian MEP's Immunity over Russia Spy Probe," Euractiv, October 15, 2015, http://www.euractiv.com/section/europe-s-east/news/parliam ent-lifts-hungarian-mep-s-immunity-over-russia-spy-probe/; Dezső András, "A Beautiful Match Made in Moscow," Index.hu, September 28, 2014, http://index.hu/belfold/2014/09/28/a_glorio us_match_made_in_russia/.

68. "Former Jobbik Sentenced for Espionage for Russia," MTI– Hungary Today, September 28, 2022, https://hungarytoday.hu/ former-jobbik-mep-sentenced-for-espionage-for-russia/.

69. Anton Shekhovtsov, *Russia and the Western Far Right: Tango Noir* (Abingdon, UK: Routledge, 2017); Maria Snegovaya, "Fellow Travelers or Trojan Horses? Similarities Across Pro-Russian Parties' Electorates in Europe," *Party Politics* 28, no. 3 (Spring 2021): 409–18, https://doi.org/10.1177/1354068821995813.

70. Aleksandr Fisher, "Trickle Down Soft Power: Do Russia's Ties to European Parties Influence Public Opinion?," *Foreign Policy Analysis* 17, no. 1 (Winter 2021), https://doi.org/10.1093/fpa/ oraa013.

71. Max Seddon and Michael Stothard, "Putin Awaits Returns on Le Pen Investment," *Financial Times*, May 4, 2017, https://www.ft.com/content/010eec62-30b5-11e7-9555-23ef563ec f9a?mhq5j=e1.

72. Anton Shekhovtsov, "'Foreign Politicians' Visit to Crimea Is Russia's Latest Disinformation Failure," *Moscow Times*, March 29, 2017, https://themoscowtimes.com/articles/foreign-politicians-visit-to-crimea-is-russias-latest-disinformation-failure-57569.

73. Alina Polyakova et al., "The Kremlin's Trojan Horses: Russian Influence in France, Germany, and the United Kingdom," Atlantic Council, November 2016, http://www.atlanticcouncil.org/ima ges/publications/The_Kremlins_Trojan_Horses_web_0228_th ird_edition.pdf.

74. Jane Bradley, "Major Donation to U.K. Conservative Party Was Flagged over Russia Concerns," *New York Times*, May 12, 2022, https://www.nytimes.com/2022/05/12/world/europe/russian-money-uk-tories.html.

75. Ali Shalchi, Claire Mills, John Woodhouse, Melanie Gower, and Neil Johnston, "Countering Russian Influence in the UK," House of Commons Library, April 1, 2022, https://commonslibrary.par liament.uk/research-briefings/cbp-9472/.

76. Mitchell A. Orenstein and R. Daniel Keleman, "Trojan Horses in EU Foreign Policy," *Journal of Common Market Studies* 55, no. 1 (2016): 87–102, https://doi.org/10.1111/jcms.12441.

77. Bálint Magyar, *Post-Communist Mafia State: The Case of Hungary* (Budapest: Central European University Press, 2016).

78. BBC, "Greece's Tsipras Condemns Sanctions Against Russia," BBC News, May 28, 2016, http://www.bbc.com/news/world-europe-36403129.http://www.bbc.com/news/world-europe-36403129.

79. Orenstein and Keleman, "Trojan Horses."

80. Petra Vejvodová, Jakub Janda, and Veronika Víchová, "The Russian Connections of Far-Right and Paramilitary Organizations in the Czech Republic," Political Capital, April 2017, http://www.polit icalcapital.hu/pc-admin/source/documents/PC_NED_country_ study_CZ_20170428.pdf

81. "The Criminal Investigation by the Join Investigative Team," Netherlands Public Prosecution Service, 2023, https://www.pro

secutionservice.nl/topics/mh17-plane-crash/criminal-investigat
ion-jit-mh17.

82. Ben Nimmo, "How MH17 Gave Birth to the Modern Russian
Spin Machine," *Foreign Policy*, September 29, 2016, https://foreig
npolicy.com/2016/09/29/how-mh17-gave-birth-to-the-modern-
russian-spin-machine-putin-ukraine/.

83. Agnia Grigas, "Legacies, Coercion, and Soft Power: Russian
Influence in the Baltic States," Chatham House Briefing Paper,
August 2012, 10.

84. Snyder, *The Road to Unfreedom*.

85. National Intelligence Council, "Assessing Russian Activities and
Intentions in Recent US Elections," Office of the Director of
National Intelligence, January 6, 2017, 4, https://www.dni.gov/
files/documents/ICA_2017_01.pdf; Steven Erlanger, "Russia's RT
Network: Is It More BBC or K.G.B.?," *New York Times*, March 8,
2017, https://www.nytimes.com/2017/03/08/world/europe/russ
ias-rt-network-is-it-more-bbc-or-kgb.html; Rosie Gray, "How
the Truth Is Made at Russia Today," Buzzfeed, March 13, 2014,
https://www.buzzfeed.com/rosiegray/how-the-truth-is-made-at-
russia-today?utm_term=.euwEAJkqK#.or57gqrzb.

86. National Intelligence Council, "Assessing Russian Activities," 4;
Erlanger, "Russia's RT Network"; Adrian Chen, "The Agency,"
New York Times, June 2, 2015, https://www.nytimes.com/2015/
06/07/magazine/the-agency.html; Lawrence Alexander, "Social
Network Analysis Reveals Full Scale of Kremlin's Twitter Bot
Campaign," Global Voices, April 2, 2015, https://globalvoices.org/
2015/04/02/analyzing-kremlin-twitter-bots/.

87. Committee on Foreign Relations, "Putin's Asymmetric Assault,"
39. See also Peter Pomerantsev, "The Kremlin's Information War,"
Journal of Democracy 26, no. 4 (2015), http://doi.org/10.1353/
jod.2015.0074.

88. Denise Clifton, "How Trump and His Allies Have Run with
Russian Propaganda," *Mother Jones*, June 5, 2017, http://www.
motherjones.com/politics/2017/06/russian-active-measures-
trump-propaganda-conspiracy-theories/.

89. Robert Orttung, Elizabeth Nelson, and Anthony Livshen, "How
Russia Today Is Using YouTube," *Washington Post*, March 23, 2015,

https://www.washingtonpost.com/news/monkey-cage/wp/2015/ 03/23/how-russia-today-is-using-youtube/; Elias Groll, "Kremlin's 'Sputnik' Newswire Is the Buzzfeed of Propaganda," *Foreign Policy*, November 10, 2014, https://foreignpolicy.com/2014/11/10/kreml ins-sputnik-newswire-is-the-buzzfeed-of-propaganda/.

90. "Nigel Farage's Relationship with Russian Media Comes Under Scrutiny," *Guardian*, March 31, 2014, https://www.theguardian. com/politics/2014/mar/31/nigel-farage-relationship-russian-media-scrutiny.

91. "Green Party Candidates to Face Off in Debate Hosted by RT (Watch Live)," RT, May 9, 2016, https://www.rt.com/usa/342 395-green-party-rt-debate/; "America to Choose Either 'Proto-Fascist' or 'Corruption Queen'—Jill Stein to RT," RT, November 2, 2017, https://www.rt.com/usa/365045-jill-stein-elections-can didates/; "The Other Guys: Meet Third-Party US Candidates for President," RT, November 7, 2016, at https://www.rt.com/usa/ 365681-us-elections-other-candidates/; "Debunking the Media's Smear Campaign Against Green Presidential Candidate Jill Stein," RT, August 25, 2016, https://www.rt.com/usa/355444-de bunking-jill-stein-smears/.

92. Peter Walker, "Russia 'Spreading Fake News About Refugees to Sow Discord in Europe' Says Ex-Spy," *Independent*, March 22, 2017, http://www.independent.co.uk/news/world/europe/russia-europe-threat-refugee-crisis-europe-aggravate-propaganda-krem lin-farenc-katrei-hungarian-spy-a7642711.html.

93. Stefan Meister, "The 'Lisa Case': Germany as a Target of Russian Disinformation," NATO, 2016, https://www.nato.int/docu/rev iew/2016/Also-in-2016/lisa-case-germany-target-russian-disinfo rmation/EN/index.htm.

94. Andy Greenberg, "How an Entire Nation Became Russia's Test Lab for Cyberwar," *Wired*, June 20, 2017, https://www.wired.com/ story/russian-hackers-attack-ukraine/.

95. Andrew Wilson, *Ukraine's Orange Revolution* (New Haven, CT: Yale University Press, 2005).

96. Mark Galeotti, "Controlling Chaos: How Russia Manages Its Political War in Europe," European Council on Foreign Affairs, September 2017, 7, http://www.ecfr.eu/page/-/ECFR228_-_CON TROLLING_CHAOS1.pdf.

97. Select Committee on Intelligence of the United States Senate, "Report of the Select Committee on Intelligence United States Senate on Russian Active Measures Campaigns and Interference in the 2016 U.S. Election: Volume 2: Russia's Use of Social Media, with Additional Views," October 10, 2019, https://www.intelligence.senate.gov/sites/default/files/documents/report_volume5.pdf; Chris O'Brien, "U.S. Senate Report on 2016 Election Details Wikileaks' Russian Ties," VentureBeat, August 19, 2020, https://venturebeat.com/business/u-s-senate-report-on-2016-election-details-wikileaks-russian-tie.

98. Stephanie Kirchgaessner, Dan Collyns, and Luke Harding, "Revealed: Russia's Secret Plan to Help Julian Assange Escape from UK," *Guardian*, September 21, 2018, https://www.theguardian.com/world/2018/sep/21/julian-assange-russia-ecuador-embassy-london-secret-escape-plan.

99. Jason Le Miere, "Russia Election Hacking: Countries Where the Kremlin Has Allegedly Sought to Sway Votes," *Newsweek*, May 9, 2017, http://www.newsweek.com/russia-election-hacking-france-us-606314; Mark Clayton, "Ukraine Election Narrowly Avoided 'Wanton Destruction' from Hackers," *Christian Science Monitor*, June 17, 2014, https://www.csmonitor.com/World/Passcode/2014/0617/Ukraine-election-narrowly-avoided-wanton-destruction-from-hackers-video.

100. Andy Greenberg, "'Crash Override': The Malware That Took Down a Power Grid," *Wired*, June 12, 2017, https://www.wired.com/story/crash-override-malware/.

101. Microsoft Digital Security Unit, "An Overview of Russia's Cyberattack Activity in Ukraine," April 27, 2022, https://query.prod.cms.rt.microsoft.com/cms/api/am/binary/RE4Vwwd.

102. Andy Greenberg, "Hackers Gain Direct Access to US Power Grid Controls," *Wired*, September 6, 2017, https://www.wired.com/story/hackers-gain-switch-flipping-access-to-us-power-systems/.

103. The White House, "Statement by President Biden on Our Nation's Cybersecurity," United States Government, March 21, 2022, https://www.whitehouse.gov/briefing-room/statements-releases/2022/03/21/statement-by-president-biden-on-our-nations-cybersecurity/.

104. Agnia Grigas, *The New Geopolitics of Natural Gas* (Cambridge, MA: Harvard University Press, 2017); Stephen F. Szabo, *Germany, Russia, and the Rise of Geo-Economics* (London: Bloomsbury, 2015).

105. Dimitar Bechev, *Rival Power: Russia in Southeast Europe* (New Haven, CT: Yale University Press, 2017).

106. Mitchell Orenstein, "Putin the Green? The Unintended Consequences of Russia's Energy War on Europe," Foreign Policy Research Institute, February 15, 2023, https://www.fpri.org/arti cle/2023/02/putin-the-green-the-unintended-consequences-of-russias-energy-war-on-europe/.

107. Jack Losh, "Is Russia Killing Off Eastern Ukraine's Warlords," *Foreign Policy*, October 25, 2016, https://foreignpolicy.com/ 2016/10/25/who-is-killing-eastern-ukraines-warlords-motor ola-russia-putin/; Pavel Kanygin, "Why Was the Separatist Leader of Donetsk Assassinated? Questions You're Too Embarrassed to Ask About Rebel Politics in Eastern Ukraine," Meduza, September 4, 2018, https://meduza.io/en/feature/2018/ 09/04/why-was-the-separatist-leader-of-donetsk-assassinated.

108. Dasha Litvinova, "Hundreds Arrested as Shocked Russians Protest Ukraine Attack," AP News, February 24, 2022, https:// apnews.com/article/russia-ukraine-vladimir-putin-europe-rus sia-moscow-9a3eab8c8cb047254c82f1839ef77b9f.

109. Dezső András and Szabolcs Panyi, "Russian Diplomats Exercised with Hungarian Cop Killer's Far-Right Gang," Index, October 28, 2016, http://index.hu/belfold/2016/10/28/russian_diplo-mats_exercised_with_hungarian_cop_killer_s_far-right_gang/.

110. Vejvodová, Janda, and Víchová, "Russian Connections"; Péter Krekó et al., "Marching Towards Eurasia: The Kremlin Connections of the Slovak Far-Right," Political Capital, January 2015, https://www.researchgate.net/publication/287218227_ Marching_towards_Eurasia_The_Kremlin_connections_of_ the_Slovak_far-right; "The Russian Connection: The Spread of Pro-Russian Policies on the European Far Right," Political Capital, March 14, 2014, http://www.riskandforecast.com/user uploads/files/pc_flash_report_russian_connection.pdf.

111. Josh Lederman, Courtney Kube, Abigail Williams, and Ken Dilanian, "U.S. Officials Suspect Russia in Mystery 'Attacks' on

Diplomats in Cuba, China," NBC News, September 11, 2018, https://www.nbcnews.com/news/latin-america/u-s-officials-suspect-russia-mystery-attacks-diplomats-cuba-china-n908141; William J. Broad, "Microwave Weapons Are Prime Suspects in Ills of U.S. Workers," *New York Times*, September 1, 2018, https://www.nytimes.com/2018/09/01/science/sonic-attack-cuba-microwave.html.

112. Mark Galeotti, "Russia's Hybrid Warfare as a Byproduct of a Hybrid State," War on the Rocks, December 6, 2016, https://warontherocks.com/2016/12/russias-hybrid-war-as-a-byproduct-of-a-hybrid-state/.

113. Galeotti, "Controlling Chaos," 7.

Chapter 3

1. Akrady Moshes, "Russia's European Policy Under Medvedev: How Sustainable Is a New Compromise?," *International Affairs* 88, no. 1 (Winter 2012): 17–30, https://doi.org/10.1111/j.1468-2346.2012.01054.x.

2. Robert Coalson, "As Merkel Heads for Russia, Moscow Is in for a Schokenhoff," Radio Free Europe / Radio Liberty, November 16, 2012, https://www.rferl.org/a/news-analysis-merkel-putin-schockenhoff/24768692.html.

3. Roderich Kiesewetter and Ingmar Zielke, "Permanent NATO Deployment Is Not the Answer to European Security," *European View* 15, no. 1 (Spring 2016): 37–45, https://doi.org/10.1007/s12290-016-0392-8.

4. Alexander J. Motyl, "The West Should Arm Ukraine," *Foreign Affairs*, February 10, 2015, https://www.foreignaffairs.com/articles/russia-fsu/2015-02-10/west-should-arm-ukraine.

5. European Union Committee, "The EU and Russia: Before and Beyond the Crisis in Ukraine," House of Lords, February 20, 2015, https://publications.parliament.uk/pa/ld201415/ldselect/ldeucom/115/115.pdf.

6. Stephen White, Margot Light, and Ian McAllister, "Russia and the West: Is There a Values Gap?," *International Politics* 42, no. 3 (2005): 314–33, https://doi.org/10.1057/palgrave.ip.8800114.

7. David J. Kramer, *Back to Containment: Dealing with Putin's Regime* (Washington, DC: McCain Institute, 2017).
8. Transcript, "Putin's Prepared Remarks at the 43rd Munich Conference on Security Policy," *Washington Post*, February 12, 2007, http://www.washingtonpost.com/wp-dyn/content/article/2007/02/12/AR2007021200555.html; Kramer, *Back to Containment*, describes the weak Bush administration response to Putin's attack on US dominance of the international system.
9. Stephen F. Szabo, *Germany, Russia, and the Rise of Geo-Economics* (London: Bloomsbury, 2015).
10. Francis Fukuyama, *The End of History and the Last Man* (New York: Free Press, 1992).
11. James Sherr, "A War of Narratives and Arms," in Keir Giles et al., *The Russian Challenge* (London: Royal Institute of International Affairs, 2015), 23–32.
12. Josh Rogin, "Germany Helped Prep Russia for War, U.S. Sources Say," *Daily Beast*, April 22, 2014, https://www.thedailybeast.com/germany-helped-prep-russia-for-war-us-sources-say.
13. Vladimir Gel'man, *Authoritarian Russia: Analyzing Post-Soviet Regime Changes* (Pittsburgh: University of Pittsburgh Press, 2015).
14. "A Scripted War," *Economist*, August 14, 2008, https://www.economist.com/node/11920992.
15. Margriet Drent, Rob Hendriks, and Dick Zandee, "New Threats, New EU, and NATO Responses," Clingendael: Netherlands Institute of International Relations, 2015, https://www.clingendael.org/sites/default/files/pdfs/New%20Threats_New%20EU_Nato%20Responses_Clingendael_July2015.pdf.
16. Hilary Appel and Mitchell A. Orenstein, *From Triumph to Crisis: Neoliberal Economic Reform in Postcommunist Countries* (New York: Cambridge University Press, 2018), ch. 5.
17. Alina Polyakova et al., "The Kremlin's Trojan Horses: Russian Influence in France, Germany, and the United Kingdom," Atlantic Council, November 2016, http://www.atlanticcouncil.org/images/publications/The_Kremlins_Trojan_Horses_web_0228_third_edition.pdf.
18. Szabo, *Germany, Russia*, 77.
19. Janusz Bugajski, *Dismantling the West: Russia's Atlantic Agenda* (Washington, DC: Potomac Books, 2009); Edward Lucas, *The New*

Cold War: Putin's Russia and the Threat to the West (New York: Palgrave Macmillan, 2008).

20. Kramer, *Back to Containment.*

21. Tuomas Forsberg, "From *Ostpolitik* to 'Frostpolitik'? Merkel, Putin, and German Foreign Policy Towards Russia," *International Affairs* 92, no. 1 (2016): 21–42; Szabo, *Germany, Russia.*

22. Ellen Barry, "Rally Defying Putin's Party Draws Tens of Thousands," *New York Times*, December 10, 2011, https://www.nytimes.com/2011/12/11/world/europe/thousands-protest-in-moscow-russia-in-defiance-of-putin.html.

23. Vladimir Gel'man, "Cracks in the Wall: Challenges to Electoral Authoritarianism in Russia," *Problems of Post-Communism* 60, no. 2 (2013): 3–10.

24. Ralf Neukirch and Matthias Schepp, "German-Russian Relations Enter a New Ice Age," *Der Spiegel*, May 30, 2012, http://www.spiegel.de/international/germany/german-and-russian-relations-are-at-an-impasse-a-835862.html.

25. Glenn Kessler, "Flashback: Obama's Debate Zinger on Romney's '1980s' Foreign Policy (Video)," *Washington Post*, March 20, 2014, https://www.washingtonpost.com/news/fact-checker/wp/2014/03/20/flashback-obamas-debate-zinger-on-romneys-1980s-foreign-policy.

26. Ali Watkins, "Obama Team Was Warned in 2014 About Russian Interference," Politico, August 14, 2017, https://www.politico.com/story/2017/08/14/obama-russia-election-interference-241547.

27. Jan Strupczewski and Paul Taylor, "Russia Is a Strategic Problem for the EU: Tusk," Reuters, December 18, 2014, http://www.reuters.com/article/us-ukraine-crisis-russia-eu-idUSKBN0JW2S620141218.

28. David Cadier, "Eastern Partnership vs Eurasian Union? The EU-Russia Competition in the Shared Neighbourhood and the Ukraine Crisis," *Global Policy* 5, no. 1 (2014), https://onlinelibrary.wiley.com/doi/full/10.1111/1758-5899.12152.

29. "Agreement on the Settlement of Crisis in Ukraine—Full Text," *Guardian*, February 21, 2014, https://www.theguardian.com/world/2014/feb/21/agreement-on-the-settlement-of-crisis-in-ukraine-full-text.

30. Rajan Menon and Eugene Rumer, *Conflict in Ukraine: The Unwinding of the Post-Cold War Order* (Cambridge, MA: MIT Press, 2015), 80.

31. Harriet Alexander and Yekaterina Kravtsova, "Vladimir Putin Held Secret Meeting to Agree Crimea Annexation Weeks Before Referendum," *Telegraph*, March 20, 2014, https://www.telegraph.co.uk/news/worldnews/vladimir-putin/10712866/Vladimir-Putin-held-secret-meeting-to-agree-Crimea-annexation-weeks-before-referendum.html.

32. Sergei Markedonov, Alexander Gushchin, and Anna Tsibulina, "The Ukrainian Challenge for Russia," Russian International Affairs Council Working Paper, 2015, https://russiancouncil.ru/common/upload/www/newsletter/ukraine24-en/.

33. Google Books Ngram Viewer.

34. Matthieu Crozet and Julian Hinz, "Collateral Damage: The Impact of the Russia Sanctions on Sanctioning Countries Exports," CEPII Working Paper no. 2016-16, June 2016.

35. Yun Chee Foo, Sabine Siebold, Bart Meijjer, Vladimir Soldatkin, and Anna Koper, "Blow to Gazprom Critics as EU Court Upholds Antitrust Settlement," Reuters, February 2, 2022, https://www.reuters.com/business/energy/eu-court-upholds-antitrust-settlement-gazprom-case-2022-02-02/.

36. Roderich Kiesewetter and Ingmar Zielke, "Permanent NATO Deployment Is Not the Answer to European Security," *European View* 15, no. 1 (Spring 2016): 37–45, https://doi.org/10.1007/s12290-016-0392-8.

37. Taras Kuzio, "Ukraine Between a Constrained EU and Assertive Russia," *Journal of Common Market Studies* 55, no. 1 (2016): 1–18.

38. Ed Gresser, "Trade Fact of the Week: Russian Share of World GDP and Trade: 1% to 2%," Progressive Policy Institute, February 23, 2022, https://www.progressivepolicy.org/blogs/trade-fact-of-the-week-russian-share-of-world-gdp-and-trade-1-to-2/.

39. Iikka Korhonen, "Sanctions and Counter-Sanctions—What Are Their Economic Effects in Russia and Elsewhere?," BOFIT Policy Brief, no. 2, Fall 2019, 3–10, http://urn.fi/URN:NBN:fi:bof-201909131464.

40. Michael Rochlitz, "Why Russia Is Lacking an Economic Strategy for the Future," *Russian Analytical Digest*, no. 285 (Summer 2022): 9–12, doi: 10.3929/ethz-b-000555473.

41. Country Fact Sheet: Russian Federation, UNCTAD World Investment Report 2017, United Nations Conference on Trade and Development, 2017, https://unctad.org/system/files/official-document/wir2017_en.pdf.

42. Rochlitz, "Why Russia Is Lacking an Economic Strategy," 9–12.

43. Markedonov, Gushchin, and Tsibulina, "Ukrainian Challenge for Russia."

44. Stephen Blank, "Georgia: The War Russia Lost," *Military Review*, no. 1 (November–December 2008): 40.

45. Mitchell A. Orenstein and R. Daniel Keleman, "Trojan Horses in EU Foreign Policy," *Journal of Common Market Studies* 55, no. 1 (2016): 87–102, https://doi.org/10.1111/jcms.12441.

46. Luke Harding, *A Very Expensive Poison: The Assassination of Alexander Litvinenko and Putin's War with the West* (New York: Knopf Doubleday, 2017).

47. Forsberg, "From *Ostpolitik* to Frostpolitik," 26. This is an excellent and detailed article on changes to German foreign policy on Russia.

48. Ian Traynor and Patrick Wintour, "Ukraine Crisis: Vladimir Putin Has Lost the Plot, Says German Chancellor," *Guardian*, March 3, 2014, https://www.theguardian.com/world/2014/mar/03/ukraine-vladimir-putin-angela-merkel-russian.

49. "Rattachement de la Crimée à la Russie: La colère de Hollande, Merkel et Obama," *L'Express*, March 18, 2014, https://www.lexpress.fr/actualite/monde/europe/rattachement-de-la-crimee-a-la-russie-la-colere-de-hollande-merkel-et-obama_1501058.html.

50. Andrew Rettman, "Italy Dangles Veto Threat on EU's Russia Sanctions," EU Observer, October 25, 2018, https://euobserver.com/foreign/143207.

51. Stefano Vergine, "Conte to Putin: EU Sanctions on Russia Make Italy 'Sad,'" EUobserver, July 5, 2019, https://euobserver.com/world/145376.

52. Somini Sengupta and Andrew E. Kramer, "Dutch Inquiry Links Russia to 298 Deaths in Explosion of Jetliner over Ukraine,"

New York Times, September 28, 2016, https://www.nytimes.com/ 2016/09/29/world/asia/malaysia-air-flight-mh17-russia-ukra ine-missile.html?mcubz=3&_r=0; Ian Neubauer, "Top AIDS Researcher Killed in Malaysia Airlines Crash," *Time*, July 17, 2014, http://time.com/3003840/malaysia-airlines-ukraine-crash-top-aids-researchers-killed-aids2014-mh17/.

53. "Flight MH17 Shot Down by a Russian-Supplied Buk Missile 'Most Convincing Scenario by Far,' Says PACE," Council of Europe, June 23, 2022, https://www.coe.int/en/web/portal/-/fli ght-mh17-shot-down-by-a-russian-supplied-buk-missile-most-convincing-scenario-by-far-says-pace.

54. Jessica Elgot, "Dutch Foreign Minister Frans Timmermans Gives Perfect Response to Horror of MH17," *Huffington Post*, July 23, 2014, http://www.huffingtonpost.co.uk/2014/07/22/speech-un-mh17_n_5609363.html.

55. Rebecca M. Nelson, "US Sanctions and Russia's Economy," CRS Report 7-5700, Congressional Research Service, February 17, 2017, 4, with updated data from World Bank.

56. Masha Hedberg, "The Target Strikes Back: Explaining Countersanctions and Russia's Strategy of Differentiated Retaliation," *Post-Soviet Affairs* 34, no. 1 (2018): 35–54, https:// doi.org/10.1080/1060586X.2018.1419623.

57. Michael Birnbaum, "Russia Bans Food Imports from U.S., E.U.," *Washington Post*, August 7, 2014, https://www.washingtonpost. com/world/russia-bans-food-imports-from-us-eu/2014/08/07/ a29f5bea-1e14-11e4-82f9-2cd6fa8da5c4_story.html?utm_term= .11bdec97d971.

58. Jason Bush, "Russia's Import-Substitution Drive Will Take Years—and May Be Misguided," Reuters, October 1, 2015, https://www. reuters.com/article/us-russia-economy-import-substitution/ russias-import-substitution-drive-will-take-years-and-may-be-misguided-idUSKCN0RV4W920151001.

59. Vladimir Alexandrovich Davydenko, Gulnara Fatykhovna Romashkina, and Ruzilya Maratovna Nasyrova, "Models of Russian Consumer Behaviour: Retail Under Crisis Pressure," *Ekonomska Misao i Praksa* [Economic Thought and Practice] (Croatia) no. 2 (2017): 697–714.

60. "Historic Inflation Russia—CPI Inflation," Inflation.EU, n.d., http://www.inflation.eu/inflation-rates/russia/historic-inflation/cpi-inflation-russia.aspx.

61. "Russia Food Inflation," Trading Economics, n.d., https://tradingeconomics.com/russia/food-inflation.

62. Nelson, *US Sanctions and Russia's Economy*.

63. International Monetary Fund, "Russian Federation: Staff Report for the 2015 Article IV Consultation," August 2015, 5.

64. Nikolaus Blome, Kai Diekmann, and Daniel Biskup, "Interview with Putin," *Bild* (Germany), November 1, 2016.

65. "Russia Faces '100 Years of Solitude' (or More), Putin Aide Says," Radio Free Europe / Radio Liberty, April 10, 2018, https://www.rferl.org/a/putin-adviser-surkov-says-russia-abandoning-hopes-integrating-with-west-loneliness-isolation-/29155700.html.

66. Vladimir Putin, "Article by Vladimir Putin 'On the Historical Unity of Russians and Ukrainians," President of Russia, July 12, 2021, http://www.en.kremlin.ru/events/president/news/66181.

67. Emma Ashford, "Not-So-Smart Sanctions: The Failure of Western Restrictions Against Russia," *Foreign Affairs* 114 (2016): 114–23.

68. Alexander J. Motyl, "The West Should Arm Ukraine," *Foreign Affairs*, February 10, 2015, https://www.foreignaffairs.com/articles/russia-fsu/2015-02-10/west-should-arm-ukraine.

69. Josep Borrell, "Yes, the Sanctions Against Russia Are Working," European Union External Action, August 26, 2023, https://www.eeas.europa.eu/eeas/yes-sanctions-against-russia-are-working_en.

70. Matina Stevis-Gridneff, "At Europe's Largest Port, Russia Sanctions Meet Their Toughest Test," *New York Times*, July 8, 2022, https://www.nytimes.com/2022/07/08/world/europe/russia-eu-sanctions-rotterdam.html.

71. Marco Siddi, "EU-Russia Energy Relations," *Handbook of Energy Governance in Europe*, Winter 2020, 6, https://doi.org/10.1007/978-3-319-73526-9_54-1.

72. Danila Bochkarev, "Gazprom Plays Ball: The Depoliticization of the European Gas Market," Eurostat, January 25, 2017, http://ec.europa.eu/eurostat/statistics-explained/index.php/File:Main_origin_of_primary_energy_imports,_EU-28,_2005-2015_(%25_of_extra_EU-28_imports)_YB17.png.

73. Szabo, *Germany, Russia*, 71.

74. Agnia Grigas, *The New Geopolitics of Natural Gas* (Cambridge, MA: Harvard University Press, 2017).

75. "Main Origin of Primary Energy Imports, EU-28, 2005–2015 (5% of Extra EU-28 Imports) YB17," Eurostat, July 12, 2017, http://ec.europa.eu/eurostat/statistics-explained/index.php/File:Main_origin_of_primary_energy_imports,_EU-28,_2005-2015_(%25_of_extra_EU-28_imports)_YB17.png.

76. Marco Siddi, "EU-Russia Energy Relations," *Handbook of Energy Governance in Europe* (Winter 2020): 1–25, https://doi.org/10.1007/978-3-319-73526-9_54-1.

77. Euractiv with Reuters, "EU Wants Same Price for Russian Gas for All Its Members: Oettinger," Euractiv, May 2, 2014, https://www.euractiv.com/section/energy/news/eu-wants-same-price-for-russian-gas-for-all-its-members-oettinger/.

78. Florent Silve and Pierre Noël, "Cost Curves for Gas Supply Security: The Case of Bulgaria," Electricity Policy Research Group Working Paper 1031, September 2010, https://www.repository.cam.ac.uk/bitstream/handle/1810/257219/cwpe1056.pdf; Reuters Staff, "Bulgaria and Romania Launch Gas Pipeline," Reuters, November 11, 2016, http://www.reuters.com/article/bulgaria-gas-romania-idUSL8N1DB2YX.

79. Bochkarev, "Gazprom Plays Ball."

80. Jacob Cohen, "Let's Drink to All the Russian Gas: How Energy Dependence Affects European Union Energy Strategy Towards Russia," Senior Honors Thesis, University of Pennsylvania, April 2018.

81. "Communication from the Commission to the European Parliament, the Council, the European Economic and Social Committee and the Committee of the Regions on an EU Strategy for Liquefied Natural Gas and Gas Storage," European Commission, February 16, 2016, 6, https://eur-lex.europa.eu/legal-content/EN/TXT/?uri=COM%3A2016%3A49%3AFIN.

82. Rachel Waldholz, Benjamin Wehrmann, and Julian Wettengel, "Ukraine War Pushes Germany to Build LNG Terminals," Clean Energy Wire, May 11, 2023, https://www.cleanenergywire.org/factsheets/liquefied-gas-does-lng-have-place-germanys-energy-future.

83. "Question and Answers on the Third Legislative Package for an Internal EU Gas and Electricity Market," European Commission, March 2, 2011, http://europa.eu/rapid/press-release_MEMO-11-125_en.htm?locale=en/; Dagmara Stoerring and Susanne Horl, "Fact Sheets on the European Union: Internal Energy Market," European Parliament, June 2017, https://www.europarl.europa.eu/factsheets/en/sheet/45/internal-energy-market.

84. Yuliya Lovochkina, Member of Parliament of Ukraine, interview by Mitchell A. Orenstein, June 13, 2017.

85. Sergei Komlev, "Third Energy Package and Its Impact on Gazprom Activities in Europe," EBC Working Committee "Energy," Gazprom, Essen, March 18, 2011, gazpromexport.ru/files/komlev_speech_essen_18_03_1124.pdf.

86. Jakob Hedenskog and Robert L. Larsson, *Russian Leverage on the CIS and the Baltic States* (Stockholm: Swedish Defence Research Agency, 2007).

87. Komlev, "Third Energy Package."

88. Reuters Staff, "Timeline—EU's Anti-Monopoly Case Against Russia's Gazprom," Reuters, October 25, 2016, https://www.reuters.com/article/idAFL8N1CV6WG.

89. Stanley Reed and Milan Schreuer, "E.U. Settles with Russia's Gazprom over Antitrust Charges," *New York Times*, May 24, 2018.

90. Benjamin Fox, "EU Launches Anti-Trust Case Against Gazprom," EUobserver, October 4, 2013, https://euobserver.com/political/121659; Simone Tagliapietra, "The EU Antitrust Case: No Big Deal for Gazprom," Bruegel, March 15, 2017, http://bruegel.org/2017/03/the-eu-antitrust-case-no-big-deal-for-gazprom/; David Sheppard and Henry Fox, "US and Russia Step Up Fight to Supply Europe's Gas," *Financial Times*, August 3, 2017, https://www.ft.com/content/352f4cac-6c7a-11e7-b9c7-15af748b60d0; Alexei Lossan, "Gazprom Recognizes EU Restrictions for the First Time," Russia Beyond the Headlines, March 29, 2016, https://www.rbth.com/business/2016/03/29/gazprom-recognizes-eu-restrictions-for-the-first-time_579955; Georgi Gotev, "Nord Stream 2 Official: We See a Lot of Smokescreens Thrown Around," Euractiv, March 23, 2017, https://www.euractiv.com/section/energy/interview/nord-stream-2-official-we-see-a-lot-of-smokescreens-thrown-around/.

91. Bobo Lo, *Russia and the New World Disorder* (London: Royal Institute of International Affairs, 2015), 86; Szabo, *Germany, Russia*.

92. "REPowerEU: A Plan to Rapidly Reduce Dependence on Russian Fossil Fuels and Fast Forward the Green Transition," European Commission, May 18, 2022, https://ec.europa.eu/commission/presscorner/detail/en/IP_22_3131.

93. Anna Herranz-Surrallés, Israel Solorio, and Jenny Fairbrass, "Renegotiating Authority in the Energy Union: A Framework for Analysis," *Journal of European Integration* 42, no. 1 (Winter 2020): 1–17, https://doi.org/10.1080/07036337.2019.1708343.

94. Mitchell Orenstein, "Putin the Green? The Unintended Consequences of Russia's Energy War on Europe," Foreign Policy Research Institute, February 15, 2023, https://www.fpri.org/article/2023/02/putin-the-green-the-unintended-consequences-of-russias-energy-war-on-europe/.

95. Orenstein, "Putin the Green?"

96. Stefan Nicola, Carol Matlack, and Birgit Jennen, "Germany Builds an Election Firewall to Fight Russian Hackers," Bloomberg, June 14, 2017, https://www.bloomberg.com/news/articles/2017-06-14/germany-builds-an-election-firewall-to-fight-russian-hackers.

97. Committee on Foreign Affairs, "EU Strategic Communication to Counteract Anti-EU Propaganda by Third Parties," European Parliament, October 14, 2016, https://www.europarl.europa.eu/doceo/document/A-8-2016-0290_EN.html.

98. "GEC Special Report: Pillars of Russia's Disinformation and Propaganda Ecosystem," United States Department of State, August 2020, https://www.state.gov/wp-content/uploads/2020/08/Pillars-of-Russia%E2%80%99s-Disinformation-and-Propaganda-Ecosystem_08-04-20.pdf.

99. Brent D. Griffiths, "Ex-Head of DHS Disinformation Board Warns the US Is 'in a Really Bleak Situation,'" *Business Insider*, July 6, 2022, https://www.businessinsider.com/nina-jankowicz-disinformation-board-mature-way-bleak-situation-2022-7; Robby Soave, "Nina Jankowicz's Faulty Record, Not Her Critics, Doomed the Disinformation Board," *Reason*, May 18, 2022, https://reason.com/2022/05/18/disinformation-board-nina-jankowicz-taylor-lorenz-pause-dhs/.

100. "Facebook to Start Disclosing Identity of Political Advertisers," Radio Free Europe / Radio Liberty, April 7, 2018, https://www.rferl.org/a/facebook-start-disclosing-identity-political-adverti ser-network-russian-election-meddling-/29151116.html.
101. Jean-Baptiste Jeangène Vilmer et al., "Information Manipulation: A Challenge for Our Democracies," report by the Policy Planning Staff (CAPS, Ministry for Europe and Foreign Affairs) and the Institute for Strategic Research (IRSEM, Ministry for the Armed Forces), Republic of France, 2018, 105–53.
102. Mark Galeotti, "Controlling Chaos: How Russia Manages Its Political War in Europe," European Council on Foreign Affairs, September 2017, 7, http://www.ecfr.eu/page/-/ECFR228_-_CONTROLLING_CHAOS1.pdf.
103. Samuel Charap and Timothy Colton, *Everybody Loses: The Ukraine Crisis and the Ruinous Contest for Post-Soviet Eurasia* (New York: Routledge, 2017).
104. Loveday Morris, John Hudson, Adela Suliman, and Alex Horton, "Warnings of Attack on Ukraine Nuclear Plant Set the World on Edge," *Washington Post*, August 19, 2022, https://www.washing tonpost.com/world/2022/08/19/zaporizhzhia-nuclear-plant-ukraine-russia/.
105. Steve Brusk and Ralph Ellis, "Russian Planes Intercepted Near U.S., Canadian Airspace," CNN, November 13, 2014, accessed May 21, 2018, at https://www.cnn.com/2014/09/19/us/russian-plane-incidents/index.html.https://www.cnn.com/2014/09/19/us/russian-plane-incidents/index.html.
106. Reuters Staff, "Russia Threatens to Aim Nuclear Missiles at Denmark Ships if It Joins NATO Shield," Reuters, March 22, 2015, https://www.reuters.com/article/us-denmark-russia/rus sia-threatens-to-aim-nuclear-missiles-at-denmark-ships-if-it-joins-nato-shield-idUSKBN0MI0ML20150322.
107. Zachary Fryer-Biggs, "British Fighter Jets Intercept Russian Bombers Once Again Taunting U.K.: Report," *Newsweek*, January 15, 2018, http://www.newsweek.com/russian-bombers-taunt-uk-again-fly-781741.http://www.newsweek.com/russian-bombers-taunt-uk-again-fly-781741.
108. Drent, Hendriks, and Zandee, "New Threats," 25.
109. NATO Public Diplomacy Division, "Defence Expenditure of NATO Countries (2010–2017)," North Atlantic Treaty

Organization, June 2017, 4, https://www.nato.int/nato_st atic_fl2014/assets/pdf/pdf_2017_06/20170629_170629-pr2 017-111-en.pdf.

110. "Donald Trump Tells NATO Allies to Pay Up at Brussels Talks," *BBC News*, May 25, 2017.

111. The Data Team, "Military Spending by NATO Members," *Economist*, February 16, 2017, https://www.economist.com/blogs/ graphicdetail/2017/02/daily-chart-11. See also Kaija Schilde, "European Military Capabilities: Enablers and Constraints on EU Power?," *Journal of Common Market Studies* 55, no. 1 (2017): 37–53.

112. Magnus Nordenman, "Lessons from Sweden's Sub Hunt," USNI News, October 28, 2014, https://news.usni.org/2014/10/28/less ons-swedens-sub-hunt.

113. Maria Sheahan and Sarah Marsh, "Germany to Increase Defence Spending in Response to 'Putin's War'—Scholz," Reuters, February 27, 2022, https://www.reuters.com/business/aerosp ace-defense/germany-hike-defense-spending-scholz-says-furt her-policy-shift-2022-02-27/.

114. Kristin Archick, "Russia's Invasion of Ukraine: European Union Responses and Implications for U.S.-EU Relations," Congressional Research Service, July 28, 2022, https://crsrepo rts.congress.gov/product/pdf/IN/IN11897.

115. Schilde, "European Military Capabilities."

116. Daniel Kochis, "Support for Montenegro's Accession to NATO Would Send a Message of Strength," Heritage Foundation, Issue Brief 4647, January 12, 2017, https://www.heritage.org/sites/ default/files/2017-01/IB4647_0.pdf.

117. Edward Wong and Lara Jakes, "NATO Won't Let Ukraine Join Soon. Here's Why," *New York Times*, March 16, 2022, https:// www.nytimes.com/2022/01/13/us/politics/nato-ukraine.html.

118. Esther Ademmer, *Russia's Impact on EU Policy Transfer to the Post-Soviet Space: The Contested Neighborhood* (London: Routledge, 2017); Julia Langbein, *Transnationalization and Regulatory Change in the EU's Eastern Neighbourhood: Ukraine Between Brussels and Moscow* (London: Routledge, 2017); László Bruszt and Julia Langbein, "Varieties of Dis-embedded Liberalism: EU Integration Strategies in the Eastern Peripheries of Europe,"

Journal of European Public Policy 24, no. 2 (2017): 297–315; Tanja A. Börzel and Frank Schimmelfennig, "Coming Together or Drifting Apart? The EU's Political Integration Capacity in Eastern Europe," *Journal of European Public Policy* 24, no. 2 (2017): 278–96; Antoaneta Dimitrova and Elitsa Kortenska, "What Do Citizens Want? And Why Does It Matter? Discourses Among Citizens as Opportunities and Constraints for EU Enlargement," *Journal of European Public Policy* 24, no. 2 (2017): 259–77.

119. Michael Emerson and Denis Cenusa, eds., *Deepening EU-Moldovan Relations: What, Why, and How?* (London: Rowman & Littlefield International, 2016).

120. Anahit Shirinyan, "What Armenia's New Agreement with the EU Means," *EUobserver*, November 24, 2017; Esther Ademmer and Yaroslav Lissovolik, "Thoughts on Inclusive Economic Integration," *Kiel Institute for the World Economy*, January 2018.

Chapter 4

1. Andrei Makhovsky, "Belarus Won't Choose Between the EU and Russia: Lukashenko," Reuters, March 23, 2016, http://www.reuters.com/article/us-belarus-eu-poland-idUSKCN0WP 1HI; Elena Korosteleva, "The EU and Belarus: Seizing the Opportunity?," Swedish Institute for Policy Studies Working Paper, November 2016, https://kar.kent.ac.uk/59637/1/Bela rus%20policy%20brief%20final%20oct%202016.pdf.

2. Korosteleva, "The EU and Belarus."

3. Yuras Karmanau, "Belarusians Wary of Being Drawn into Russia's War in Ukraine," *PBS NewsHour*, April 26, 2023, https://www.pbs.org/newshour/world/belarusians-wary-of-being-drawn-into-russias-war-in-ukraine.

4. Omer Bartov and Eric D. Weitz, eds., *Shatterzone of Empires: Coexistence and Violence in the German, Habsburg, Russian, and Ottoman Borderlands* (Bloomington: Indiana University Press, 2013).

5. Taras Kuzio, "Viktor Pinchuk Wants Ukraine to Capitulate to Russia," *Euromaidan Press*, January 4, 2017, http://euromaid anpress.com/2017/01/04/victor-pinchuk-wants-ukraine-to-cap itulate-to-russia-crimea-donbas/.

6. "Abkhazia Profile—Overview," BBC, August 27, 2015, http://www.bbc.com/news/world-europe-18175394.

7. AFP News Agency, "New Armenian Prime Minister Assures Putin of 'Strategic Alliance,'" Radio Free Europe / Radio Liberty, May 14, 2018, https://www.rferl.org/a/pashinian-putin-meeting-sochi/29226096.html.

8. Margarita Antidze, "Armenia, Azerbaijan Closer to War over Nagorno-Karabakh than at Any Time Since 1994," Reuters, June 1, 2017, https://www.reuters.com/article/armenia-azerbaijan-conflict-idUSL8N1IY402; Rovshan Ibrahimov and Mehmet Fatih Oztarsu, "Causes of the Second Karabakh War: Analysis of the Positions and the Strength and Weakness of Armenia and Azerbaijan," *Journal of Balkan and Near Eastern Studies* 24, no. 4 (2022): 595–613, https://doi.org/10.1080/19448953.2022.2037862.

9. David R. Cameron and Mitchell A. Orenstein, "Post-Soviet Authoritarianism: The Influence of Russia in Its 'Near Abroad,'" *Post-Soviet Affairs* 28, no. 1 (2017): 1–44; Ian Bond, "Contested Space: Eastern Europe Between Russia and the EU," Centre for European Reform, March 2017, http://www.cer.eu/sites/default/files/pb_eastern_part_IB_9march17.pdf.

10. T. J. Chisinau, "Why Has Russia Banned Moldovan Wine?," *Economist*, November 25, 2013, https://www.economist.com/blogs/economist-explains/2013/11/economist-explains-18.

11. "Russia Is Destroying Its Food," Stratfor, August 11, 2015, https://worldview.stratfor.com/article/russia-destroying-its-food.

12. Denis Cenusa et al., "Russia's Punitive Trade Policy Measures Towards Ukraine, Moldova, and Georgia," Centre for European Policy Studies, September 2014, 7, http://aei.pitt.edu/54994/1/WD_300_Punitive_Trade_Measures_by_Russia.pdf.

13. Cenusa et al., "Russia's Punitive Trade Policy."

14. "Bringing Plurality and Balance to the Russian Language Media Space," European Endowment for Democracy, June 25, 2015, https://www.democracyendowment.eu/news/bringing-plurality-1/; Peter Pomerantsev, "The Kremlin's Information War," *Journal of Democracy* 26, no. 4 (2015), http://doi.org/10.1353/jod.2015.0074.

15. Peter Pomerantsev, *Nothing Is True and Everything Is Possible: The Surreal Heart of the New Russia* (New York: PublicAffairs, 2014).

16. "Ukraine Bans Russian Media Outlets, Websites," Committee to Protect Journalists, May 17, 2017, https://cpj.org/2017/05/ukra ine-bans-russian-media-outlets-websites.php.

17. Robert C. Blitt, "Russia's 'Orthodox' Foreign Policy: The Growing Influence of the Russian Orthodox Church in Shaping Russia's Policies Abroad," Penn Law: Legal Scholarship Repository, November 28, 2011, http://scholarship.law.upenn.edu/cgi/view content.cgi?article=1058&context=jil; Stanislav Zlenko, "Trust to Social Institutions," Kyiv International Institute of Sociology, February 1, 2017, http://kiis.com.ua/?lang=eng&cat=repo rts&id=678&page=1; Bureau of Democracy, Human Rights, and Labor, "Belarus: International Religious Freedom Report 2005," US Department of State, 2005, https://www.state.gov/j/ drl/rls/irf/2005/51542.htm; Central Intelligence Agency, "The World Factbook: Religions," June 5, 2023, https://www.cia.gov/ the-world-factbook/countries/world/#:~:text=Christian%20 31.1%25%2C%20Muslim%2024.9%25,15.6%25%20(2020%20 est.).

18. Igor Munteanu, interview with Mitchell A. Orenstein, Chisinau, June 2017.

19. James J. Coyle, "Ukrainians Desert Russian Orthodox Church en Masse," *Newsweek*, June 25, 2016, http://www.newsweek.com/ ukrainian-desert-russian-orthodox-church-en-masse-474357.

20. Roman Olearchyk and Max Seddon, "Ukraine's Orthodox Church Emerges from Russia's Shadow," *Financial Times*, September 29, 2018, https://www.ft.com/content/1bdfb854-c26e-11e8-95b1- d36dfef1b89a.

21. Hilary Appel and Mitchell A. Orenstein, *From Triumph to Crisis: Neoliberal Economic Reform in Postcommunist Countries* (New York: Cambridge University Press, 2018).

22. Michael Emerson and Denis Cenusa, eds., *Deepening EU-Moldovan Relations: What, Why, and How?* (London: Rowman & Littlefield International, 2016).

23. Strategic Communications, "Eastern Partnership," European Union, October 10, 2016, https://www.eeas.europa.eu/eeas/east ern-partnership_en.

24. Béla Galgóczi, "Why Central and Eastern Europe Needs a Pay Rise," Working Paper 2017.01, European Trade Union Institute,

2017 https://www.etui.org/publications/working-papers/why-central-and-eastern-europe-needs-a-pay-rise.

25. Ecaterina Locoman, "Explaining Variations in International Alignments," PhD diss., Department of Political Science, Rutgers University, 2018.

26. Pleshakov, Constantine, *The Crimean Nexus: Putin's War and the Clash of Civilizations* (Yale University Press, 2017)

27. Information and Communication Department of the Secretariat of the CMU, "Ukraine and Moldova Have Intensified a Dialogue on Topical Issues of Political and Economic Cooperation—Outcomes of Negotiations of Heads of Government," State Sites of Ukraine, October 6, 2017, https://www.kmu.gov.ua/en/news/250331167.

28. Henry Foy, "Moldova Voters Face Stark Choice Between East and West," *Financial Times*, November 27, 2014, https://www.ft.com/content/4a4f7dea-7647-11e4-a777-00144feabdc0.

29. Gergana Noutcheva, "Whose Legitimacy? The EU and Russia in Contest for the Eastern Neighbourhood," *Democratization* 25, no. 2 (2018), https://www.tandfonline.com/doi/full/10.1080/13510347.2017.1363186.

30. Yuliya Lovochkina, Member of Parliament of Ukraine, interview by Mitchell A. Orenstein, June 13, 2017.

31. Noutcheva, "Whose Legitimacy?"

32. Vladimir Putin, "Orthodox-Slavic Values: The Foundation of Ukraine's Civilisational Choice Conference," President of Russia, July 27, 2013, http://en.kremlin.ru/events/president/news/18961.

33. Vladimir Putin, "On the Historical Unity of Russians and Ukrainians," President of Russia, July 12, 2022. http://www.en.kremlin.ru/events/president/news/66181.

34. "Russia Faces '100 Years of Solitude' (or More), Putin Aide Says," Radio Free Europe / Radio Liberty, April 10, 2018, https://www.rferl.org/a/putin-adviser-surkov-says-russia-abandoning-hopes-integrating-with-west-loneliness-isolation-/29155700.html.

35. Rating Group Ukraine, "Public Opinion Survey Residents of Ukraine, May 28–June 14, 2016," Center for Insights in Survey Research, International Republican Institute, 2016, http://www.

iri.org/sites/default/files/wysiwyg/2016-07-08_ukraine_poll_
shows_skepticism_glimmer_of_hope.pdf.

36. "Opportunities and Challenges Facing Ukraine's Democratic
Transition," National Democratic Institute, January 4–16, 2023,
https://www.ndi.org/sites/default/files/January_2023_Ukraine_
wartime_survey_ENG.pdf.

37. Tom Balmforth, "As Ukraine Says 'Farewell Unwashed Russia,'
Putin Says Take Care in 'Gay' Europe," Radio Free Europe / Radio
Liberty, June 15, 2017, https://www.rferl.org/a/putin-unwashed-
russia-poroshenko-ukraine-gay/28557438.html.

38. Luke Hurst, "Revolt, Repression, and Reprisals: A Look Back
at a Year of Turmoil in Belarus," Euronews, September 9, 2021,
https://www.euronews.com/2021/08/09/revolt-repression-and-
reprisals-a-look-back-at-a-year-of-turmoil-in-belarus.

39. Mariusz Maszkiewicz, "State Ideology in Belarus—Main
Problems and Concepts," unpublished manuscript, University of
Cardinal Stephan Wyszynski, Warsaw, 2012; Natalia Leshchenko,
"The National Ideology and the Basis of the Lukashenka Regime
in Belarus," *Europe-Asia Studies* 60, no. 8 (2008): 1419–33.

40. Maxim Edwards, "Moldova's New President: His Bark Is Worse
than His Bite," *World Policy*, November 28, 2016.

41. Jorge Libereiro, "Approved! EU Countries Endorse Ukraine and
Moldova as Official Candidates to Join Bloc," Euronews, June 29,
2022, https://www.euronews.com/my-europe/2022/06/23/appro
ved-eu-countries-endorse-ukraine-and-moldova-as-official-can
didates-to-join-bloc.

42. Denis Cenusa, "Geopolitical Games Expected Ahead of Moldova's
2018, Elections," Foreign Policy Research Institute, October 10,
2017, https://www.fpri.org/article/2017/10/geopolitical-games-
expected-ahead-moldovas-2018-elections/.

43. Cenusa, "Geopolitical Games Expected."

44. Center for Insights in Survey Research, "National Survey of
Moldova," International Republican Institute: 57, https://www.
iri.org/wp-content/uploads/2023/09/Survey-Moldova-2023_C
ISR.pdf

45. "Former Moldovan PM Jailed for Nine Years," Radio Free
Europe / Radio Liberty, June 27, 2016, https://www.rferl.org/

a/moldova-former-prime-minister-filat-jailed-9-years/27823
377.html.

46. David Cadier and Samuel Charap, "The Polarisation of Regional Politics: The Impact of the EU-Russia Confrontation on Countries in the Common Neighborhood," in *Damage Assessment: EU-Russia Relations in Crisis*, ed. Łukasz Kulesa, Ivan Timofeev, and Joseph Dobbs, European Leadership Network and Russian International Affairs Council, June 15, 2017, http://www.europe anleadershipnetwork.org/damage-assessment-eu-russia-relati ons-in-crisis_4846.html.

47. Pleshakov, *Crimean Nexus*, 16.

48. Lucan A. Way, "Weak States and Pluralism: The Case of Moldova," *East European Politics and Societies* 17, no. 3 (2003).

49. Cadier and Charap, "Polarisation of Regional Politics."

50. Andrew Osborne, "Inside the Fantasy Home of the £3.5bn Politician," *Telegraph*, November 27, 2011, https://www.telegr aph.co.uk/culture/art/art-features/8917730/Inside-the-fantasy-home-of-the-3.5bn-politician.html.

51. "Georgia—Trade," European Commission, n.d., https://policy. trade.ec.europa.eu/eu-trade-relationships-country-and-region/ countries-and-regions/georgia_en. The EU-Georgia Association Agreement was signed June 27, 2014.

52. Regis Gente, "Bidzina Ivanishvili, a Man Who Plays According to Russian Rules?," *Caucasus Survey* 1, no. 1 (2013): 117–26, https://doi.org/10.1080/23761199.2013.11417276; Christopher Caldwell, "Back in the USSR? Georgia Elects an Oligarch," *Weekly Standard*, October 22, 2012, Hans Gutbrod and Nana Papiashvili, "Georgian Attitudes to Russia: Surprisingly Positive," *Russian Analytical Digest* 68, no. 9 (2009): 8–12, http://home.gwu.edu/ ~cwelt/Russian_Analytical_Digest_68.pdf.

53. Francis Fukuyama and Nino Evgenidze, "Russia Is Winning in Georgia: America Needs to Get Tough with Tbilisi," *Foreign Affairs*, April 6, 2023, https://www.foreignaffairs.com/georgia/rus sia-united-states-winning-georgia.

54. Régis Genté, "A Broken Dream: The Oligarch, Russia, and Georgia's Drift from Europe." European Council on Foreign Relations, December 21, 2022.

55. "Ukrainian Intelligence Accuses Georgia of Allowing Russia to Dodge Sanctions," *OC Media*, April 5, 2022, https://oc-media. org/ukrainian-intelligence-accuses-georgia-of-allowing-russia-to-dodge-sanctions/.

56. Korosteleva, "The EU and Belarus."

57. Stanislav Markus and Volha Charnysh, "The Flexible Few: Oligarchs and Wealth Defense in Developing Democracies," *Comparative Political Studies* 50, no. 12 (2017): 1632–65, http:// journals.sagepub.com/doi/abs/10.1177/0010414016688000.

58. Maria Levcenko, "Vlad Plahotniuc: Moldova's Man in the Shadows," Open Democracy, February 25, 2016, https://www. opendemocracy.net/en/odr/vlad-plahotniuc-moldova-s-man-in-shadows/; "Prime," Wikipedia (Russian edition), accessed September 28, 2017, https://ru.wikipedia.org/wiki/Prime; "Canal 2," Point, n.d., https://point.md/ru/tv/2plus; "Разное," Canal 3, n.d., http://www.canal3.md/ru/raznoe.html. PublikaTV broadcasts (Kremlin-owned) Russia 24, among others: "Publika TV," Wikipedia (Russian edition), accessed September 28, 2017, https://ru.wikipedia.org/wiki/Publika_TV.

59. Henry Pope, "US Treasury Sanctions Kremlin Political Assets in Moldova," Organized Crime and Corruption Reporting Project, October 31, 2022. https://www.occrp.org/en/daily/16967-u-s-treasury-sanctions-kremlin-political-assets-in-moldova.

60. Mariana Rață, "Money, Businesses, and Interests of Igor Dodon and 'Crucial' Alliances of PD-PSRM," Centrul de Investigații Jurnalistice, October 16, 2016, https://anticoruptie.md/en/electi ons-2016/money-businesses-and-interests-of-igor-dodon-and-crucial-alliances-of-pd-psrm.

61. Reuters Staff, "Moldova Declares Russian Deputy PM Rogozin Persona Non Grata," Reuters, August 2, 2017, http://www.reut ers.com/article/us-moldova-rogozin/moldova-declares-russ ian-deputy-pm-rogozin-persona-non-grata-idUSKBN1AI1MZ; "Moldova Expels Five Russian Diplomats," Al-Jazeera, May 29, 2017, http://www.aljazeera.com/news/2017/05/moldova-expels-russian-diplomats-170529175133505.html; Ana Maria Touma, "Moldovan President Ridiculed After Putin Joke," *Balkan Insight*, June 6, 2017, https://balkaninsight.com/2017/06/06/moldo

van-president-ridiculed-after-putin-joke-06-05-2017/; Eugen Tomiuk, "Despite Russian Allegations, Moldova's Dodon Finds No Fault with Training Base," *Radio Free Europe / Radio Liberty*, August 14, 2017, https://www.rferl.org/a/moldova-dodon-refu tes-russia-rt-allegations-military-base/28676040.html.

62. Amanda Paul, "The EU in the South Caucasus and the Impact of the Russia-Ukraine War," *The International Spectator* 50, no. 3 (September 2015): 30–42, DOI:10.1080/03932729.2015.1054223; "EU-Azerbaijan Relations," European Union, November 16, 2021, https://eeas.europa.eu/headquarters/headquarters-home page_en/4013/EU-Azerbaijan%20relations; "Azerbaijan Seeks a Balance Between Russia and the West," Stratfor, June 18, 2014, https://www.stratfor.com/geopolitical-diary/azerbaijan-seeks-balance-between-russia-and-west.

63. Economist Intelligence Unit, "Armenia Joins Eurasian Union," *Economist*, October 14, 2014, http://country.eiu.com/article. aspx?articleid=592382843; Hrant Kostanyan, "EU-Armenian Relations: Seizing the Second Chance," Centre for European Policy Studies, October 31, 2016, https://www.ceps.eu/publicati ons/eu-armenian-relations-seizing-second-chance.

64. Hayk Paronyan and Ruben Elamiryan, "Armenian Foreign Policy Between Eurasian and European Integration Models," *Eastern Journal of European Studies* 12, no. 1 (2021).

65. Bartov and Weitz, *Shatterzone of Empires*.

Chapter 5

1. Ruth Fraňková, "Zeman: Russian Television Lies on 1968 Invasion of Czechoslovakia," *Radio Praha International*, June 3, 2015, https://english.radio.cz/zeman-russian-television-lies-1968-invasion-czechoslovakia-8258186.

2. Jakub Janda, "How Czech President Miloš Zeman Became Putin's Man," *Observer*, January 26, 2018, http://observer.com/2018/ 01/how-czech-president-milos-zeman-became-vladimir-put ins-man/.

3. Martina Čermáková, "MfD: Russian Lukoil Pays Huge Debt of Zeman's Key Aide Nejedlý," *Prague Daily Monitor*, November 7,

2016, https://praguemonitor.com/news/07/11/2016/2016-11-07-mfd-russian-lukoil-pays-huge-debt-zemans-key-aide-nejedly/.

4. Neil MacFarquhar, "How Russians Pay to Play in Other Countries," *New York Times*, December 30, 2016, https://www.nytimes.com/2016/12/30/world/europe/czech-republic-russia-milos-zeman.html.

5. Karel Janicek, "Czech President Milos Zeman Leaves, Opponents Celebrate," ABC News, March 8, 2023, https://abcnews.go.com/International/wireStory/czech-president-milos-zeman-leaves-opponents-celebrate-97704337.

6. Mitchell A. Orenstein and R. Daniel Keleman, "Trojan Horses in EU Foreign Policy," *Journal of Common Market Studies* 55, no. 1 (2016): 87–102, https://doi.org/10.1111/jcms.12441.

7. Balázs Orbán, "Guest Post: Hungary Tries to Balance Between Russia and EU," *Financial Times*, February 16, 2015, http://blogs.ft.com/beyond-brics/2015/02/16/guest-post-hungary-tries-to-balance-between-russia-and-eu/; Rick Lyman, "Putin Swaggers into Hungary as Europe Worries About U.S.," *New York Times*, February 2, 2017, https://www.nytimes.com/2017/02/02/world/europe/vladimir-putin-hungary.html.

8. Jakob Hedenskog and Robert L. Larsson, *Russian Leverage on the CIS and the Baltic States* (Stockholm: Swedish Defence Research Agency, 2007).

9. Dimitar Bechev, *Rival Power: Russia in Southeast Europe* (New Haven, CT: Yale University Press, 2017).

10. Vija Pakalkaite, "Lithuania's Strategic Use of EU Energy Policy Tools: A Transformation of Gas Dynamics," Oxford Institute for Energy Studies, September 2016, 13, https://www.oxfordenergy.org/wpcms/wp-content/uploads/2016/09/Lithuanias-Strategic-Use-of-EU-Energy-Policy-Tools-A-transformation-of-Gas-Market-Dynamics-NG-111.pdf.

11. Tsvetana Paraskova, "After Poland, Lithuania Becomes U.S. LNG Buyer," *Pipeline & Gas Journal*, June 27, 2017, https://pgjonline.com/2017/06/27/after-poland-lithuania-becomes-u-s-lng-buyer/.

12. Independent Balkan News Agency, "Bulgaria-Romania Gas Interconnector Pipeline Finished," *Sofia Globe*, November

11, 2016, https://sofiaglobe.com/2016/11/11/bulgaria-roma
nia-gas-interconnector-pipeline-finished/. See also Bechev,
Rival Power.

13. Vladimir Milov, "Can South Stream Be Revived?," Bulgaria
Analytica, July 8, 2016, https://bulgariaanalytica.org/en/2016/07/
08/can-south-stream-be-revived/.

14. Bechev, *Rival Power*, 215.

15. Milov, "Can South Stream Be Revived?"; Jim Yardley and Jo
Becker, "How Putin Forged a Pipeline Deal That Derailed,"
New York Times, December 30, 2014, https://www.nytimes.com/
2014/12/31/world/europe/how-putin-forged-a-pipeline-deal-
that-derailed-.html.

16. Georgi Gotev, "Russian MP: We Will Buy Bulgaria, We Already
Bought Half of the Coast," Euractiv, September 20, 2016, https://
www.euractiv.com/section/central-europe/news/russian-mp-
we-will-buy-bulgaria-we-already-bought-half-of-the-coast/.

17. "Russian Ambassador Says Hungary Could Become Regional
Gas Distribution Hub," Daily News Hungary, March 23, 2015,
https://dailynewshungary.com/russian-ambassador-says-hung
ary-could-become-regional-gas-distribution-hub/.

18. Andrew Byrne and Neil Buckley, "EU Approves Hungary's
Russian-Financed Nuclear Station," *Financial Times*, March 6,
2017, https://www.ft.com/content/0478d38a-028a-11e7-ace0-
1ce02ef0def9.

19. Euractiv.com with Reuters, "Putin and Orbán Contemplate
Stronger Energy Ties," Euractiv, February 18, 2015, http://www.
euractiv.com/section/central-europe/news/putin-and-orban-
contemplate-stronger-energy-ties/.

20. "Annual Report of the Security Information Service for 2014,"
Security Information Service, September 4, 2015, https://www.
bis.cz/aktuality/vyrocni-zprava-bezpecnostni-informacni-slu
zby-za-rok-2014-10754362.html.

21. Bechev, *Rival Power*; Yardley and Becker, "How Putin Forged a
Pipeline Deal."

22. Jacob Cohen, "Let's Drink to All the Russian Gas: How Energy
Dependence Affects European Union Energy Strategy Towards
Russia," Senior Honors Thesis, University of Pennsylvania,
April 2018.

23. Agnia Grigas, "Compatriot Games: Russian-Speaking Minorities in the Baltic States," *World Politics Review*, October 21, 2014, http://www.worldpoliticsreview.com/articles/14240/compatriot-games-russian-speaking-minorities-in-the-baltic-states.

24. Timothy Snyder, *The Road to Unfreedom: Russia, Europe, America* (New York: Tim Duggan Books, 2018).

25. Maria Snegovaya, "Fellow Travelers or Trojan Horses? Similarities Across Pro-Russian Parties' Electorates in Europe," *Party Politics* 28, no. 3 (2022): 409–18.

26. Łukasz Wenerski and Michal Kacewicz, "Russian Soft Power in Poland: The Kremlin and Pro-Russian Organizations," ed. Lóránt Győri, Political Capital, April 2017, http://www.politicalcapital.hu/pc-admin/source/documents/PC_NED_country_study_PL_20170428.pdf.

27. Wenerski and Kacewicz, "Russian Soft Power."

28. Dezső András and Szabolcs Panyi, "Russian Diplomats Exercised with Hungarian Cop Killer's Far-Right Gang," Index, October 28, 2016, http://index.hu/belfold/2016/10/28/russian_diplomats_exercised_with_hungarian_cop_killer_s_far-right_gang/; Andrew Higgins, "Intent on Unsettling E.U., Russia Taps Foot Soldiers from the Fringe," *New York Times*, December 24, 2016, https://www.nytimes.com/2016/12/24/world/europe/intent-on-unsettling-eu-russia-taps-foot-soldiers-from-the-fringe.html.

29. Grigorij Mesežnikov and Radovan Bránik, "Hatred, Violence and Comprehensive Military Training: The Violent Radicalisation and Kremlin Connections of Slovak Paramilitary, Extremist and Neo-Nazi Groups," ed. Lóránt Győri, Political Capital, April 2017, https://politicalcapital.hu/pc-admin/source/documents/PC_NED_country_study_SK_20170428.pdf.

30. Péter Krekó, Lóránt Győri, and Edit Zgut, "From Russia with Hate: The Activity of Pro-Russian Extremist Groups in Central-Eastern Europe," ed. Lóránt Győri, Political Capital, April 2017, https://politicalcapital.hu/pc-admin/source/documents/PC_NED_summary_analysis_EN_20170428.pdf.

31. Radovan Geist, "Russia Targets Slovakia as the Weakest Link in V4," Euractiv, March 16, 2017, https://www.euractiv.com/section/central-europe/news/russian-targets-slovakia-as-the-weakest-link-in-v4/; "Demand for Right-Wing Extremism Index

(DEREX)," *Political Capital*, November 11, 2016, http://www. politicalcapital.hu/hireink.php?article_read=1&article_id=315.

32. Katarína Klingová and Daniel Milo, "Vulnerability Index: Subversive Russian Influence in Central Europe," GLOBSEC Policy Institute, 2017, https://www.globsec.org/what-we-do/ publications/vulnerability-index-subversive-russian-influence- central-europe.

33. E.L., "Orbán and the Wind from the East," *Economist*, November 14, 2011, https://www.economist.com/blogs/easternapproaches/ 2011/11/hungarys-politics.

34. Bálint Magyar, *Post-Communist Mafia State: The Case of Hungary* (Budapest: Central European University Press, 2016).

35. Alexander Motyl, "Viktor Orban's Dilemma: Turn Towards the West or Remain with Putin," *The Hill*, April 26, 2023, https://theh ill.com/opinion/international/3971272-viktor-orbans-dilemma- turn-toward-the-west-or-remain-with-putin/.

36. Stanislav Kuvaldin, "Why Russia Keeps Insisting That Poland Is Preparing to Partition Ukraine," Carnegie Endowment for International Peace, December 7, 2022, https://carnegieendowm ent.org/politika/88585.

37. Zoltan Simon, "How EU Is Withholding Funding to Try to Rein In Hungary, Poland," *New York Times*, January 2, 2023, https:// www.washingtonpost.com/business/how-eu-is-withholding- funding-to-try-to-rein-in-hungary-poland/2022/12/30/ba364 1fc-8818-11ed-b5ac-411280b122ef_story.html.

38. Szabolcs Panyi, "Hungarian Secret Agent Reveals in Detail How Serious the Russian Threat Is," Index, March 21, 2017, http:// index.hu/belfold/2017/03/21/hungarian_secret_agent_reveals_ how_serious_the_russian_threat_is/.

39. "Annual Report of the Security Information Service for 2015," Security Information Service, September 1, 2016, https://www. bis.cz/annual-reports/annual-report-of-the-security-informat ion-service-for-2015-442e6079.html.

40. Katarína Klingová, "Information War Monitor for Central Europe: June 2017 Part 1," GLOBSEC Policy Institute, July 5, 2017, https://www.globsec.org/what-we-do/publications/information- war-monitor-central-europe-june-2017-part-1-0.

41. Klingová and Milo, "Vulnerability Index."

42. Mitchell Orenstein, "Transformation of the European Union After Russia's Attack on Ukraine," *Journal of European Integration* 45, no. 3 (2023).

43. Thomas Frear, Łukasz Kulesa, and Ian Kearns, "Dangerous Brinkmanship: Close Military Encounters Between Russia and the West in 2014," European Leadership Network, November 2014, http://www.europeanleadershipnetwork.org/medialibrary/2014/11/09/6375e3da/Dangerous%20Brinkmanship.pdf; Thomas Frear, "List of Close Military Encounters Between Russia and the West, March 2014–March 2015," European Leadership Network, March 12, 2015, http://www.europeanleadershipnetwork.org/medialibrary/2015/03/11/4264a5a6/ELN%20Russia%20-%20West%20Full%20List%20of%20Incidents.pdf.

44. Matthew Dey, "Russia 'Simulates' Nuclear Attack on Poland," *Telegraph*, November 1, 2009, http://www.telegraph.co.uk/news/worldnews/europe/poland/6480227/Russia-simulates-nuclear-attack-on-Poland.html.

45. Mariusz Antoni Kaminski and Zdzislaw Sliwa, "Poland's Threat Assessment: Deepened, Not Changed," *Prism* 10, no. 2 (March 10, 2023), https://ndupress.ndu.edu/Media/News/News-Article-View/Article/3323942/polands-threat-assessment-deepened-not-changed/.

46. Samuel Osborne, "Russian Naval Activity in Europe 'Exceeds Cold War Levels' Says Nato Admiral," *Independent*, April 10, 2017, http://www.independent.co.uk/news/world/europe/russia-navy-europe-cold-war-levels-nato-admiral-michelle-howard-warships-submarines-aircraft-a7675771.html.

Chapter 6

1. Thomas Risse and Nelli Babayan, "Democracy Promotion and the Challenges of Illiberal Regional Powers: Introduction to the Special Issue," *Democratization* 22, no. 3 (2015): 381–99.

2. Larry Wolff, *Inventing Eastern Europe: The Map of Civilization on the Mind of the Enlightenment* (Stanford, CA: Stanford University Press, 1994), 4.

3. Nina Jankowicz, *How to Lose the Information War: Russia, Fake News, and the Future of Conflict* (London: I. B. Taurus, 2020);

Mason Clark, "Russian Hybrid Warfare," Institute for the Study of War, September 2020, https://www.understandingwar.org/rep ort/russian-hybrid-warfare.

4. Georgy Tadtaev, "Сепаратисты Техаса рассказали о своих 'российских' контактах в Facebook" [Texas separatists spoke about their "Russian" contacts on Facebook], РБК, September 15, 2017, http://www.rbc.ru/rbcfreenews/59bb26fe9a7947d77 e25d2c5; Pavel Kazarnovsky, "СМИ рассказали о попытках 'фабрики троллей' устроить митинг в США" [The media talked about the attempts of the 'factory trolls' to arrange a rally in the United States], РБК, September 12, 2017, http://www.rbc. ru/politics/12/09/2017/59b7b88a9a79475a418953dd.

5. Jon Swaine and Luke Harding, "Russia Funded Facebook and Twitter Investments Through Kushner Investor," *Guardian*, November 5, 2017, https://www.theguardian.com/news/2017/ nov/05/russia-funded-facebook-twitter-investments-kushner-investor.

6. Timothy Snyder, *The Road to Unfreedom: Russia, Europe, America* (New York: Tim Duggan Books, 2018), 124.

7. Janko Roettgers, "Accused of Spreading Propaganda, RT Gets Deplatformed," Protocol, March 2, 2022, https://www.protocol. com/entertainment/rt-ban-roku-apple-directv.

8. Mona Elswah and Philip N. Howard, "'Anything That Causes Chaos': The Organizational Behavior of Russia Today (RT)," *Journal of Communication* 70, no. 5 (2020): 623–45.

9. Natalya Kanevskaya, "How the Kremlin Wields Its Soft Power In France," Radio Free Europe / Radio Liberty, June 24, 2014, https:// www.rferl.org/a/russia-soft-power-france/25433946.html.

10. Kanevskaya, "How the Kremlin Wields."

11. Yair Rosenberg, "Friends Don't Let Friends Vote for Jill Stein," *Tablet*, August 10, 2016, https://www.tabletmag.com/scroll/210 549/friends-dont-let-friends-vote-for-jill-stein.

12. Andrew Feinberg, "My Life at a Russian Propaganda Network," Politico, August 21, 2017, http://www.politico.com/magazine/ story/2017/08/21/russian-propaganda-sputnik-reporter-215511.

13. Jim Rutenberg, "RT, Sputnik, and Russia's New Theory of War," *New York Times*, September 13, 2017, https://www.nytimes. com/2017/09/13/magazine/rt-sputnik-and-russias-new-the

ory-of-war.html; National Intelligence Council, "Assessing Russian Activities and Intentions in Recent US Elections," Office of the Director of National Intelligence, January 6, 2017, 4, https://www.dni.gov/files/documents/ICA_2017_01.pdf; Katie Zavadski, "Putin's Propaganda TV Lies about Its Popularity," *Daily Beast*, September 17, 2015, http://www.thedailybeast.com/putins-propaganda-tv-lies-about-its-popularity.

14. Clint Watts and Andrew Weisburd, "How Russia Wins an Election," Politico, December 13, 2016, http://www.politico.com/magazine/story/2016/12/how-russia-wins-an-election-214524; Jankowicz, *How to Lose*.

15. Ben Knight, "Teenage Girl Admits Making Up Migrant Rape Claim That Outraged Germany," *Guardian*, January 31, 2016, https://www.theguardian.com/world/2016/jan/31/teenage-girl-made-up-migrant-claim-that-caused-uproar-in-germany.

16. Adrian Chen, "The Agency," *New York Times*, June 2, 2015, https://www.nytimes.com/2015/06/07/magazine/the-agency.html.

17. Bridge R., "911 Reasons Why 9/11 Was (Probably) an Inside Job," *RT*, June 28, 2010, http://rt.com/usa/911-attack-job/; Ilya Yablokov, "Conspiracy Theories as a Russian Public Diplomacy Tool: The Case of *Russia Today* (*RT*)," *Politics* 35, nos. 3–4 (2015), https://doi.org/10.1111/1467-9256.12097.

18. Oliver Bullough, "Inside Russia Today: Counterweight to the Mainstream Media, or Putin's Mouthpiece?," *New Statesman*, May 10, 2013, http://www.newstatesman.com/world-affairs/world-affairs/2013/05/inside-russia-today-counterweight-mainstream-media-or-putins-mou.

19. Margaret Vice, "Publics Worldwide Unfavorable Toward Putin, Russia," Pew Research Center, August 16, 2017, http://www.pewglobal.org/2017/08/16/publics-worldwide-unfavorable-toward-putin-russia/.

20. Rob Garver, "Global Public Perception of Russia's Leadership Eroded Sharply in 2022," Voice of America News, April 25, 2023, https://www.voanews.com/a/global-public-perception-of-russias-leadership-eroded-sharply-in-2022/7064927.html.

21. Robert S. Mueller III, "Report on the Investigation into Russian Interference in the 2016 Presidential Election," US Department of Justice, 2019.

22. Andrew Wilson, *Ukraine's Orange Revolution* (New Haven, CT: Yale University Press, 2005).

23. Michael Riley and Jordan Robertson, "Russian Cyber Hacks on U.S. Electoral System Far Wider than Previously Known," Bloomberg, June 13, 2017, https://www.bloomberg.com/news/articles/2017-06-13/russian-breach-of-39-states-threatens-future-u-s-elections.

24. Damien Sharkov, "France's Front National Accepts €9M Loan from Russian Bank," *Newsweek*, November 25, 2014, http://www.newsweek.com/frances-front-national-accepts-eu9m-loan-russian-bank-286999.

25. Marine Turchi and Mathias Destal, "Le Pen–Putin Friendship Goes Back a Long Way," EUobserver, April 22, 2017, https://euobserver.com/elections/137629.

26. Emilio Ferrera, "Disinformation and Social Bot Operations in the Run Up to the 2017 French Presidential Election," University of Southern California, Information Sciences Institute, 2017, https://arxiv.org/ftp/arxiv/papers/1707/1707.00086.pdf.

27. Allison Stanger, "The Mueller Report Confirms It: Assange Is Not a Whistle Blower or a Journalist," *Washington Post*, April 22, 2019, https://www.washingtonpost.com/opinions/2019/04/22/mueller-report-confirms-it-assange-is-not-whistleblower-or-journalist/; "The Julian Assange Show," *RT*, https://www.rt.com/tags/the-julian-assange-show/.

28. Reuters, "Emmanuel Macron's Campaign Team Bans Russian News Outlets from Events," *Guardian*, April 27, 2017, https://www.theguardian.com/world/2017/apr/27/russia-emmanuel-macron-banned-news-outlets-discrimination.

29. Stefan Wagstyl, "German Politics: Russia's Next Target?," *Financial Times*, January 29, 2017, https://www.ft.com/content/31a5758c-e3d8-11e6-9645-c9357a75844a; Patrick Beuth et al., "Cyberattack on the Bundestag: Merkel and the Fancy Bear," Zeit Online, May 12, 2017, http://www.zeit.de/digital/2017-05/cyberattack-bundestag-angela-merkel-fancy-bear-hacker-russia/seite-4.

30. Gregory Krieg and Joshua Berlinger, "Hillary Clinton: Donald Trump Would Be Putin's 'Puppet,'" CNN, October 20, 2016, http://www.cnn.com/2016/10/19/politics/clinton-puppet-vladimir-putin-trump/index.html.

31. Ashley Parker and David E. Sanger, "Donald Trump Calls on Russia to Find Hillary Clinton's Missing Emails," *New York Times*, July 27, 2016, https://www.nytimes.com/2016/07/28/us/politics/ donald-trump-russia-clinton-emails.html.

32. Mueller, "Report," 36.

33. Luke Harding, *Collusion: Secret Meetings, Dirty Money, and How Russia Helped Donald Trump Win* (New York: Vintage, 2017).

34. Maggie Haberman and Jonathan Martin, "Paul Manafort Quits Donald Trump's Campaign after a Tumultuous Run," *New York Times*, August 19, 2016, https://www.nytimes.com/2016/08/20/ us/politics/paul-manafort-resigns-donald-trump.html; Andrew E. Kramer, Mike McIntire, and Barry Meier, "Secret Ledger in Ukraine Lists Cash for Donald Trump's Campaign Chief," *New York Times*, August 14, 2016, https://www.nytimes.com/2016/08/ 15/us/politics/paul-manafort-ukraine-donald-trump.html.

35. Rajeev Syal, "Brexit: Foreign States May Have Interfered in Vote, Report Says," *Guardian*, April 12, 2017, https://www.theg uardian.com/politics/2017/apr/12/foreign-states-may-have-interfered-in-brexit-vote-report-says; Neil Barnett, "United Kingdom: Vulnerable but Resistant," in Alina Polyakova et al., "The Kremlin's Trojan Horses: Russian Influence in France, Germany, and the United Kingdom," Atlantic Council, November 2016, https://www.atlanticcouncil.org/in-depth-research-reports/ report/kremlin-trojan-horses/#uk.

36. Dan Sabbagh, Luke Harding, and Andrew Roth, "Russia Report Reveals UK Government Failed to Investigate Kremlin Interference," *Guardian*, July 21, 2020, https://www.theguardian. com/world/2020/jul/21/russia-report-reveals-uk-government-failed-to-address-kremlin-interference-scottish-referendum-brexit.

37. Snyder, *The Road to Unfreedom*, 126.

38. Patrick Foster, "Kremlin-Backed Broadcaster RT Offers Nigel Farage His Own Show," *Telegraph*, September 7, 2016, http:// www.telegraph.co.uk/news/2016/09/07/kremlin-backed-broa dcaster-rt-offers-nigel-farage-his-own-show/.

39. Carole Cadwalladr and Peter Jukes, "Arron Banks 'Met Russian Officials Multiple Times Before Brexit Vote,'" *Guardian*, June 9, 2018, https://www.theguardian.com/politics/2018/jun/09/

arron-banks-russia-brexit-meeting; Carole Cadwalladr, "Arron Banks: 'Brexit Was a War. We Won. There's No Turning Back Now,'" *Guardian*, April 2, 2017, https://www.theguardian.com/politics/ 2017/apr/02/arron-banks-interview-brexit-ukip-far-right-trump-putin-russia; Jim Waterson, "Major UKIP Donor Says 'KGB Man' Took Him to Russian Embassy," Buzzfeed, November 1, 2016, https://www.buzzfeed.com/jimwaterson/major-ukip-donor-says-kgb-man-took-him-to-russian-embassy?utm_term=.pcPAPW aEg#.llMj85kZl; Luke Harding, "Offshore Secrets of Brexit Backer Arron Banks Revealed in Panama Papers," *Guardian*, October 16, 2016, https://www.theguardian.com/world/2016/oct/15/panama-papers-reveal-offshore-secrets-arron-banks-brexit-backer.

40. Polyakova et al., "The Kremlin's Trojan Horses."

41. Stephanie Kirchgaessner, "Former Farage Aide Gives US Information in Plea Deal, Court Files Show," *Guardian*, June 7, 2017, https://www.theguardian.com/politics/2017/jun/07/former-nigel-farage-aide-us-information-plea-deal-court-files-george-cottrell.

42. Benjamin Novak, "Jobbik MEP Accused of Spying for Russia," *Budapest Beacon*, May 17, 2014, https://budapestbeacon.com/job bik-mep-accused-of-spying-for-russia/.

43. Reuters Staff, "Bulgaria's Borisov Names New Coalition Government," Reuters, March 26, 2017, https://www.reuters. com/article/us-bulgaria-government/bulgarias-borisov-names-new-coalition-government-idUSKBN17Z0XO; Clive Leviev-Sawyer, "Bulgaria's GERB, United Patriots Announce Agreement on Governance Programme for Coalition Government," *Sofia Globe*, April 13, 2017, http://sofiaglobe.com/2017/04/13/bulgar ias-gerb-united-patriots-announce-agreement-on-governance-programme-for-coalition-government-2/.

44. Catherine Belton, Souad Mekhennet, and Shane Harris, "Kremlin Tries to Build Antiwar Coalition in Germany, Documents Show," *Washington Post*, April 21, 2023, https://www.washingtonpost. com/world/2023/04/21/germany-russia-interference-afd-wage nknecht/.

45. Snyder, *The Road to Unfreedom*, 128.

46. Anton Shekhovtsov, *Russia and the Western Far Right: Tango Noir* (Abingdon, UK: Routledge, 2017).

47. Laas Leivat,"Western Thugs Advancing the Kremlin's Bid," *Estonian Life*, no. 38 (September 18, 2020), https://eestielu.com/ western-thugs-advancing-the-kremlin-s-bid/.

48. Andrew Rettman, "Fight Club: Russian Spies Seek EU Recruits," EUobserver, May 26, 2017, https://euobserver.com/foreign/ 137990.

49. Mark Galeotti, "Crimintern: How the Kremlin Uses Russia's Criminal Networks in Europe," European Council on Foreign Relations, April 18, 2017, http://www.ecfr.eu/publications/summ ary/crimintern_how_the_kremlin_uses_russias_criminal_net works_in_europe.

50. Snyder, *The Road to Unfreedom*, 290.

51. Conor Friedersdorf, "Is Russia Behind a Secession Effort in California?," *Atlantic*, March 1, 2017, https://www.theatlantic. com/politics/archive/2017/03/is-russia-behind-a-secession-eff ort-in-california/517890/.

52. Katy Murphy, "'Calexit' Campaign Dropped as Leader Bolts for Russia," *Mercury News*, April 17, 2017, http://www.mercurynews. com/2017/04/17/calexit-leaders-drop-ballot-measure-to-break-from-the-u-s/.

53. Murphy, "'Calexit' Campaign."

54. Graham Keeley, "Russia Meddled in Catalonia Independence Referendum, Says German Intelligence Boss," *The Times* (London), May 16, 2018, https://www.thetimes.co.uk/article/rus sia-meddled-in-catalonia-vote-p6g5nttpm.

55. Wagstyl, "German Politics."

56. Roman Goncharenko, Mikhail Bushuev, and Olga Tikhomirova, "Petersburg Dialogue Forum in Jeopardy," Deutsche Welle, May 28, 2021, https://www.dw.com/en/german-russian-petersburg-dialogue-forum-in-jeopardy-over-ngo-ban/a-57706360.

57. "Russian-German Dialogue Forum Founded by Putin and Schroeder Is Closed," *Ukrainska Pravda*, April 20, 2023, https:// www.pravda.com.ua/eng/news/2023/04/20/7398783/.

58. Polyakova et al., "The Kremlin's Trojan Horses."

59. Maria Snegovaya, "Russian Propaganda in Germany: More Effective Than You Think," *American Interest*, October 17, 2017, https://www.the-american-interest.com/2017/10/17/russian-pro paganda-germany-effective-think/.

60. Stephanie Kirchgasessner, "Italy's Five Star Movement Part of Growing Club of Putin Sympathisers in the West," *Guardian*, January 5, 2017, https://www.theguardian.com/world/2017/jan/05/five-star-movement-beppe-grillo-putin-supporters-west; "Meloni Pushes for Ukraine, Moldova, Balkans European Integration," Decode39, June 1, 2023, https://decode39.com/6914/meloni-ukraine-moldova-balkans-european-integration/.

61. Thomas Frear, Łukasz Kulesa, and Ian Kearns, "Dangerous Brinkmanship: Close Military Encounters Between Russia and the West in 2014," European Leadership Network, November 2014, http://www.europeanleadershipnetwork.org/medialibrary/2014/11/09/6375e3da/Dangerous%20Brinkmanship.pdf; Thomas Frear, "List of Close Military Encounters Between Russia and the West, March 2014–March 2015," European Leadership Network, March 12, 2015, http://www.europeanleadershipnetwork.org/medialibrary/2015/03/11/4264a5a6/ELN%20Russia%20-%20West%20Full%20List%20of%20Incidents.pdf

62. Andrew Naughtie, "NATO Jets Scrambled to Intercept Russian Aircraft in Norway and Baltics," Euronews, April 26, 2023, https://www.euronews.com/2023/04/26/nato-jets-scrambled-to-intercept-russian-aircraft-in-norway-baltic.

63. Laura Smith-Spark, "Why Is Russia Sending Bombers Close to U.S. Airspace?," CNN, July 27, 2015http://www.cnn.com/2015/07/27/world/us-russia-bombers-intentions/index.html; "Russia Simulated an Attack on Denmark," The Local, October 31, 2014, https://www.thelocal.dk/20141031/russia-simulated-a-military-%20attack-on-denmark.

64. Rachel S. Cohen, "Spike in Russian Aircraft Intercepts Straining Air Force Crews in Alaska, Three-Star Says," *Air Force Times*, April 28, 2021, https://www.airforcetimes.com/news/your-air-force/2021/04/28/spike-in-russian-aircraft-intercepts-straining-air-force-crews-in-alaska-three-star-says/.

65. Elisabeth Braw, "How to Deal with Russian Information Warfare? Ask Sweden's Subhunters," Defense One, April 3, 2018, https://www.defenseone.com/ideas/2018/04/how-deal-russian-information-warfare-ask-sweden/147154/.

66. Reuters Staff, "Russia Threatens to Aim Nuclear Missiles at Denmark Ships if It Joins NATO Shield," Reuters, March 22,

2015, https://www.reuters.com/article/us-denmark-russia/rus
sia-threatens-to-aim-nuclear-missiles-at-denmark-ships-if-it-
joins-nato-shield-idUSKBN0MI0ML20150322; Ian Johnston,
"Russia Threatens to Use 'Nuclear Force' over Crimea and the
Baltic States," *Independent*, April 1, 2015, http://www.independ
ent.co.uk/news/world/europe/russia-threatens-to-use-nuclear-
force-over-crimea-and-the-baltic-states-10150565.html.

67. "France Boosts Military Spending amid War in Ukraine,"
Associated Press, April 4, 2023, https://apnews.com/article/fra
nce-boosts-military-spending-amid-ukraine-war-db213e964b2ff
26f3d87e7a4a3ba0cdc.

68. Daniel Boffey, "Defence Spending in Western and Central Europe
Tops Last Year of Cold War," *Guardian*, April 23, 2023, https://
www.theguardian.com/world/2023/apr/24/defence-spending-in-
western-and-central-europe-tops-last-year-of-cold-war.

69. Lauren Sukin, "Rattling the Nuclear Saber: What Russia's Nuclear
Threats Really Mean," Carnegie Endowment for International
Peace, May 4, 2023, https://carnegieendowment.org/2023/05/
04/rattling-nuclear-saber-what-russia-s-nuclear-threats-rea
lly-mean-pub-89689.

70. Mitchell Orenstein, "Putin the Green? The Unintended
Consequences of Russia's Energy War on Europe," Foreign Policy
Research Institute, February 15, 2023, https://www.fpri.org/arti
cle/2023/02/putin-the-green-the-unintended-consequences-of-
russias-energy-war-on-europe/.

71. Risse and Babayan, "Democracy Promotion"; Tanja A. Borzel,
"The Noble West and the Dirty Rest? Western Democracy
Promoters and Illiberal Regional Powers," *Democratization* 22,
no. 3 (2015): 519–35.

72. James Crisp, "Macron Warns of European 'Civil War' over
Growing East-West Divide," *Telegraph*, April 17, 2018, https://
www.telegraph.co.uk/news/2018/04/17/macron-warns-europ
ean-civil-war-growing-east-west-divide/.

73. Fred Hiatt, "McMaster Warned Against Officials Who 'Glamorize
and Apologize' for Dictators. Hmm," *Washington Post*, April 8,
2018, https://www.washingtonpost.com/opinions/were-in-a-bat
tle-to-defend-democracy--and-trump-is-on-the-wrong-side/
2018/04/08/0ba0abfc-39b0-11e8-9c0a-85d477d9a226_story.html.

74. Adam Davidson, "Trump's Business of Corruption," *New Yorker*, August 21, 2017, https://www.newyorker.com/magazine/2017/08/21/trumps-business-of-corruption.
75. Craig Unger, "Trump's Russian Laundromat," *New Republic*, July 13, 2017.
76. Scott Horsley, "Is Trump the Toughest Ever on Russia?," NPR, July 20, 2018, https://www.npr.org/2018/07/20/630659379/is-trump-the-toughest-ever-on-russia.

Chapter 7

1. Timothy Snyder, *The Road to Unfreedom: Russia, Europe, America* (New York: Tim Duggan Books, 2018), 94.
2. Robert Legvold, *Return to the Cold War* (Cambridge, UK: Polity Press, 2016).
3. John J. Mearsheimer, "Why the Ukraine Crisis Is the West's Fault: The Liberal Delusions That Provoked Putin," *Foreign Affairs*, September–October 2014, 1–12; Joshua R. Itzkowitz Shifrinson, "Deal or No Deal? The End of the Cold War and the U.S. Offer to Limit NATO Expansion," *International Security* 40, no. 4 (Spring 2016): 7–44; Samuel Charap and Timothy Colton, *Everybody Loses: The Ukraine Crisis and the Ruinous Contest for Post-Soviet Eurasia* (New York: Routledge, 2017).
4. Mary Sarotte, *The Struggle to Create Post–Cold War Europe* (Princeton, NJ: Princeton University Press, 2009).
5. Dmitri Trenin, *Should We Fear Russia?* (Cambridge: Polity Press, 2016); Dmitri Trenin, *Post-Imperium: A Eurasian Story* (Washington, DC: Carnegie Endowment for International Peace, 2011); Celeste Wallander, "Russian Transimperialism and Its Implications," *Washington Quarterly* 30, no. 2 (Spring 2007): 107–22; Bobo Lo, *Russia and the New World Disorder* (London: Royal Institute of International Affairs, 2015), 101.
6. Gerald Toal, *Near Abroad: Putin, the West, and the Contest over Ukraine and the Caucasus* (Oxford: Oxford University Press, 2017).
7. Many facets of the Putin era were already on display at Moscow State University in the fall of 2000: rising anti-Western sentiment, pervasive corruption, and efforts to dominate democracy through

propaganda. Courses and students had already shifted from pro-Western to anti-Western in the course of a year. Students commented to me that they used to support Western democracy and values, but now they saw that the West had subverted Russia during the 1990s, and they had adopted a more nationalistic outlook. They told me about massive and organized corruption at the university. While some outstanding students were admitted to the university after succeeding on rigorous placement tests, others paid bribes for admission, for grades, to pass exams, and to get jobs and job recommendations after. Students knew exactly who the scholarship students were. Ten years later, I learned that the dean of the faculty that I worked with, Alexey Surin, was removed from his position in 2010 after his twenty-six-year-old daughter, also on the faculty, was accused of accepting a 35,000-euro admission bribe ("MGU Lecturer Quits in Bribe Case," *Moscow Times*, May 13, 2010, http://old.themoscowtimes.com/sitemap/free/2010/5/article/mgu-lecturer-quits-in-bribe-case/405856.html/). Dean Surin was also responsible for reversing the decline of the 1990s, turning the faculty into a high-quality academic institution, and building an impressive new facility for the faculty of public administration. At the time, one of the faculty's biggest problems was that it had invested heavily in teaching Western approaches to public administration, but was facing competition from a new school of "political technology" that taught the dark arts of winning and manipulating democratic elections, associated with Gleb Pavlovsky, a Kremlin-connected political scientist and media guru of the Putin administration.

8. Associated Press, "Putin: Soviet Collapse a 'Genuine Tragedy,'" NBC News, April 25, 2005, http://www.nbcnews.com/id/7632057/ns/world_news/t/putin-soviet-collapse-genuine-tragedy/.

9. "Russian Federation," The World Bank | Data, 2017, http://data.worldbank.org/country/russian-federation. Russia's GDP in 1989 was $506.5 billion. In 1999, at the lowest point of recession, it had fallen to $195.9 billion; Kristen Ghodsee and Mitchell A. Orenstein, *Taking Stock of Shock: Social Consequences of the 1989 Revolutions* (Oxford: Oxford University Press, 2021).

10. "Russian Federation," The World Bank | Data, 2017, http://data.worldbank.org/country/russian-federation. In 1989, Russia's total

life expectancy (for men and women) at birth was 69.2 years. In 1994, it had fallen to 64.5 years.

11. Taras Kuzio, "Ukraine Between a Constrained EU and Assertive Russia," *Journal of Common Market Studies* 55, no. 1 (2016): 1–18; "An Open Letter to the Obama Administration from Central and Eastern Europe," Radio Free Europe / Radio Liberty, July 16, 2009, https://www.rferl.org/a/An_Open_Letter_To_The_Obama_Administration_From_Central_And_Eastern_Eur ope/1778449.html.

12. Mitchell A. Orenstein, "Vladimir Putin: An Aspirant Metternich?," Foreign Policy Research Institute, January 2015, https://www.fpri. org/docs/orenstein_on_putin_1.pdf.

13. Richard Weitz, "The Rise and Fall of Medvedev's European Security Treaty," German Marshall Fund of the United States, May 29, 2012.

14. Sergei Karaganov, "Goals for Russia," Russia in Global Affairs, August 28, 2006, http://eng.globalaffairs.ru/pubcol/n_7095.

15. Samuel Huntington, *The Clash of Civilizations and the Remaking of World Order* (New York: Simon and Schuster, 1996).

16. Timothy Snyder, *On Tyranny: Twenty Lessons from the Twentieth Century* (New York: Tim Duggan Books, 2017).

17. Jaroslav Hašek, *The Good Soldier Svejk and His Fortunes in the World War* (New York: Penguin Classics, 2005).

18. Mitchell A. Orenstein, "The European Union's Transformation After Russia's Attack on Ukraine," *Journal of European Integration* 45, no. 3 (2023): 333–342, https://doi.org/10.1080/07036337.2023.2183393.

19. "Russia's War on Ukraine Is Changing Europe," *Economist*, June 7, 2023, https://www.economist.com/europe/2023/06/07/russias-war-on-ukraine-is-changing-europe.

20. Gavin Wilde and Justin Sherman, "Targeting Ukraine Through Washington: Russian Electoral Interference, Ukraine, and the 2024 US Election," Atlantic Council, March 14, 2022, https:// www.atlanticcouncil.org/in-depth-research-reports/issue-brief/ targeting-ukraine-through-washington/; Lee Drutman and Sean McFate, "The Real Winners of the 2024 Election Could Be China and Russia," *Time*, December 21, 2022, https://time.com/6242 314/real-winners-of-the-2024-election-could-be-china-and-russia/.

21. Graeme Massie and Io Dodds, "Ukraine Tells 'Clown' Tucker Carlson to Check His Facts After Pro-Kremlin Rant in First Twitter Show," *Independent*, June 8, 2023, https://ca.sports.yahoo.com/news/ukraine-tells-clown-tucker-carlson-185332801.html.

22. Nikita Smagin, "Is the Blossoming Relationship Between Russia and the UAE Doomed?," Carnegie Endowment for International Peace, April 13, 2023, https://carnegieendowment.org/politika/89531.

23. Casey Michel, "How the West Undermines Its Own Sanctions," *The Atlantic*, March 9, 2022.

24. Richard Pérez-Peña, "Britain Signals Harder Look at Wealthy Russians and Russian Wealth," *New York Times*, March 29, 2018, https://www.nytimes.com/2018/03/29/world/europe/uk-britain-russia-russian-wealth-putin.html.

25. Zeeshan Aleem, "The UK Could Seriously Punish Russia for the Spy Attack. Here's Why It Probably Won't," Vox, March 16, 2018, https://www.vox.com/world/2018/3/16/17123918/russia-nerve-agent-attack-uk-sanctions-spy-skripal.

26. UK Parliament, "Moscow's Gold: Russian Corruption in the UK," May 21, 2018, https://publications.parliament.uk/pa/cm201719/cmselect/cmfaff/932/93206.htm#_idTextAnchor022.

27. Jane Bradley, "Major Donation to U.K. Conservative Party Was Flagged over Russia Concerns," *New York Times*, May 12, 2022, https://www.nytimes.com/2022/05/12/world/europe/russian-money-uk-tories.html.

28. Julian Clover, "EU Issues Ban on Russian TV Channels," Broadband TV News, February 28, 2022, https://www.broadbandtvnews.com/2022/02/28/eu-issues-ban-on-russian-tv-channels/; Kari Paul, "RT Videos Spreading Ukraine Disinformation on YouTube Despite Ban—Report," *Guardian*, February 22, 2023, https://www.theguardian.com/media/2023/feb/22/rt-ban-youtube-videos-google-disinformation.

29. Reid Standish, "Russia's Neighbors Respond to Putin's 'Hybrid War,'" *Foreign Policy*, October 12, 2017, http://foreignpolicy.com/2017/10/12/russias-neighbors-respond-to-putins-hybrid-warlat via-estonia-lithuania-finland/.

30. Sarah Perez, "Facebook's New Authorization Process for Political Ads Goes Live in the US," Tech Crunch, April 23, 2018, https://

techcrunch.com/2018/04/23/facebooks-new-authorization-proc
ess-for-political-ads-goes-live-in-the-u-s/.

31. David Klepper, "Twitter Changes Stoke Russia, Chinese
Propaganda Surge," *AP News*, April 24, 2023, https://apnews.
com/article/twitter-russia-china-elon-musk-ukraine-2eedeabf7
d555dc1d0a68b3724cfdd55.

32. "Australia Passes Foreign Meddling Laws amid China Tensions,"
Business Times, June 29, 2018, https://www.businesstimes.com.
sg/government-economy/australia-passes-foreign-meddling-
laws-amid-china-tensions.

33. European Union Committee, "The EU and Russia: Before and
Beyond the Crisis in Ukraine," House of Lords, February 20, 2015,
https://publications.parliament.uk/pa/ld201415/ldselect/ldeu
com/115/115.pdf, 96; see also Michael E. O'Hanlon, *Beyond NATO:
A New Security Architecture for Eastern Europe* (Washington, DC:
Brookings Institution Press, 2017), 2.

34. David J. Kramer, *Back to Containment: Dealing with Putin's
Regime* (Washington, DC: McCain Institute, 2017).

35. Ivan Krastev and Gleb Pavlovsky, "The Arrival of Post-Putin
Russia," European Council on Foreign Relations Policy Brief,
March 1, 2018, http://www.ecfr.eu/publications/summary/the_a
rrival_of_post_putin_russia.

36. Trenin, *Should We Fear Russia?*

37. Philip Oltermann, Rosie Scammell, and Gordon Darroch, "Brexit
Causes Resurgence in Pro-EU Leanings Across Continent,"
Guardian, July 8, 2016, https://www.theguardian.com/world/
2016/jul/08/brexit-causes-resurgence-in-pro-eu-leanings-acr
oss-continent.

38. Mitchell A. Orenstein and R. Daniel Keleman, "Trojan Horses in
EU Foreign Policy," *Journal of Common Market Studies* 55, no. 1
(2016): 87–102, https://doi.org/10.1111/jcms.12441.

39. Alessandra Stanley, "Moscow Journal: The Americans Who Saved
Yeltsin (or Did They?)," *New York Times*, July 9, 1996, http://
www.nytimes.com/1996/07/09/world/moscow-journal-the-
americans-who-saved-yeltsin-or-did-they.html; Jennifer Wilson,
"Spinning Hillary: A History of America and Russia's Mutual
Meddling," *Guardian*, August 3, 2016, https://www.theguardian.

com/world/2016/aug/03/spinning-hillary-a-history-of-america-and-russias-mutual-meddling.

40. Eliot A. Cohen, "It's Not Enough for Ukraine to Win. Russia Has to Lose," *The Atlantic*, May 19, 2023, https://www.theatlantic.com/ideas/archive/2023/05/ukraine-victory-russia-defeat/674112/.

41. Mark Blyth, *Austerity: The History of a Dangerous Idea* (Oxford: Oxford University Press, 2013).

42. Ulrich Speck, "How the EU Sleepwalked into a Conflict with Russia," Carnegie Europe, July 10, 2014, https://carnegieeurope.eu/2014/07/10/how-eu-sleepwalked-%20into-conflict-with-russia-pub-56121.

INDEX

Figures are indicated by an italic *f* following the page number.